IMAGES
of America

MINGO JUNCTION

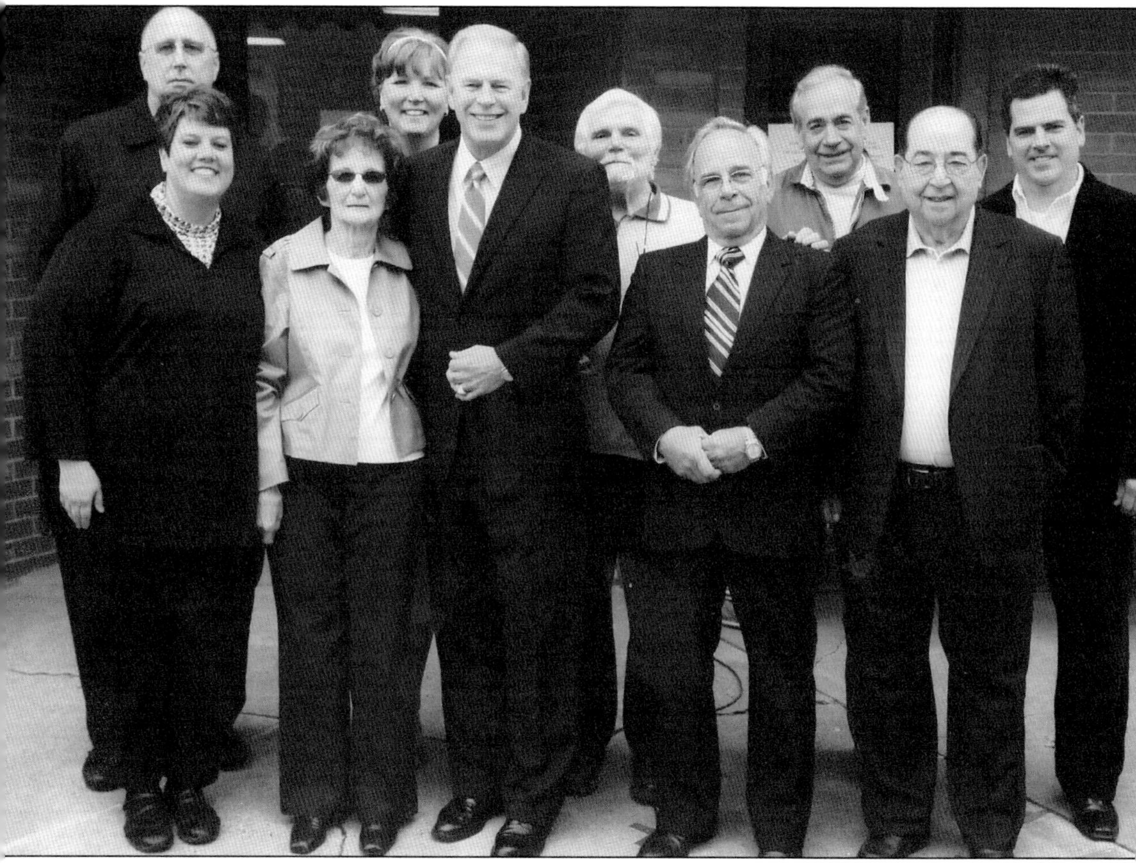

Gov. Ted Strickland Visits. Ohio governor Ted Strickland paid one of many visits to Mingo Junction on March 17, 2010. Mingo was part of his original district as a congressman. Seen here from left to right are city officials (first row) Vickie Peckins, Sophie Schoolcraft, Strickland, Mayor Dominic Chappano, and former mayor John "Wiz" Fabian; (second row) John Bracone, Judy Ruckman, city auditor Guy Mason, Jim Morrocco, and Mike Dicarlo. (Courtesy Sophie [Dojonovic] Schoolcraft.)

On the Cover: Mingo builds for the future. This photograph of the construction of the new Mingo City Building on Commercial and Potter Streets was taken on April 17, 1955. The building was dedicated January 15, 1956. Dressed in a suit to the right is Mayor Benny Leone and city and county officials. (Courtesy Leone family.)

IMAGES
of America

MINGO JUNCTION

Larry Smith and Guy Mason

ARCADIA
PUBLISHING

ISBN 978-0-7385-8340-2

Published by Arcadia Publishing
Charleston, South Carolina

Printed in the United States of America

Library of Congress Control Number: 2010936053

For all general information, please contact Arcadia Publishing:
Telephone 843-853-2070
Fax 843-853-0044
E-mail sales@arcadiapublishing.com
For customer service and orders:
Toll-Free 1-888-313-2665

Visit us on the Internet at www.arcadiapublishing.com

To the people of Mingo Junction, Ohio, who made this book possible.

"It's a long time between trains now, / but we know one will arrive.
In the simple grace of people / we learn how to survive."

—Larry Smith, from "A Long Time Between Trains"

Contents

Acknowledgments

We began with the encouragement of our Arcadia editor Melissa Bassilone, who guided us well throughout. At the Schiappa Public Library in Steubenville, Ohio, Sandy Day and Deb Stanley shared their advice and images. Unlike many American images books generated from stored research in libraries or historical societies, this book's primary source has been its many citizens who prized and preserved the town's images in shared stories and old photographs. Their doors and their albums were opened to us, and we thank them.

Certain town historians emerged, including Darlene Hoff of the Mingo Women's Club and coeditor and coauthor (along with Margaret Novotny) of the 1970 *Bicentennial History of Mingo Junction, Ohio*. We thank author-editor Darlene Hoff for permission to use images from this book. She shared her stores of information, and their book (out of print) has proven an invaluable resource. We thank Martha Sisler and Deb Stanley for their work on school history. As word traveled of our project, two collectors of vintage postcards, Madeline (Brinskey) Campbell and Sondra (White) Hyde, emerged to share their store of period photographs, as did Paula (Kendrach) Kopcha. City treasurer Sophie (Dojonovic) Schoolcraft and Mary (Visnic) Drzayich grew up in the early Mingo Bottoms area, and both proved a treasure of history. Joanne (Peeler) Sogan shared her close knowledge and images of the townspeople as did one of its photographers, Bea (Petroskey) Daily. Kay (Keenan) Kuebeler shared her family's vintage railroad and trolley images. John Grantonic—age 93—provided rare *c.* 1900 images and his sense of history, understanding, and zeal. We also thank our classmate and mayor, Dominic "Noony" Chappano, for his support.

Larry Smith thanks family members Charles Ferroni, Mary Alice (Ferroni) Mitchell, and David Smith for images and advice. Guy Mason recognizes his uncle Lou DelGallo and sister-in-law Martha (Vasich) Trombetta, who provided history and images. We both married Mingo girls in Ann (Zaben) Smith and Mary Ann (Vasich) Mason, and we thank them for their insights and understanding during this engrossing project.

Perhaps more than anyone, Eileen (Hagerty) Moody and husband Ron supplied us with vintage photographs of families, workers, and businesses. Her book on St. Agnes Catholic School and Church proved valuable. The citizens of Mingo Junction, like those on the cover, came together to build this town again through its images.

Unless otherwise noted, all images appear courtesy of the authors, Larry Smith and Guy Mason.

Introduction

Mingo Junction, Ohio, is a strong working-class town in the upper Ohio River Valley. Its rich mix of ethnicities and races goes back 250 years to when the Mingo Indians of the Seneca tribe made camps along Cross Creek in the Mingo Bottoms area. An abducted white girl, Mary Jemison, grew up there where Chief John Logan once led his people. George Washington camped in this area during his explorations of 1770. Early settlement came with trappers and frontier families like that of Joseph Ross, friend to Lewis Wetzel and Daniel Boone. By the early 1800s, settlers farmed the area and were visited by Christian missionaries. In 1806, they met Jonathan "Johnny Appleseed" Chapman, who came to the Georges Run area, south of town.

Industrialization came about with the first railroads—the Steubenville and Indiana in 1853 and the Pennsylvania in 1855. Mingo had become a junction, and during the Civil War, troops trained in the Mingo Bottoms area. Not without disasters, the area witnessed the train wreck of 1878 near the Cross Creek railroad bridge and the offshore crash of the *Scioto* and *John Lomas* excursion ships in 1882. When Rev. Layman Potter sold his lower locust grove to capitalists in 1869, the town was soon laid out into 117 lots and incorporated, with William C. Loyd as its first mayor, in 1883. The Ironworks along Mingo's Commercial Street in 1872 brought the town's first real industry. Iron and steel foundries and a nail factory brought new traffic by rail and river barge. Coal was at hand, so mining flourished. Mingo's chief industry—and that of all the Ohio River Valley—is the steel industry; the town was the seat of the Carnegie Steel Mill, then Wheeling Steel, and then the Wheeling-Pittsburgh Steel Mill for over 100 years, and it is presently home to Severstal Mills. The town rises and falls with the steel industry, and as a strong union town, Mingo has endured long strikes and shutdowns. Through the care of those who kept old photographs and postcards, the reader today is able to go inside the mills and meet the workers up close.

With all this growth came schools, the earliest in 1842, so that education was valued and became a force for development and cultural assimilation as new waves of immigrant families arrived. This book will look at the various public schools along with St. Agnes Catholic School, which began in 1898. Churches in the town have reflected the cultural heritage of its population, and the early Presbyterian and Methodist churches were soon joined by Roman Catholic, Slovak Presbyterian, Russian Orthodox, Greek Catholic, Serbian Eastern Orthodox, Baptist Byzantine Catholic, and Baptist churches. While the churches supported close groups of people, they also built community, and the reader will see how schools and churches worked together.

Images of America: *Mingo Junction* is built around the town's chief features and takes a close look at its history—including its survival through years of annual flooding from the Ohio River. Readers will visit the town industries of coal, oil, and steel; tour the downtown businesses and parks, schools, and churches; explore the daily life of its people; and meet some of its famous athletes, musicians, and artists. In the final chapter, readers will get a candid look at some of the many films made in Mingo Junction—the most famous being 1978's Academy Award-winning *The Deer Hunter.*

Among the athletes featured in these pages are two men who played for the Pittsburgh Steelers (Pirates) in the 1930s—Arthur "Jake" Strutt and George "Bunco" Kakasic—and Chicago Bears football star Joe Fortunato. Ohio State's Woody Hayes began his coaching days here under head coach and friend John Muth. Musicians include singing groups The Antones, The Stereos, Buddy Sharp and the Shakers, The Mingo Men (Savoys), and Bobby Parissi of Wild Cherry. The reader will meet the colorful Spud Hughes, adventurer and inventor of menthol cigarettes; Bill "Lil' Squirt" Albaugh, who served as mascot and spokesperson for the Squirt soda company for 35 years; and learn of Bea (Petroskey) Daily's work as a national photographer. Prominent about the town are its educators, public officials, doctors, and clergy. A long history of active social organizations marks the community, as well as a colorful history of years of bootlegging and gambling.

This book portrays Mingo Junction as it was and as it remains: a rich and colorful community with a strong character. Though Mingo may resemble many of the river towns of the upper Ohio and West Virginia Panhandle, it has its own personality and appeal. It is a place where people know each other by first and last names. The busy crowd seen on this book's cover at the construction of the new Mingo City Building reveals a town of hardworking people with their feet firmly planted on the streets of their town.

One

HISTORY

Mingo Junction links its present and future with its historic past. As one of the earliest villages in Ohio, Mingo was the base of the Ohio Seneca tribe of the Mingo Indians that lived along the rich Bottoms area where Cross Creek meets the Ohio River. The tribe was led for a time by Chief John Logan. In 1770, a young George Washington and his troops camped near Potter Spring. This period was followed by the arrival of frontier hunters, trappers, scouts, and eventually, the town's first settlers.

Large family farms developed around 1800, owned by the Meade, Peeler, Hill, Miller, Wells, Bailie, and Potter families. Ohio achieved statehood in 1803, and soon afterwards, Johnny Appleseed visited the Georges Run area. During the Civil War, the Mingo Bottoms served as a training camp for Union troops. By 1871, descendents of Lyman Potter bought up lands and divided the town into 117 lots. Schools and churches soon followed, and the town grew as railroads, coal, oil, and ironworks came to Mingo. In 1880, Auction Iron and Steel Company set up a bar mill, nail factory, and steel plant. Commercial Street welcomed hotels, dry goods, and grocery stores. By 1883, the town of Mingo Junction—formerly part of the Steubenville Township—was incorporated, with William C. Loyd as its first mayor.

Of historical record are two disasters: a train wreck in 1878 and the 1882 sinking of the *Scioto* excursion ship off Mingo's shores. Though the Ohio River served as ready transportation for industry, it also plagued the town with its recurring floods that would spread through the mill and streets of the town. Labor unions evolved with the steel industry. In 1919, union spokesperson Mother Jones came to town to encourage the workers. Succeeding waves of immigrant laborers and their families became a regular feature of the town.

Mingo has its darker sides as well; during the 1920s and 1930s, the town witnessed the reach of the Mafia's Black Hand and the narrow shadow of the Ku Klux Klan. "Gambling" as one citizen declares, "has always been a part of this town." And yet, as Fr. Daniel Coffey declares in his 1921 biography, *A Mill Town Pastor*, "All I can say is, these people are too good to me. I would not change them for any people I know. I am perfectly contented in Mingo."

The town's history has been preserved by local historian Anna Brettell, by the recent work of Eileen (Hagerty) Moody and Deb Stanley, and by the efforts of Darlene Hoff and the Mingo Women's Club.

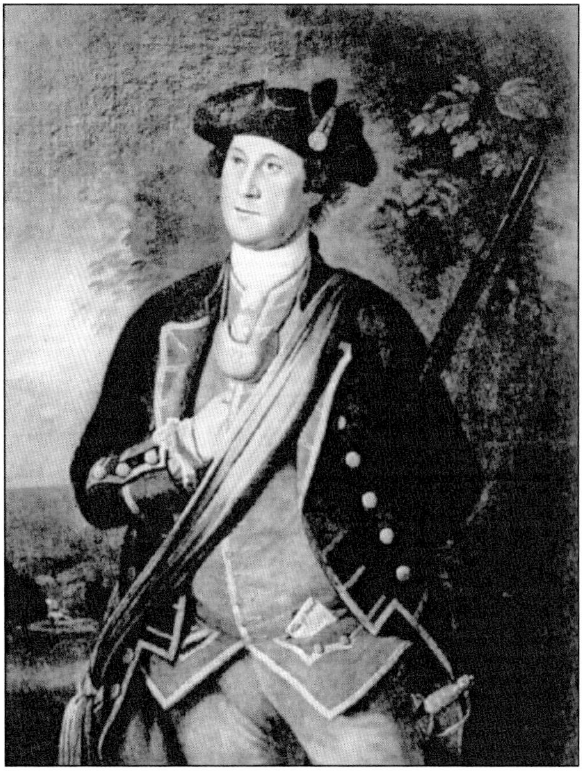

GEORGE WASHINGTON SLEPT HERE. Col. George Washington and his small band of troops camped in a snowy Mingo Town in October and November 1770. He drank from Potter Spring; a marker commemorates the event. Washington's troops had come from Fort Pitt following the Ohio River and scouting the territory for surveying claims. He wrote that Mingo was then inhabited by members of the Six Nations—and by wild geese and turkeys. In his journal, he comments on the commercial possibilities of the river town and notes that local Native Americans trade furs there. Washington is seen as a young man in this painting by C. W. Peale.

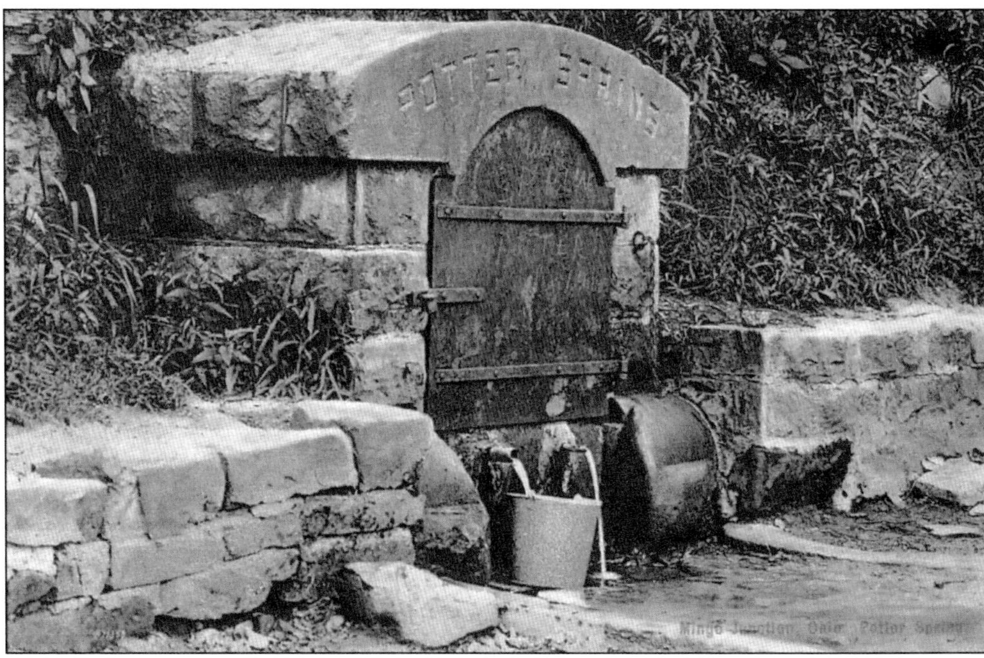

POTTER MEMORIAL SPRING. This early 1900 photograph of the spring shows the central structure located at the base of the hill above Commercial Street near the Potter Memorial Presbyterian Church. (Courtesy Darlene Hoff, originally published in *Bicentennial History of Mingo Junction, Ohio.*)

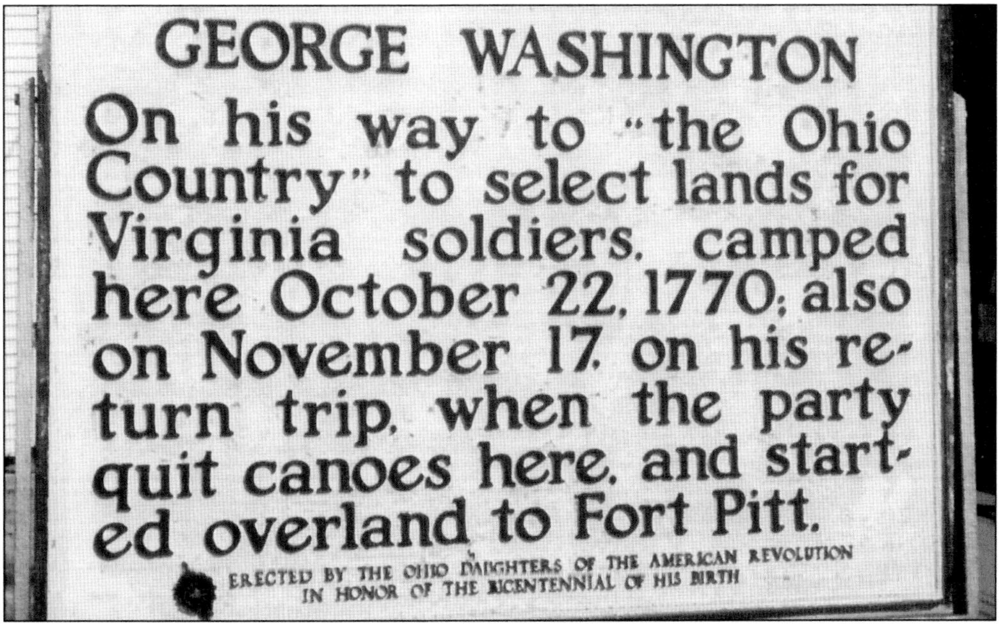

George Washington's Journal, 1770. "October 22. Reached Mingo Town abt 29 Miles by my Computation. Mingo Town was an Indian village several miles below Steubenville. Monday 22d. At the distance of about 8 Miles we came to the Mouth of Yellow Creek opposite to, or rather below, which appears to be a long bottom of very good Land, and the Assent to the Hills apparently gradual . . . About 7 Miles from the last Mentioned Creek 28 from our last Incampment, and about 75 from Pittsburg, we came to the Mingo Town Situate on the West side the River a little above the Cross Creeks. This place contains abt. Twenty Cabbins, & 70 Inhabitants of the Six Nation . . . The Water from little Beaver Creek to Mingo Town, in general, is swifter than we found it the preceding day, & without any shallows . . . The Hills, which come close to the River opposite to each bottom are steep; & on the side in view, in many places, Rocky & cragged; but said to abound in good land on the Top." Below, the Potter Memorial Spring site is seen in the late 1980s as part of a beautification project by the Mingo Women's Club and the city. (Below, courtesy Darlene Hoff.)

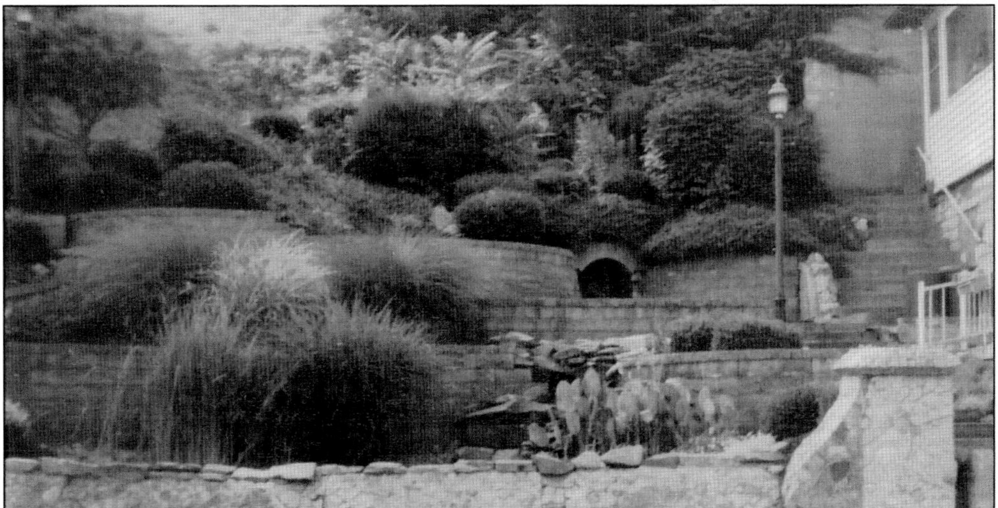

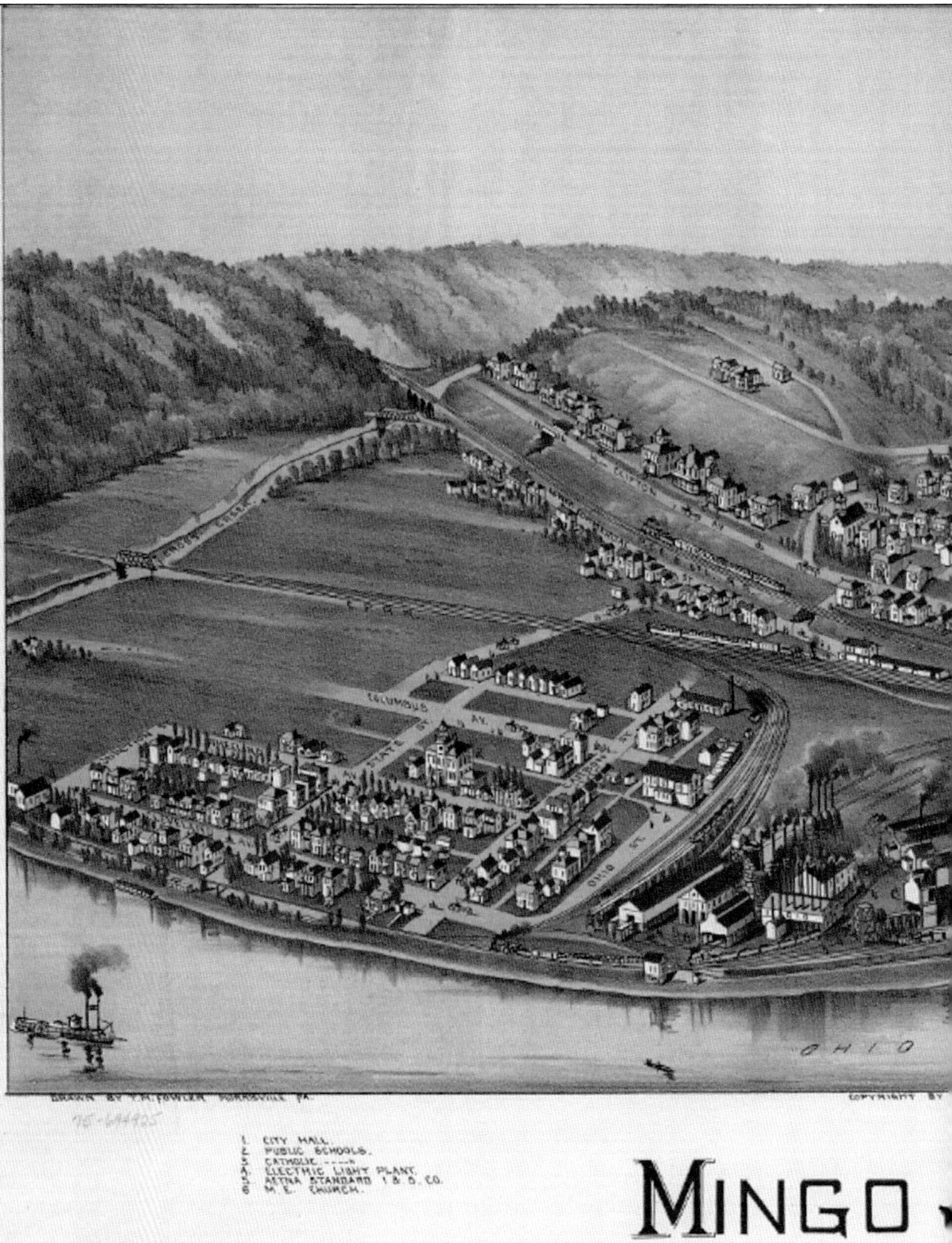

Map of Mingo Junction, 1899. This map of Mingo Junction drawn by T. M. Fowler of Morrisville, Pennsylvania, in 1899 is extremely accurate and reflects the town's basic layout in its hill neighborhoods, its village streets, and business district along Commercial Street. It also

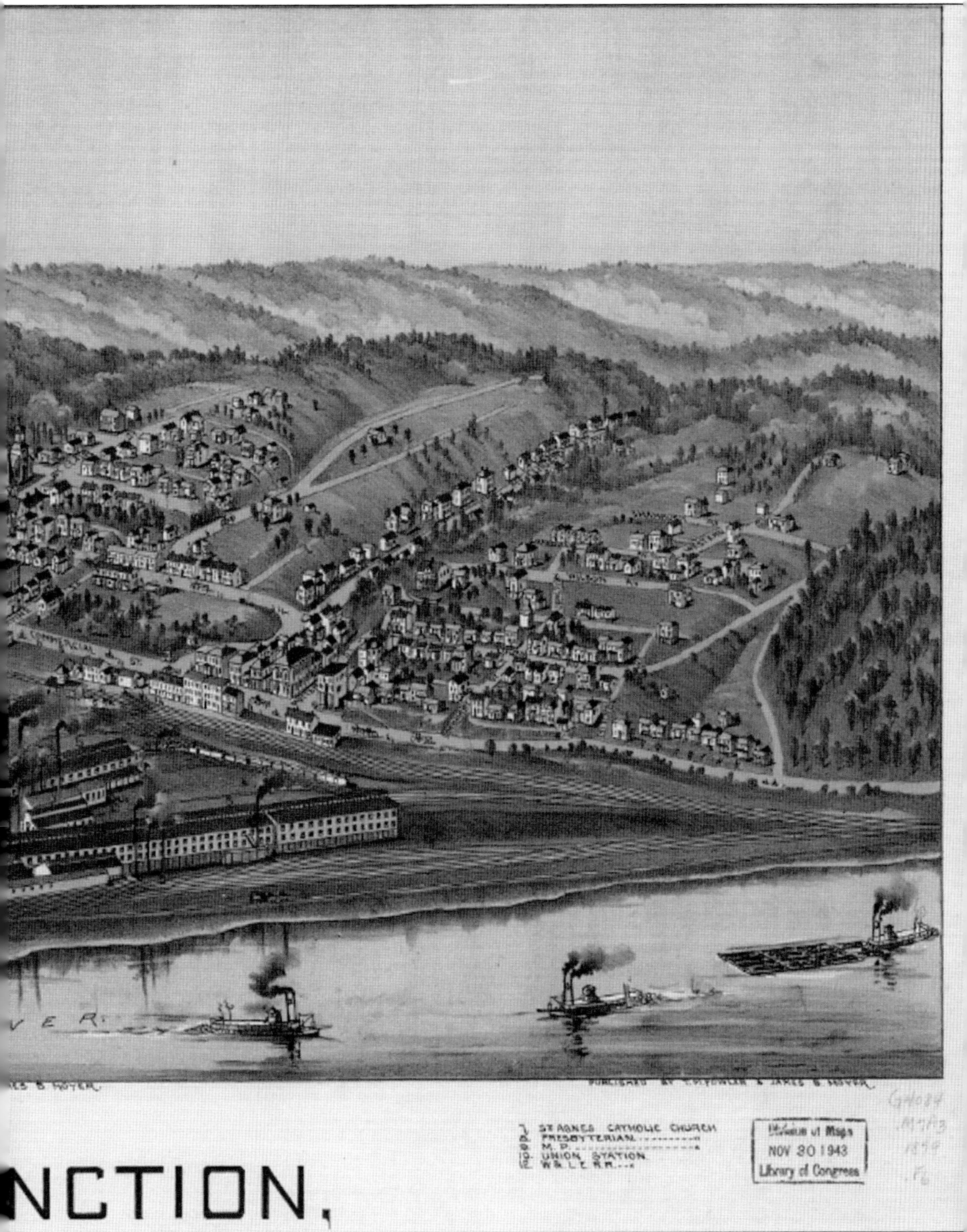

reveals the turn of century importance of the Mingo Bottoms area with its Logan School and Methodist Protestant Church (later Serbian Orthodox Church) near the expanding steel mill industry. (Courtesy Library of Congress.)

"Mingo Junction" As it is now named, is at present the site of a thrifty and prosperous village, designed for a town in the near future. The location referred to, including the property known as Potter's farm, and also the Mean's farm, was purchased, to the extent of six hundred acres, in 1800, by the Rev. Lyman Potter, and his son-in-law, Mr. Jasper Murdock, the former, at the time, being a missionary from the Presbyterian church through Ohio and Pennsylvania. At his death the property was divided into two farms. . . . Daniel [Potter] Jr., at present a lumber merchant in Steubenville, in company with Mr. Abrahams, and Mr. Robert Sherrard, banker also of Steubenville, were made executors of the estate. These gentlemen, under date of June 1871, engaged the services of a surveyor and had the nucleus of the town laid out, consisting of forty-five lots. Mr. Elisha P. Potter next opened up an addition of twenty-five lots. . . . while in December, 1872, Mr. D. Potter and Mr. R. Sherrard, further added a second addition of forty-seven lots—this making the sum total of one hundred and seventeen lots submitted for building upon. It was the fact of the fine iron works being erected at this point that induced the idea of laying out a town, which works run successfully down to 1878, then stood idle for a considerable time, but opened up again brighter than ever in September last, under a new firm known as Mingo Iron Works Company. In 1872, a neat frame Presbyterian church was put up, at a cost of $2,500 at which the Rev. S. Forbes at present [1880] officiates, while the M. E.[Methodist] Church has also a mission here. A very nice public school was built in 1873, at a cost of $3,000, and is well attended. For several years lots sold freely, and fetched good prices, but in consequence of the recent stoppage of the iron works for some twelve to eighteen months, the real estate market in that locality has been exceedingly inactive—a state of affairs, however, that does not appear likely to continue. Nor should we [o]mit to state that about 1871-1872, there was a neat railroad depot erected here, at which there is express and Western Union telegraph agencies, and accommodations for passengers traveling the Cleveland and Pittsburgh or Pittsburgh, Cincinnati and St. Louis railroads, while the station house is used for a post office, Mr. Robert Turner being in charge of the united departments conducted in the building. The iron works company have a mine in operation, with a shaft 238 feet deep, near the depot, which produces an excellent quality of coal from veins varying from two feet to three feet in thickness. On the Means farm there is also a capital drift mine, hence there is no lack of fuel in the neighborhood. In the village there is a hotel, run by mine host A. Carson, and there are also several stores—including a dry goods and notion house by Mrs. Hirshfield, a grocery and dry good store by Mr. David Simpson, and groceries by Mrs. McClusky, P. Goff, &c. In fact, with its railroad and river facilities, an ample supply of coal and abundant excellent water—ready access to Steubenville, and the advantage of a most healthy location, teeming with historical associations, we see every reasonable prospect of this favored spot of centuries ago, yet securing equal popularity in future with certainly enjoyed in the past.

TOWN HISTORY. J. A. Caldwell records the town's history in his *History of Belmont and Jefferson Counties, Ohio, and Incidental Historical Collections*, published in 1880 by the West Virginia Historical Publishing Company.

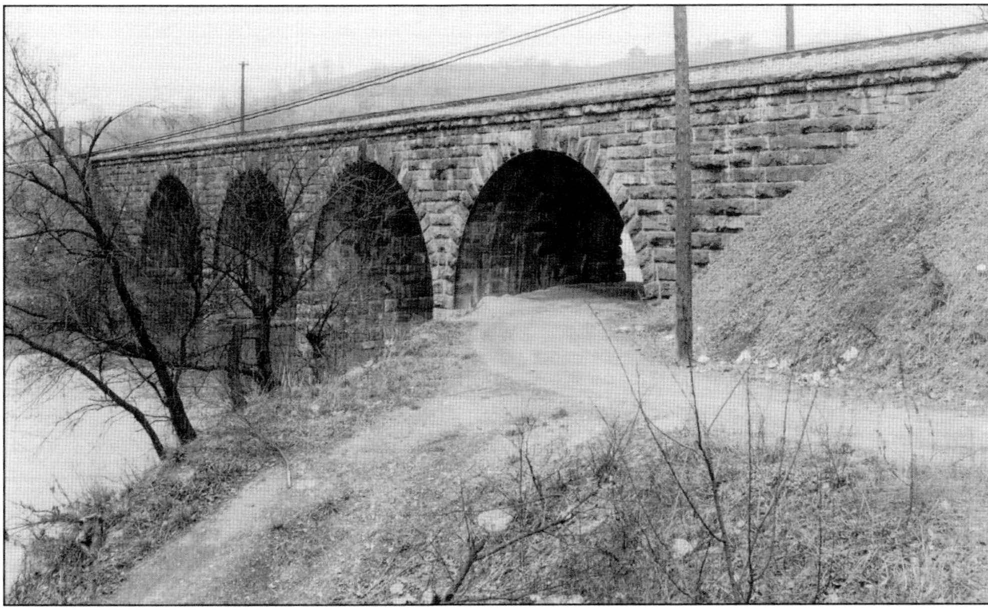

Train Wreck. In 1878, the town witnessed its first rail disaster when two trains going east and west on the same track collided just west of this Pennsylvania Stone Railroad Bridge over Cross Creek. Over 30 were injured, and 14 persons were killed. (Courtesy John Grantonic.)

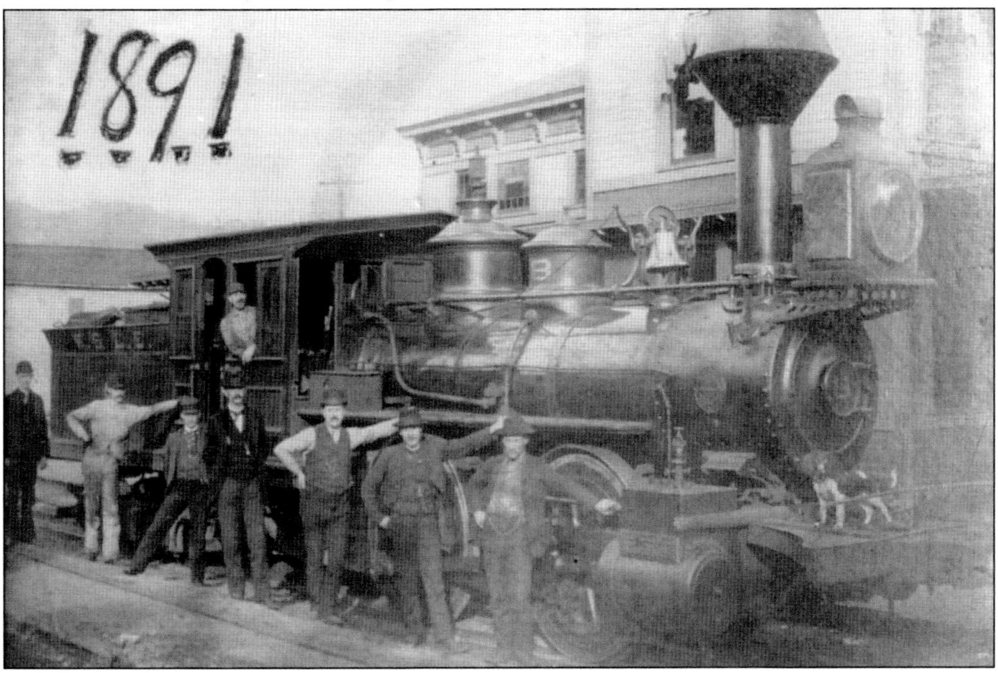

A Railroad Junction. The first railroads came early to Mingo, making it an industrial center and a junction. First came the Steubenville and Indiana Railroad in 1853, for which three locomotives were transported to Mingo by river barge from Pittsburgh. At one point, there were both freight and passenger stations in the town. This 1891 photograph shows the first rail engine entering the steel mill railroad yard. In the image is engineer William James Keys, in the bowler hat, third from right. (Courtesy Charles Roy Keys and Kay [Keenan] Kuebeler.)

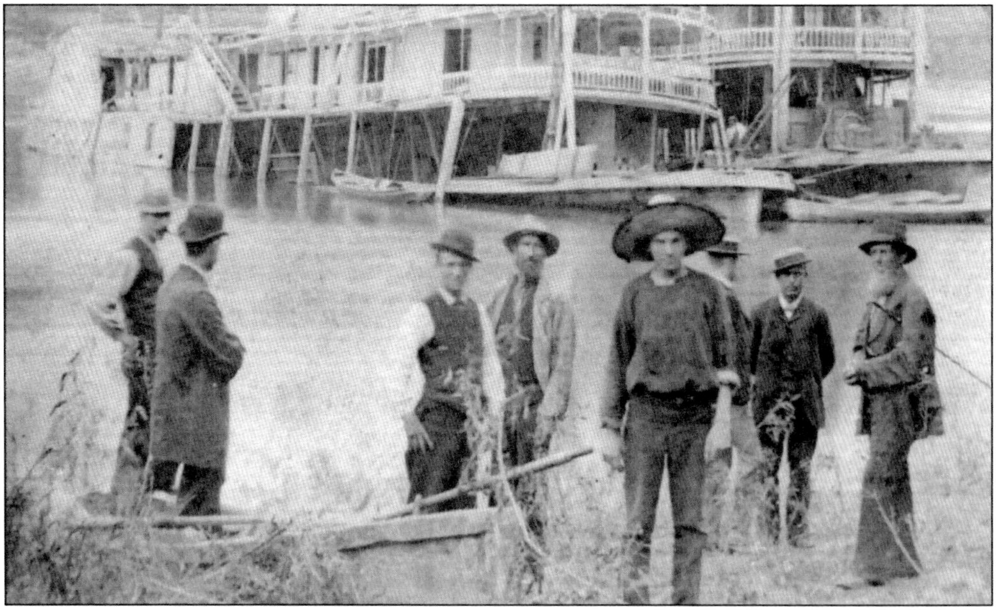

CRASH OF THE EXCURSION RIVERBOATS *SCIOTO* AND *JOHN LOMAS*. Around 8:00 p.m. on July 4, 1882, offshore from Mingo Junction, the *John Lomas* and *Scioto* collided. The *Scioto* was overloaded with some 450 passengers. Both boats were going at full steam and had signaled each other, but confusion resulted in the collision. The *Scioto* was coming upstream from its excursion, and the Lomas was headed downstream. The *Scioto* sank within 15 minutes, and the *Lomas* and surrounding fishing boats rescued many of its passengers, yet at least 75 passengers drowned, including the son of the *Scioto*'s captain, Thad Thompson. According to one report of the scene, "The watchman said he had little idea how many passengers were aboard. There were certainly 400 and possibly upwards of 500. The scene when the collision occurred was simply indescribable, the women running about, clinging to each other and to the men, screaming for their children, their husbands or friends, and the men, their panic increased by the screaming of the women, were unable to collect their wits so as to do anything intelligibly." Below is an artist's rendering of the 1882 *Scioto* and *Lomas* ship disaster that appeared in the area newspapers. (Both courtesy Sondra [White] Hyde; above, originally published in *Wheeling Intelligencer*, July 1882.)

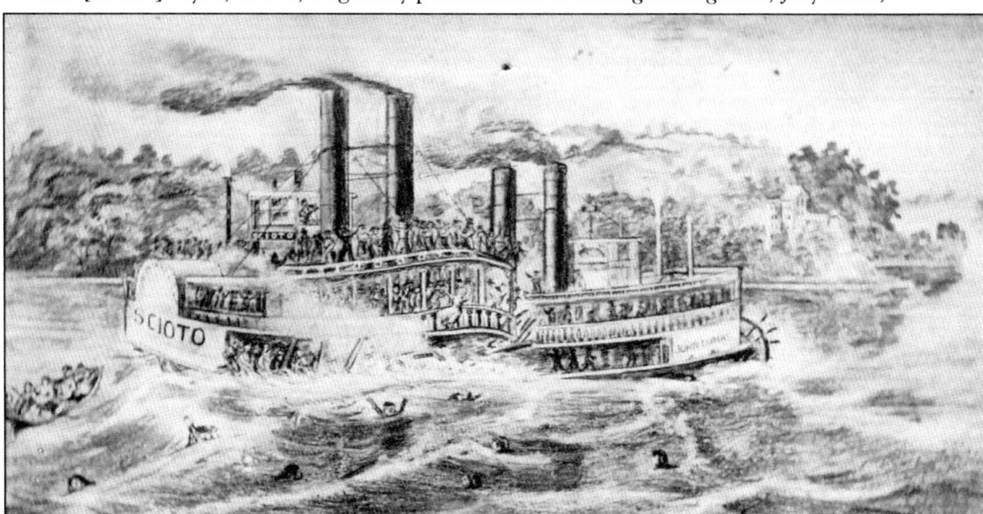

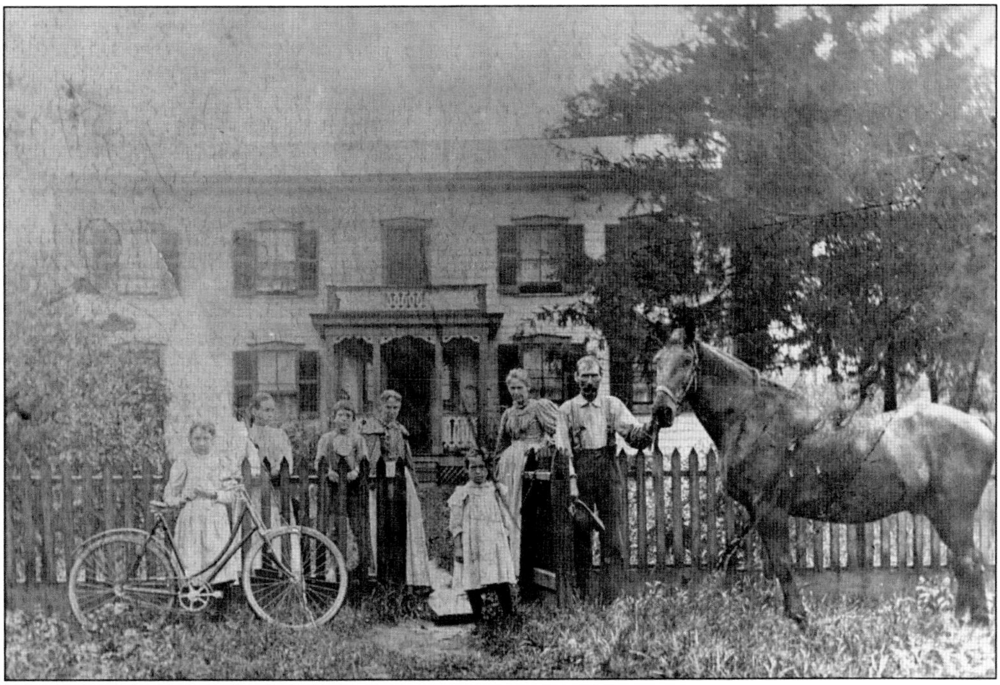

Old Houses. Pictured above is the Adam Peeler house around 1899. On what would become Peeler Street are, from left to right, Kit (with bicycle), Mary, future Mingo chief of police Sam, Elizabeth, Cassie (in foreground), and parents Agnes and Adam Peeler (holding horse). In the picture below is Willa Thompson's home, one of the oldest houses in Mingo. (Above, courtesy Joanne [Peeler] Sogan.)

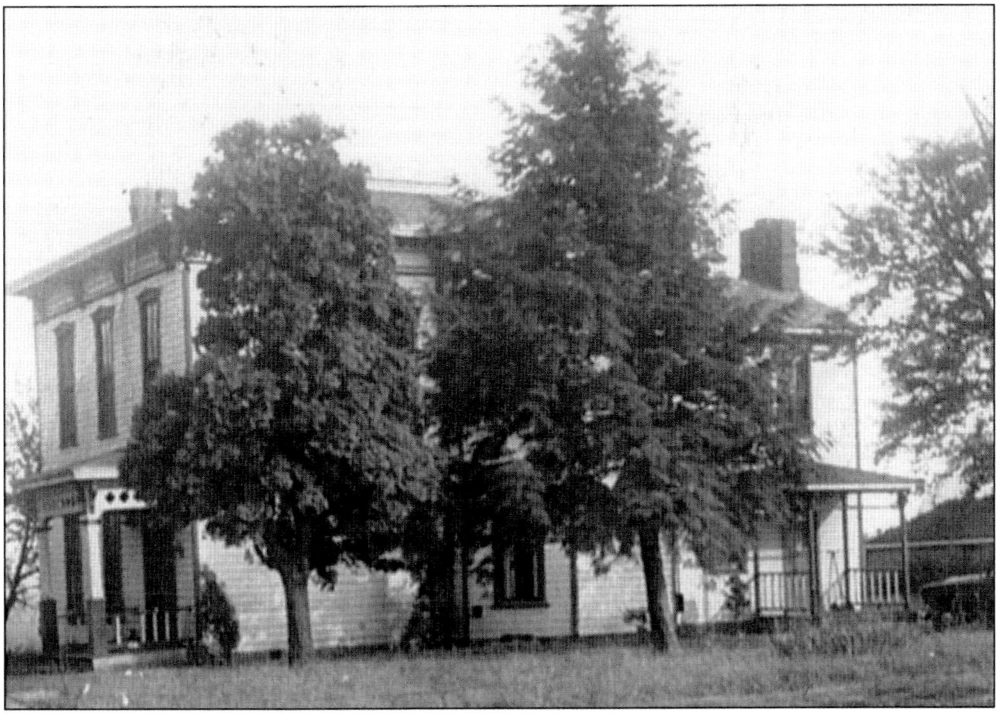

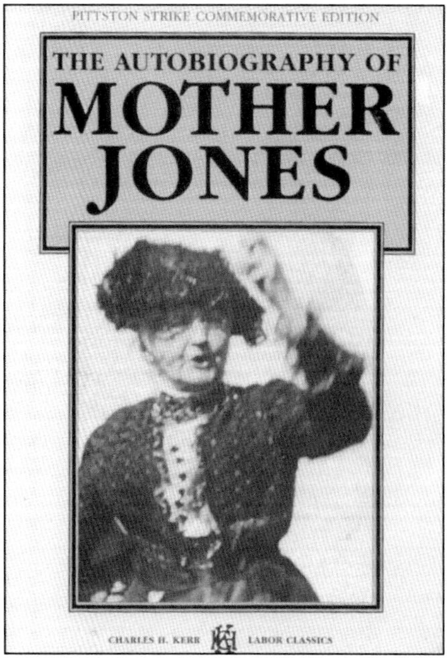

UNION ADDRESS. Mary Harris "Mother" Jones (1830–1930), was known as a "warrior for justice" and an "angel for miners." After losing her family to yellow fever and her home to a fire in Chicago, she became an itinerant reformer and advocate for workers and their families. In 1919, while on a tour of striking mill towns, she came to Mingo Junction and delivered a speech outside of the mill gates. (Both courtesy Charles H. Kerr Publishing.)

222 LIFE OF MOTHER JONES

I was speaking in Mingo. There was a big crowd there. Most of them were foreigners but they would stand for hours listening to the speakers, trying to fit the English words to the feelings in their hearts. Their patient faces looked up into mine. Slag, the finely powdered dust of the steel mills, was ground into the furrows of their foreheads, into the lines about their mouths. The mark of steel was indelibly stamped upon them. They belonged to steel, branded as are cattle on the plains by their owners.

I said to them, "Steel stock has gone up. Steel profits are enormous. Steel dividends are making men rich over night. The war—your war—has made the steel lords richer than the emperors of old Rome. And their profits are not from steel alone but from your bodies with their innumerable burns; their profits are your early old age, your swollen feet, your wearied muscles. You go without warm winter clothes that Gary and his gang may go to Florida to warm their blood. You puddle steel twelve hours a day! Your children play in the muck of mud puddles while the children of the Forty Thieves take their French and dancing lessons, and have their fingernails manicured!"

The Town's Story. *A Mill Town Pastor: The Story of a Witty and Valiant Priest* is the biography of Rev. Daniel A. Coffey, who served the St. Agnes Roman Catholic congregation from 1904 to 1916. This rich biography from his friend Rev. Joseph P. Conroy conveys both the personality of the man and the character of the town. Coffey came to Mingo from Bridgeport, Ohio, and worked as a link between the workers and the mill managers, particularly Supt. George Wisener. Coffey also worked on social reform for the workers and aided them in times of need, such as the flood of 1913. When he passed away in 1916, he was replaced by his good friend Rev. Joseph Dooley, who served from 1916 to 1953.

A MILL TOWN PASTOR

THE STORY OF A WITTY AND VALIANT PRIEST

BY

REV. JOSEPH P. CONROY, S.J.

BENZIGER BROTHERS

NEW YORK CINCINNATI CHICAGO

BENZIGER BROTHERS

PUBLISHERS OF BENZIGER'S MAGAZINE

1921

From A *Mill Town Pastor*
by John Conroy (1921)

CHAPTER IX

THE MILLS OF MEN

IF you travel by rail eastward out of Denison, Ohio, you will observe the grade steadily rising toward the hills along the Ohio River. If your journey is by night, then after the last upward plunge of the train, you sweep around a quick, dipping curve, out of the dark rocky gaps and the black woods on either hand, into what at first glance looks like a night scene in fairy land.

Thousands of lights, like fireflies, pick out the inky blackness. Along both sides of the river, far as the eye can reach, the scene is that of a vast summer garden, hung with Japanese lanterns. Here and there, great bursts of luminous smoke and vapor, copper-colored and pink and purplish white, rise into the air like huge flowered fireworks. A stranger to this locality might suppose it to be a spacious pleasure park until as he looked he would see a huge serpent of fire uncoil from some hidden nest and fling himself venomously up into the night,

98

The Mills of Men 99

stabbing at the darkness with swift tongues of flame. And in the glare that lit up the scene for a moment, he could see that it was very far from being a garden of pleasure. He has been looking at the electric lights and the furnace fires of the mills and factories of Mingo.

The Ohio Valley, meaning by that word the northeastern portion of Ohio, is probably the busiest spot on earth. From Pittsburgh down to Wheeling on both sides of the Ohio, there is one crowding succession of iron foundries, glass factories, steel mills, coal mines, tin works, potteries, oil wells. Within arm's reach all around these are the great plants for the manufacture of automobile tires and all manner of accessories. This entire system goes day and night, without intermission. It is labor on an epic scale. A bird's-eye view of the district would make Homer look about for new similes to visualize multitudes in action; and a "close-up" would very likely give Milton some further ideas for the early books of Paradise Lost and even send Dante back to retouch his Inferno.

Mingo Junction gives us as good a cross section of the Valley as any we could have. It is not as large a town as many others in the ...

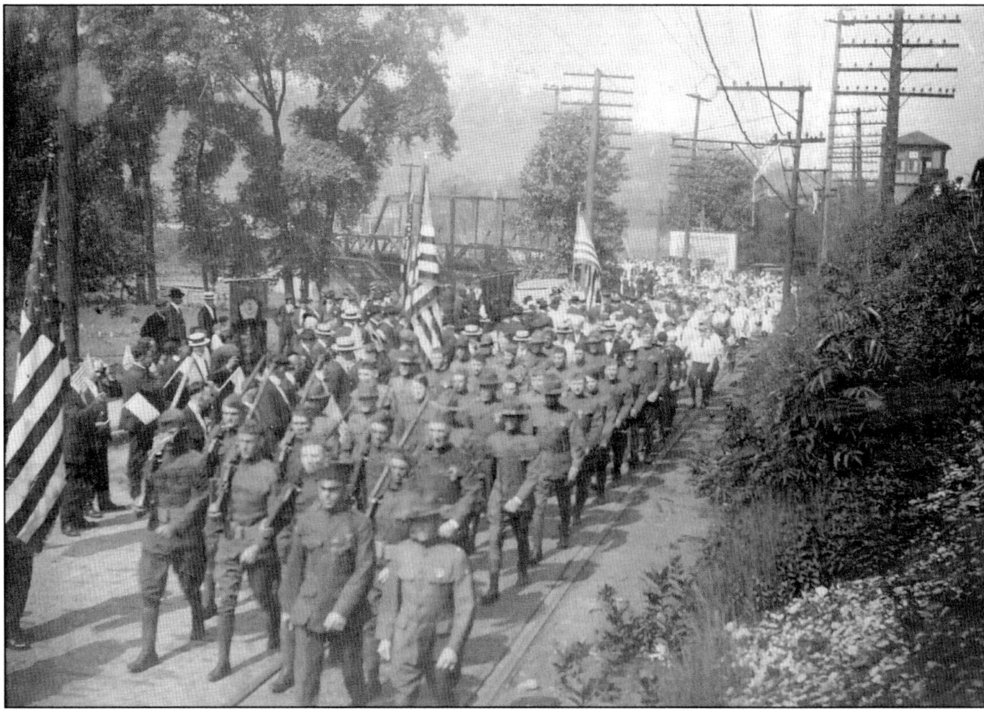

Parade at the End of World War I. Just as the end of the Civil War was celebrated largely in the town at Lyman Potter's farm, so were returning Marine troops from World War I in 1919 as they came parading through town with Capt. Joe Grantonic at the lead (above, bottom right). They passed over Cross Creek Bridge along the Mingo Bottoms area and headed up South Commercial Street. The photograph below shows the parade as it continued through town to North Commercial Street with crowds and dog leading. (Above, courtesy John Grantonic; below, courtesy Eileen [Hagerty] Moody.)

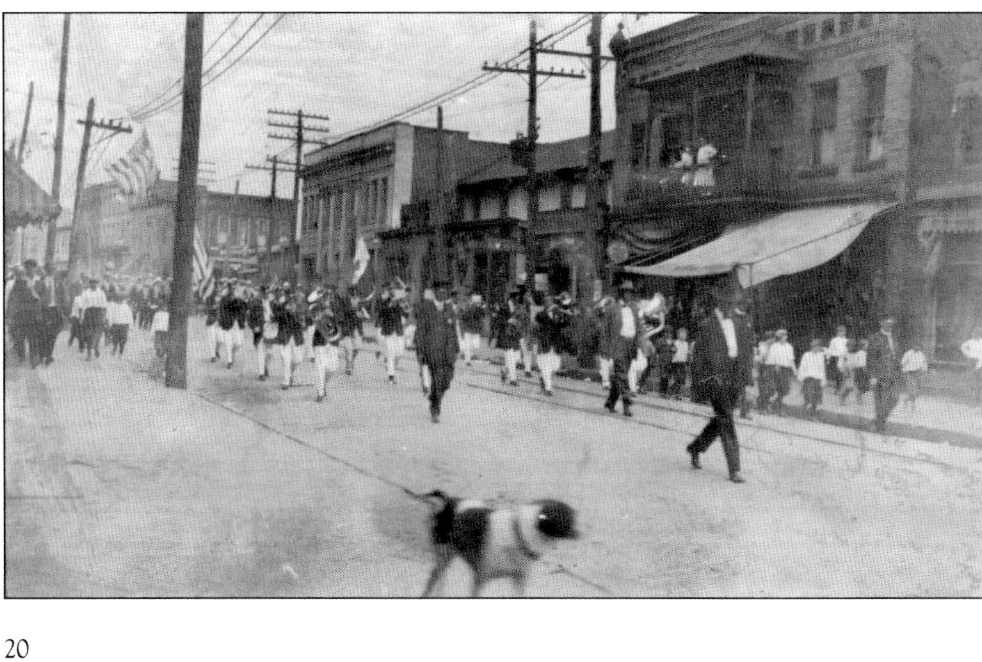

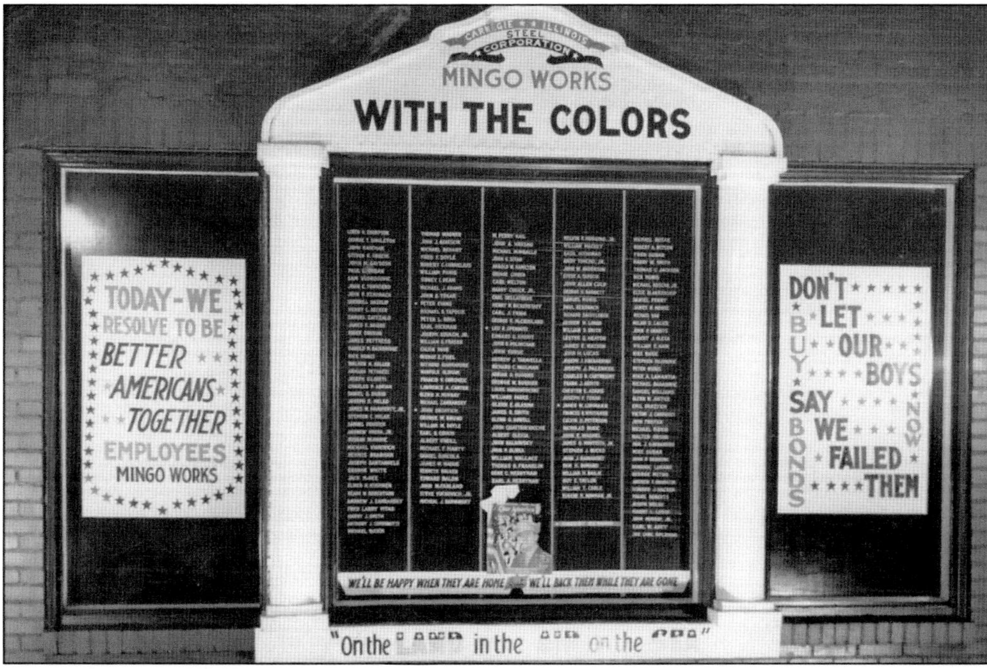

World Wars Monuments. The marker above was located near the Carnegie-Illinois mill gates and the Pennsylvania Railroad Station during World War I. Note the appeal to support the troops; the mill was commended for supplying steel plates for battleships and submarines. The photograph below shows the present-day monument to the soldiers from Korea, Vietnam, and the Gulf, Iraq, and Afghanistan Wars, which is located on Commercial Street near the post office and is maintained by the Mingo American Legion. (Above, courtesy John Buchmelter; below, courtesy Steve Roby.)

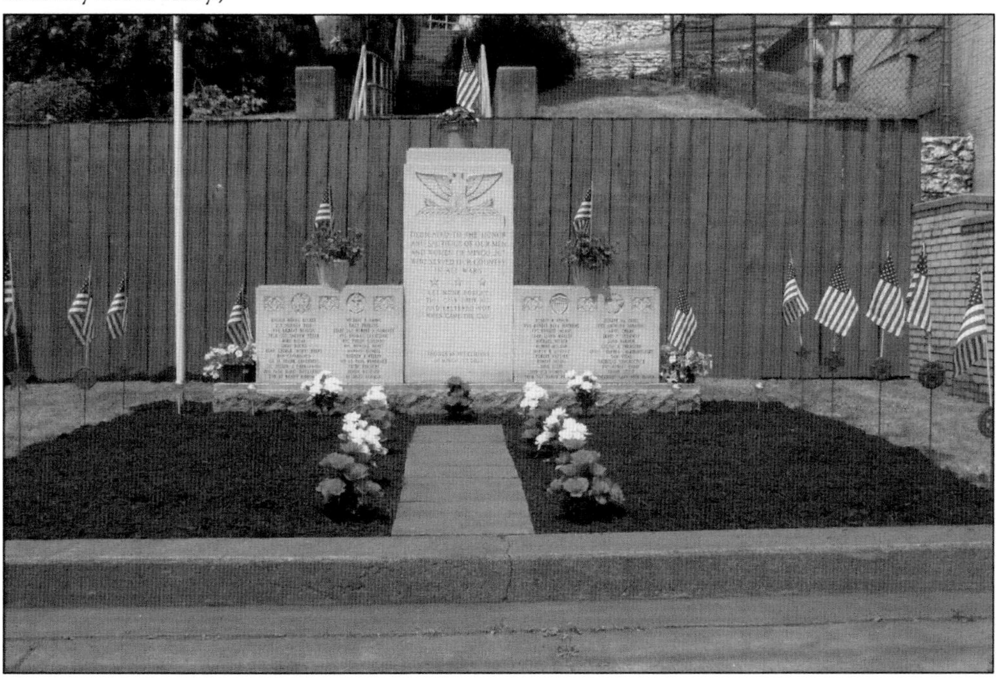

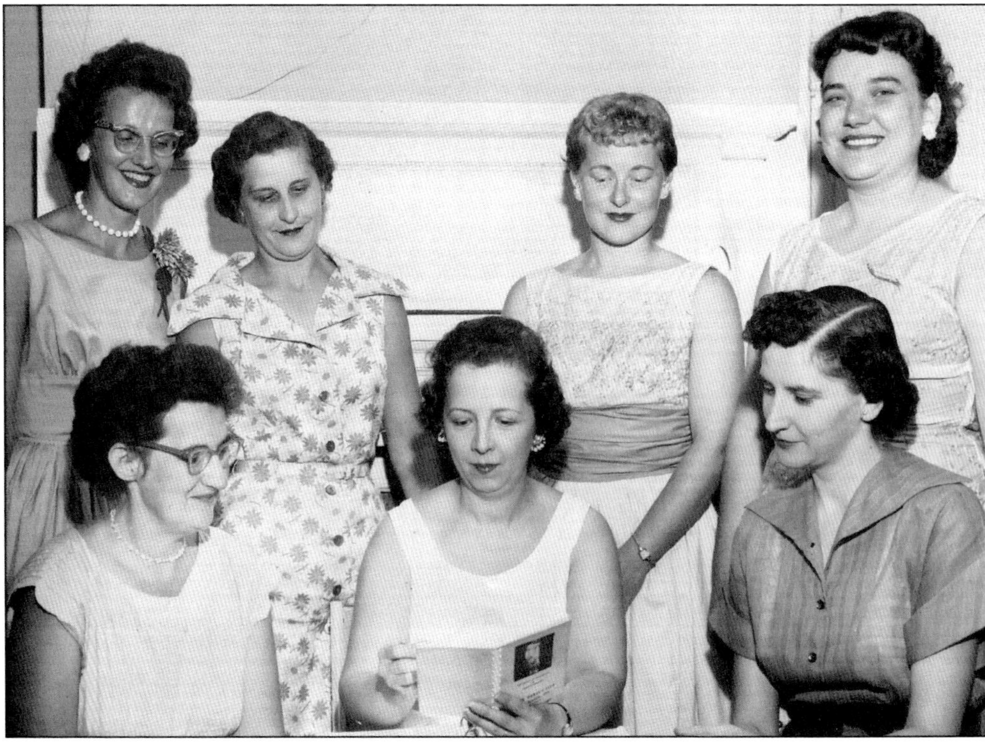

Mingo Women's Club Serves Town's History. This long-standing organization has been the most active group in preserving Mingo Junction history and in working for its beautification with projects at Potter Memorial Spring and beautification of town signs and highways. They also were responsible for publishing the 1937 *History of Mingo Junction* by Anna Brettell, and its members worked as editors of *The Bicentennial History of Mingo Junction* (1970) and helped organize the historical pageant *Echoes in Our Valley* in 1976. Shown here in 1959 from left to right are (seated) Jean Townsend, Darlene Hoff, and Mary Jane Scott; (standing) Mary Alice Trombetta, Mary Agnes Sheline, Mary Gordon, and Marge Swisher. (Courtesy Darlene Hoff, Mary Alice Trombetta, and Mingo Women's Club.)

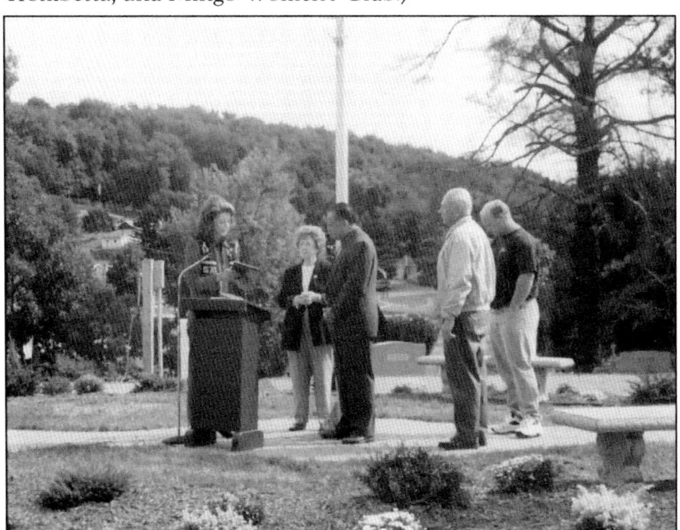

Dedication of Oakland Cemetery Park. The town's beautification and landscaping project for the cemetery and Aracoma Park was conducted by the Mingo Women's Club and the town in 2001. Honored here at the cemetery by Kathy (Valuska) Maguschak are, from left to right, Darlene Hoff, Sam Shorac, landscaper Bud Novak, and an unidentified man. (Courtesy Darlene Hoff and Mingo Women's Club.)

Two

THE TOWN'S CHURCHES

The many churches of Mingo Junction mark its landscape and reveal its rich cultural mix. One of the town's five hills, Church Hill, has served as the site of three of its large churches as well as Mingo's public and parochial schools. The churches have acted as cultural and community centers, and their ministers and priests have typically acted as spokespersons for their largely immigrant, working-class congregations, as exemplified by Fr. Daniel Coffey's service to St. Agnes Catholic Church, depicted in *A Mill Town Priest* by Joseph Conroy.

The 1770–1870 period witnessed Christian missionaries and circuit riders visiting the Mingo Bottoms area, preaching to Native Americans and frontier families. By 1880, the lands of one of those Presbyterian missionaries, Rev. Lyman Potter, were plotted into the town's original lots. In 1873, Potter Memorial Presbyterian Church became the town's first church building, erected on a rise above Commercial Street and the site of Potter Spring. In 1874, the First Methodist Protestant Church began from a group of citizens who had been meeting at the Pennsylvania Railroad Station. Their first church was erected in Mingo Bottoms. In 1883, the large Methodist Episcopal Church was built at its present site on St. Clair Avenue. In 1885, Mingo saw a Catholic mission movement, followed by the construction of a small church in 1889 on St. Clair Avenue, which established its St. Agnes Catholic School.

A pattern was thus established in which a group of citizens would gather, meet in houses or other public buildings, then organize and erect a church. This model was followed by succeeding ethnically identified groups of immigrants. In 1895, the Slovak Presbyterian Church began through an immigration chain from Austria. In 1905, St. Andrew Russian Orthodox and Greek Catholic Church was established, followed in 1906 by Holy Resurrection Serbian Eastern Orthodox Church in the Mingo Bottoms. Another Slovakian congregation developed the St. John the Baptist Byzantine Catholic Church in 1917 and erected a church in 1927. The Harmony Methodist group erected its first church building in 1909 in Deandale, and the First Baptist Church began in 1923 at several sites in the Bottoms.

The 1957–1960 construction of highway Route 7 through the town forced the razing and rebuilding of Harmony Methodist Church and the razing of the Slovak Presbyterian Church, which subsequently merged with the Potter Memorial Presbyterian Church into the First United Presbyterian Church, located on McLister Avenue in the Hillsboro area where Raynes Methodist Church was also constructed in 1961. Today churches remain at the heart of the Mingo Junction community.

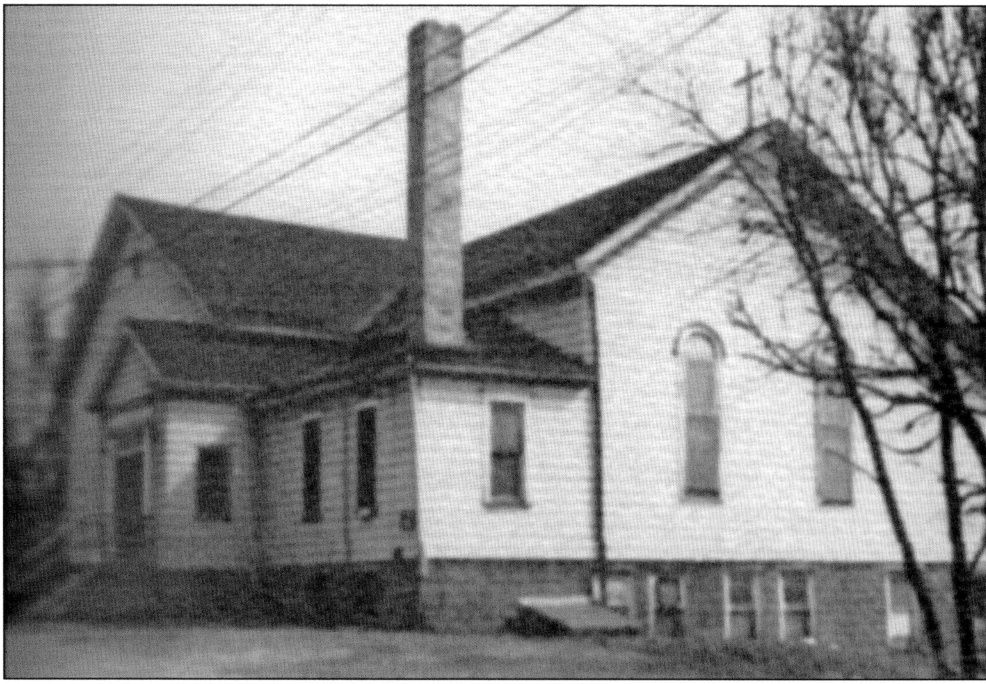

Potter Memorial Presbyterian Church. The town's first church began in 1872 when a group of 16 charter members petitioned the regional presbytery for recognition. On this site overlooking Commercial Street and the Ohio River Valley, a church was built in 1873 at a cost of $2,500 and dedicated on August 17. The first minister was Rev. T. V. Milligan, and early church elders included Adam Peeler Sr., John H. Adams, Elizha P. Potter, William M. Hill, and J. H. Erwin.

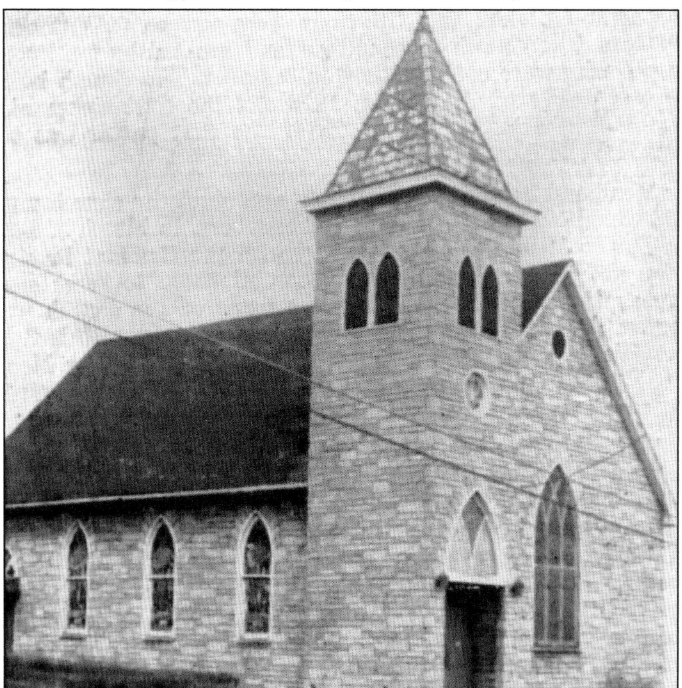

State's First Slovak Presbyterian Church. Begun in 1895 by Slovakian immigrants from the Austria region, the congregation met in members' homes and the basement of the Methodist and Presbyterian churches for 15 years. After this, chartered by the state as the first Slovak Presbyterian Church in Ohio, they erected their own building in 1910 under the guidance of Rev. William Regnemer, followed by Revs. John Bartko and George P. Folta. (Courtesy Darlene Hoff, originally published in *Bicentennial History of Mingo Junction, Ohio.*)

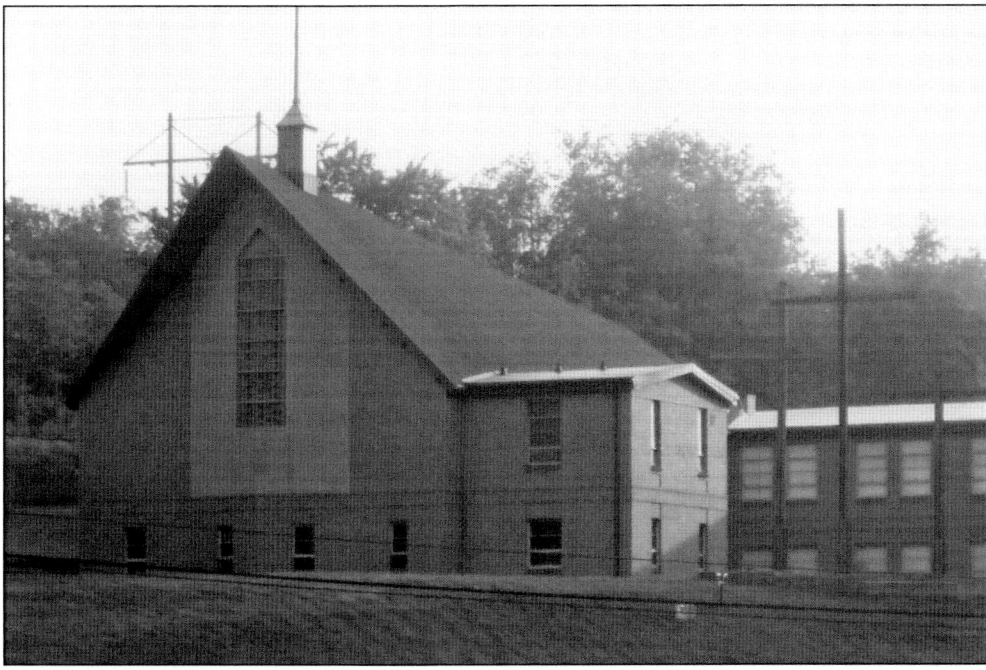

TWO CHURCHES MERGE INTO FIRST UNITED PRESBYTERIAN CHURCH. In 1960, the Potter Memorial Presbyterian Church and the Slovak Presbyterian Church merged leadership and membership, and in 1963, this new church was erected on McLister Avenue in the Hillsboro area. The Reverend Moss Rutan was the minister. The Slovak Presbyterian Church had been razed during the construction of Ohio Route 7. The photograph below shows the wood-and-brick interior of the First United Presbyterian Church. (Below, courtesy First United Presbyterian Church.)

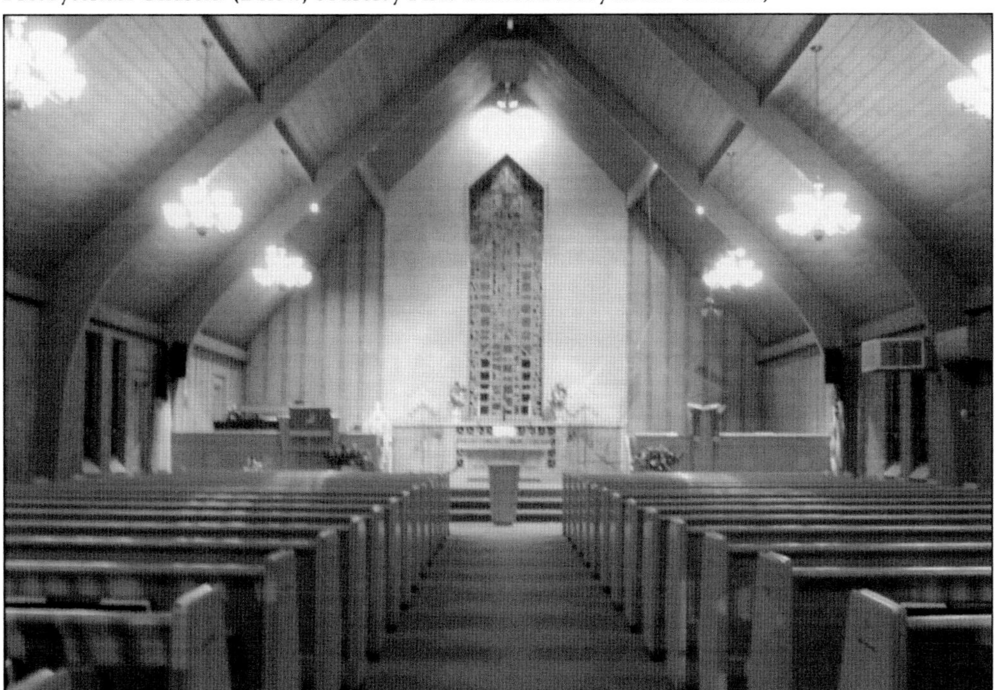

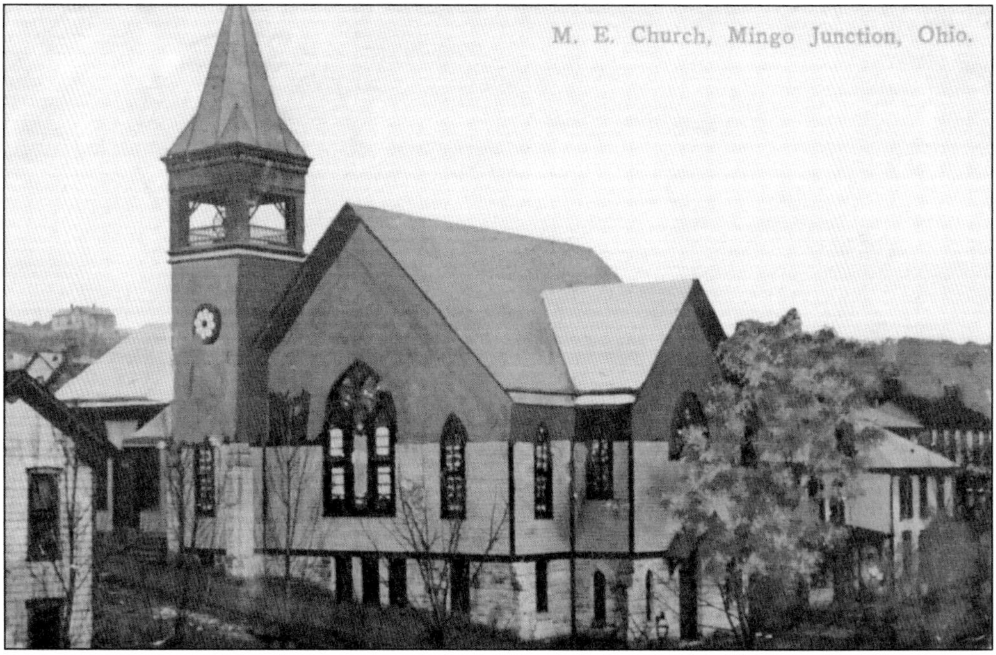

First Methodist Episcopal Church. This congregation evolved from the efforts of Mingo schoolteacher Bernard Herron with the aid of the Reverend Shearer from Wellsburg, West Virginia. The group first met in the Pennsylvania Railroad station; after revival meetings in 1875, Rev. A. W. Gruber was given charge of the congregation. In 1883, they built their first church for $2,300. It was enlarged in 1897 under the direction of Rev. J. S. Jackson at a cost of $7,500 and was enlarged again in 1929 under Rev. A. I. Cox at a cost of $11,500. Many faith and social groups have been active in the church, and in 1917, after a school fire, the church basement was used for school classrooms. The photograph below shows the large pipe organ that Andrew Carnegie presented to the church around 1902. (Both courtesy Madeline [Brinskey] Campbell.)

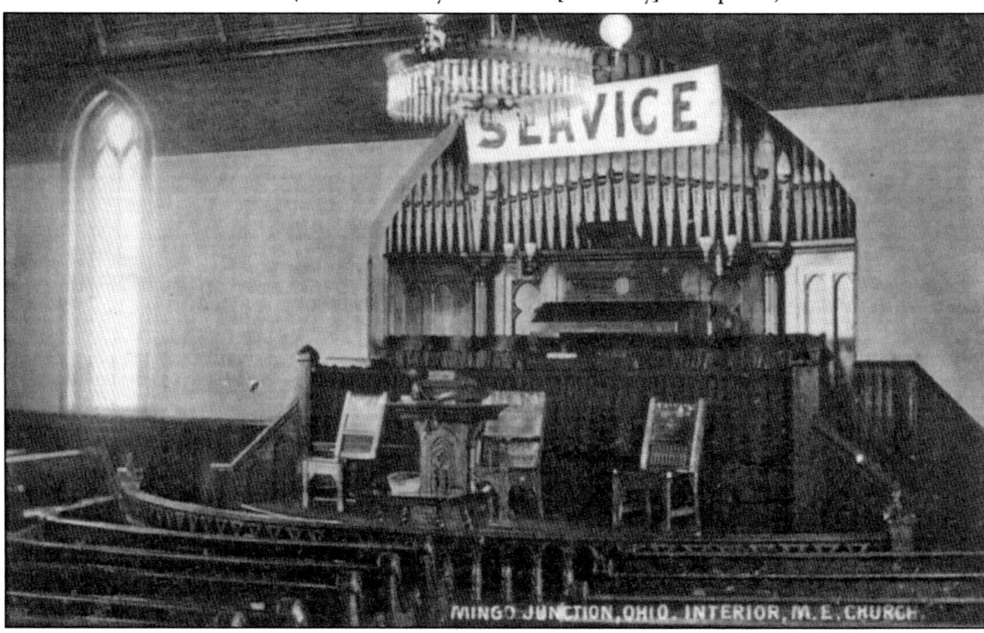

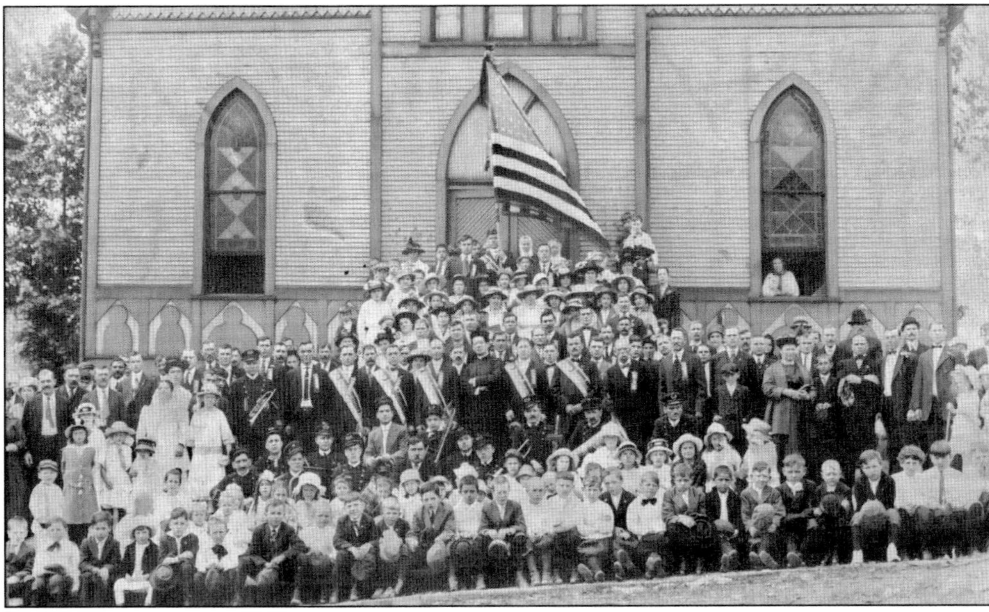

St. Agnes Roman Catholic Church. Following a period where Mingo served as a Catholic mission site linked to St. Francis Church of Toronto, Ohio, a church was built in 1889 on St. Clair Avenue across from the Methodist Episcopal church. The pastor then was Fr. Walter Ross, followed by Fr. John Meade, Fr. Daniel Coffey, and Msgr. Joseph F. Dooley, who led the congregation from 1916 to 1953, a period that included the construction of the large St. Agnes church building. The lower image shows the town's first parochial school, built in 1898 on the corner of Steuben and St. Clair Streets. Grades 1–12 were first taught by the Sisters of Charity from Nazareth, Kentucky; after 1902, classes were taught by the Franciscan Sisters of Charity. When this photograph was taken in 1955, a new school building had been erected on Murdock and Peeler Streets for grades one through eight. (Above, courtesy Nick Trausch; below, courtesy Eileen [Hagerty] Moody.)

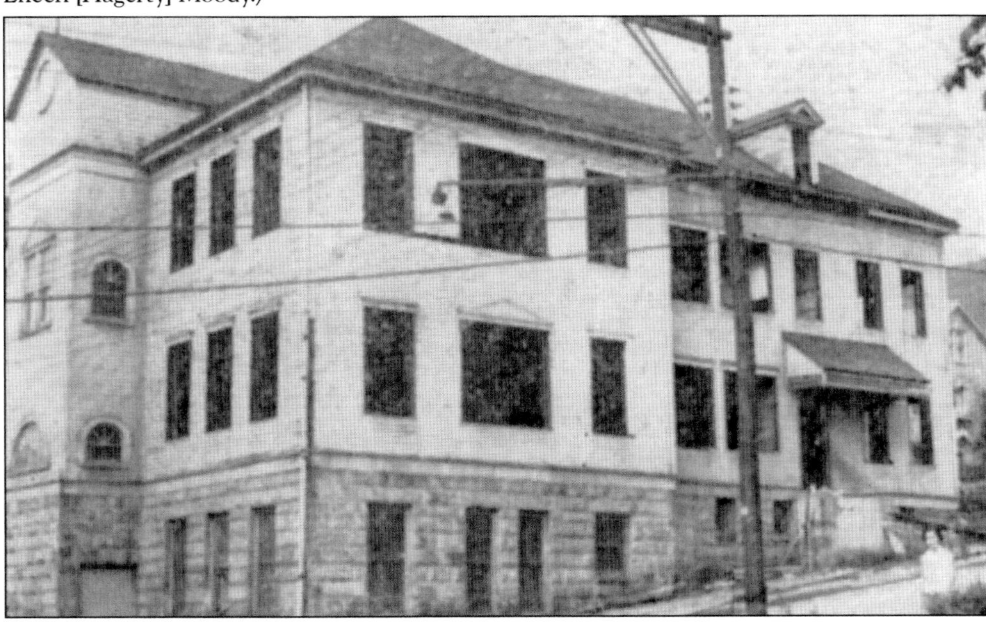

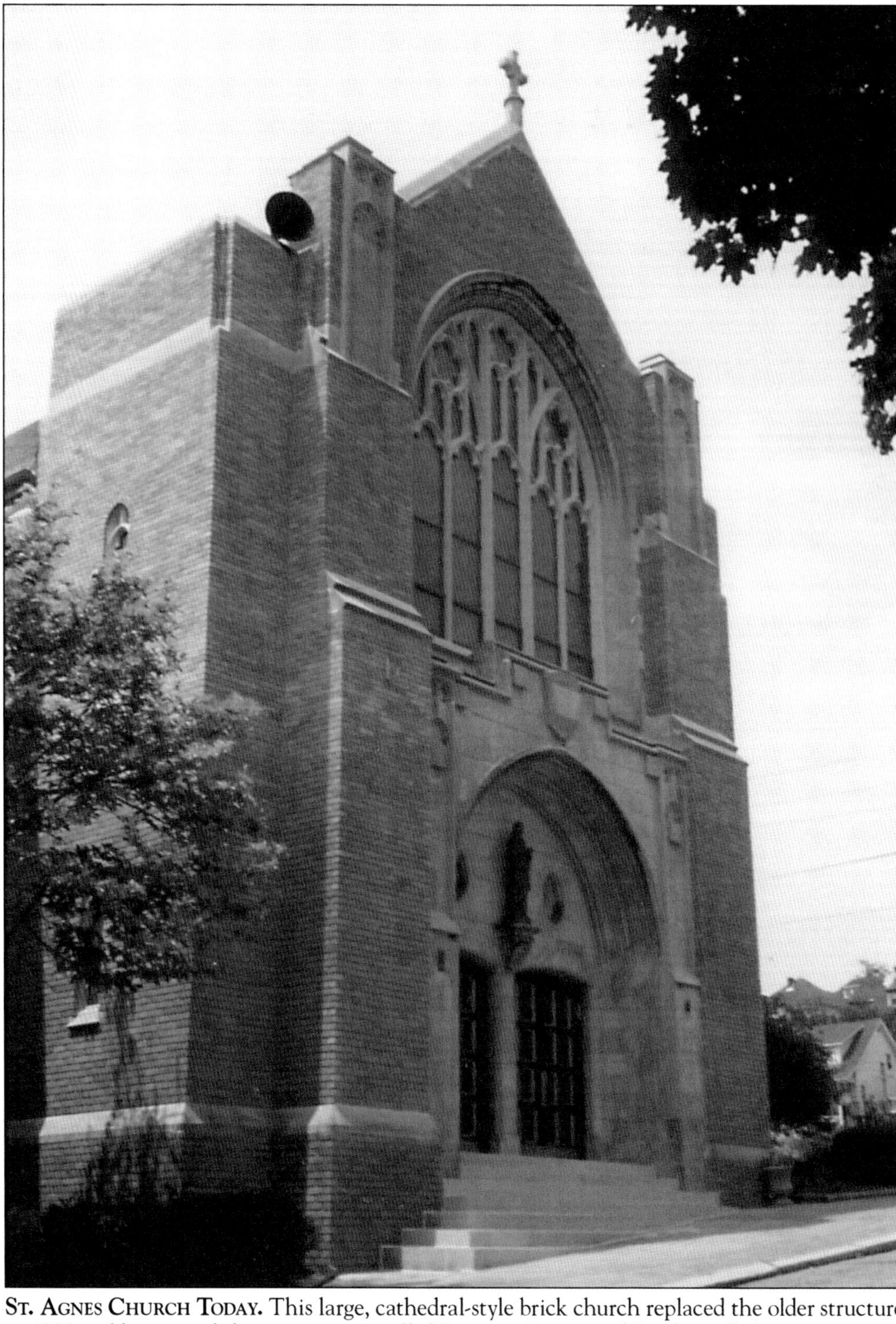

St. Agnes Church Today. This large, cathedral-style brick church replaced the older structure in 1923 and has served the community well. (Courtesy Diocese of Steubenville.)

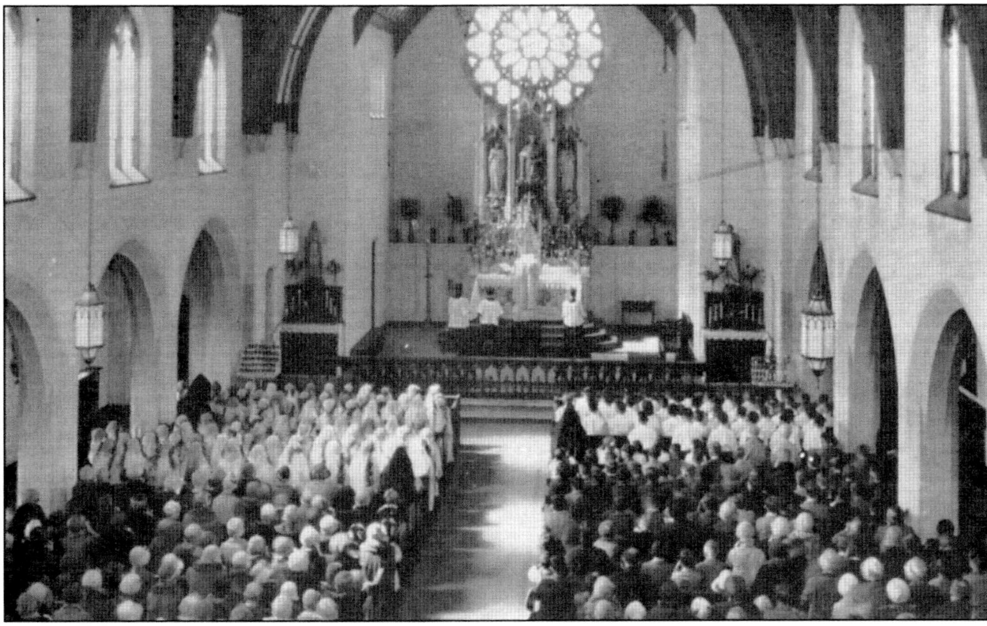

St. Agnes Dedication. The cathedral ceiling and long hall of the main church building houses a large number of people, as evidenced in this church dedication ceremony. St. Agnes's basement, like most of those in the town's churches, also serves as a location for community events. (Courtesy Eileen [Hagerty] Moody.)

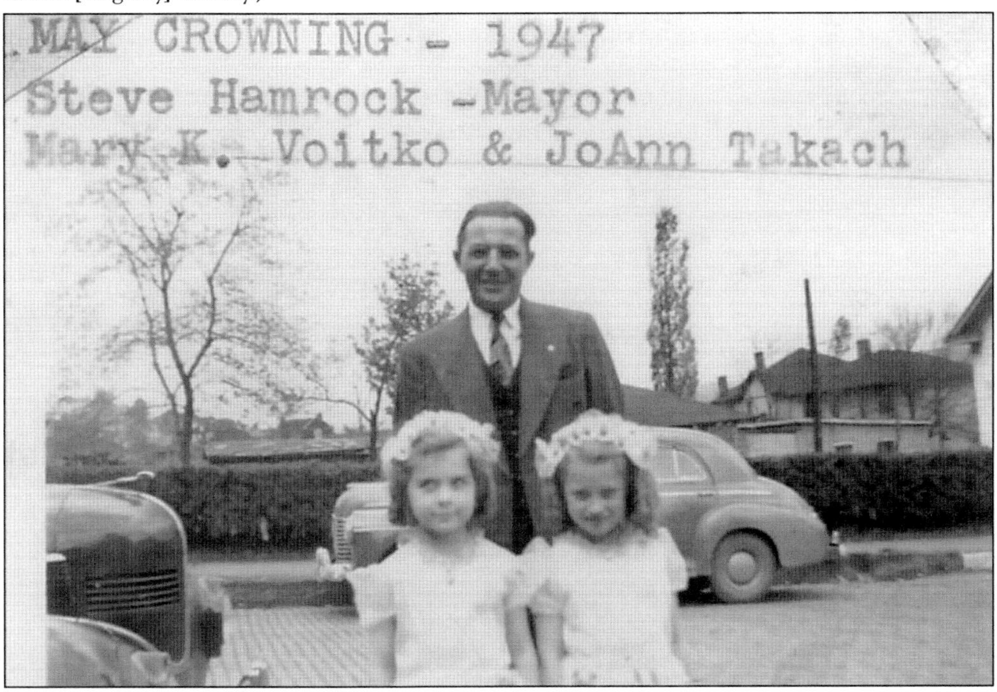

May Crowning Ceremony. As the photograph indicates, the annual May Crowning at St. Agnes Church was a large community event in which youngsters paraded while parents and neighbors watched in awe. Pictured here are Mayor Steve Hamrock and young students Mary K. Voitko (left) and JoAnn Takach. (Courtesy JoAnn [Seville] Takach.)

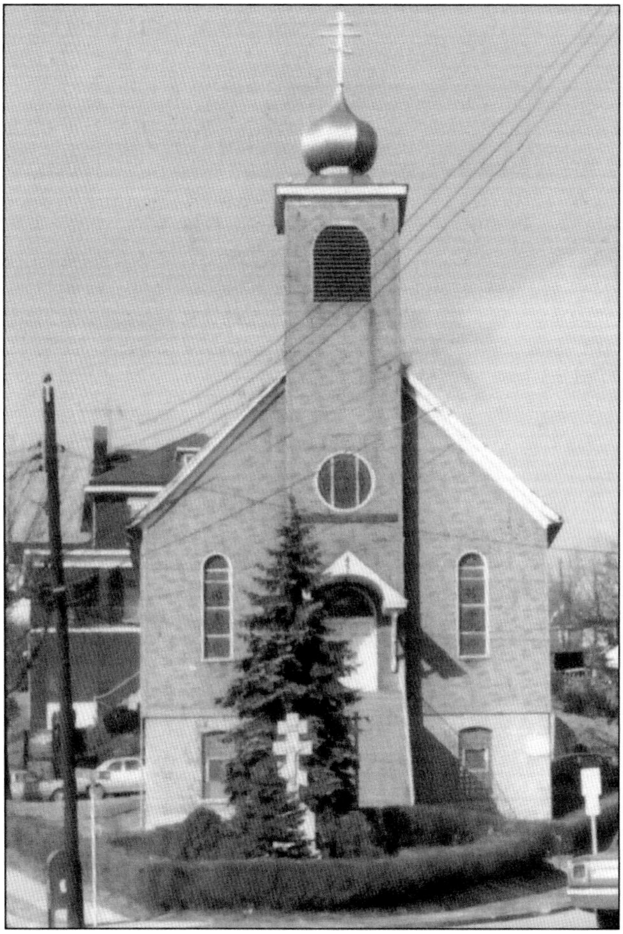

St. Andrew Russian Orthodox and Greek Catholic Church. As one of the earliest immigrant churches, St. Andrew held early meetings in homes, followed by the construction of this church on Reservoir Hill in 1906. This first building was at the corner of Lincoln and Stanton Avenues. Fr. Alexis Toth was pastor, and among early organizers were Stephen Kundrat, Michael Olexia, John Halechak, John Sabol, and Michael Andrachak. The photograph below shows the new St. Andrew's church, built in 1998 near the St. Andrews Cemetery at the top of Reservoir Hill. John Kopcha is the present minister. (Both courtesy Fr. John Kopcha.)

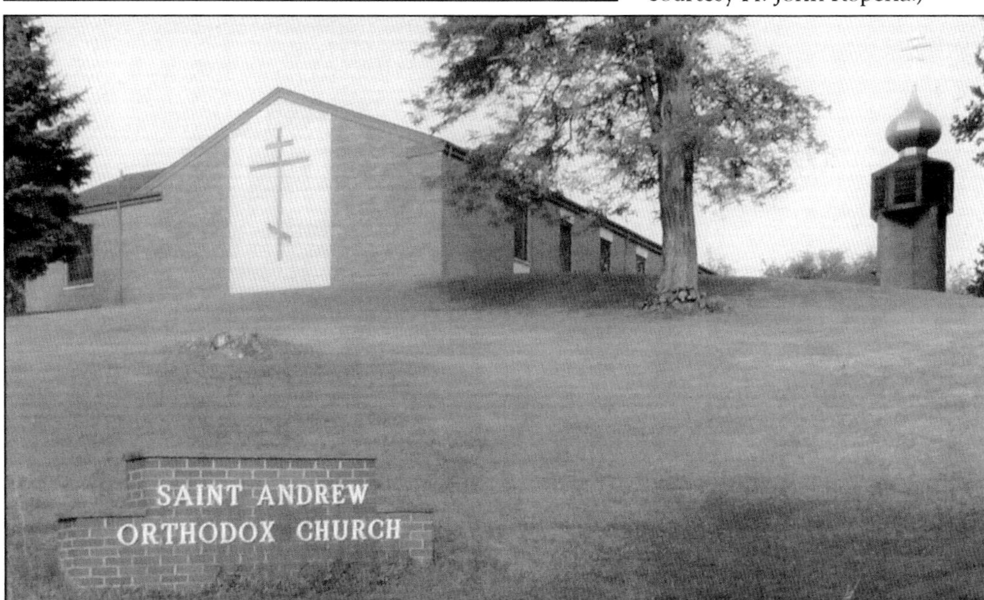

HOLY RESURRECTION SERBIAN EASTERN ORTHODOX CHURCH. This church building located in the Mingo Bottoms area was purchased from the Methodist Protestant Church in August of 1906. It became a center for the Serbian Eastern Orthodox faith, drawing its congregation from as far west as Columbus; as far east as Burgettstown, Pennsylvania; as far south as Marietta; and as far north as Toronto, Ohio. The parish's first priest was Fr. Savo Voyvodich. When the Wheeling-Pittsburgh mills expanded in 1945, the church was sold, and in 1947, its altar was moved to a new church building in Steubenville. (Courtesy Florence [Grantonic] Hirkala.)

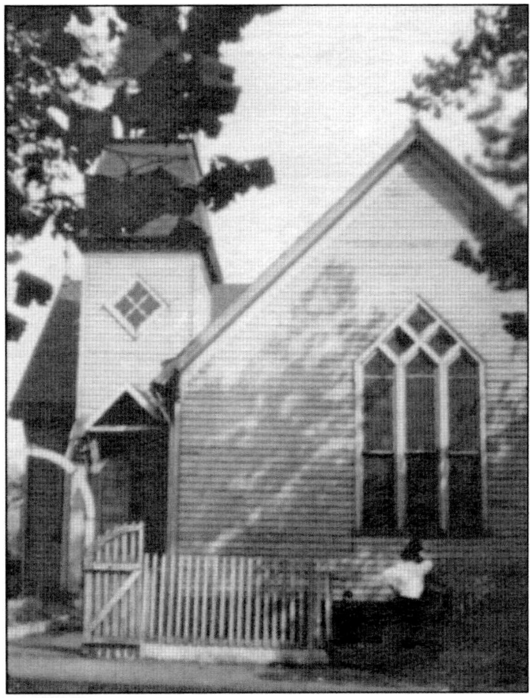

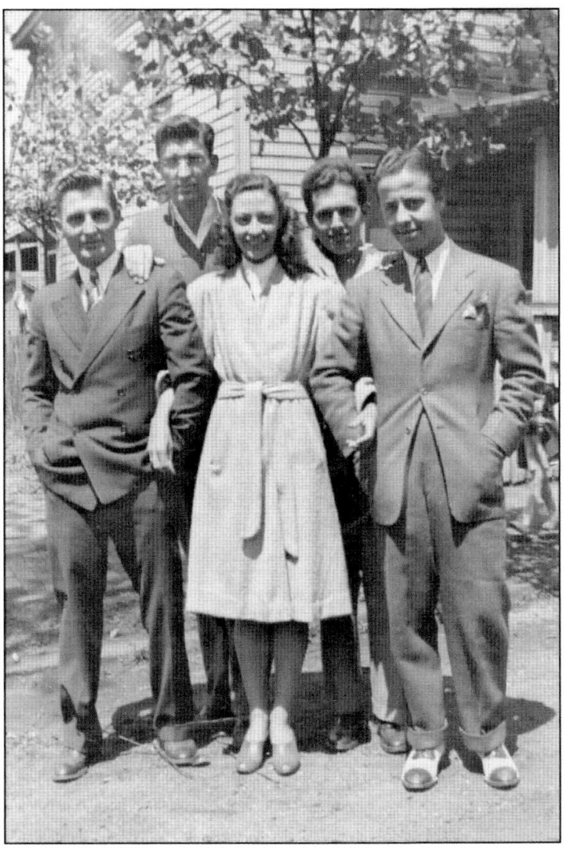

GOING TO CHURCH IN THE BOTTOMS. Pictured in their Sunday best in the 1940s outside the Holy Resurrection Serbian Eastern Orthodox Church are, from left to right, Emil Drzayich, "Stretch" Vujonovich, Babs Zatezalo, Mike Busic, and Nick Vukovic. (Courtesy Mary [Visnic] Drzayich.)

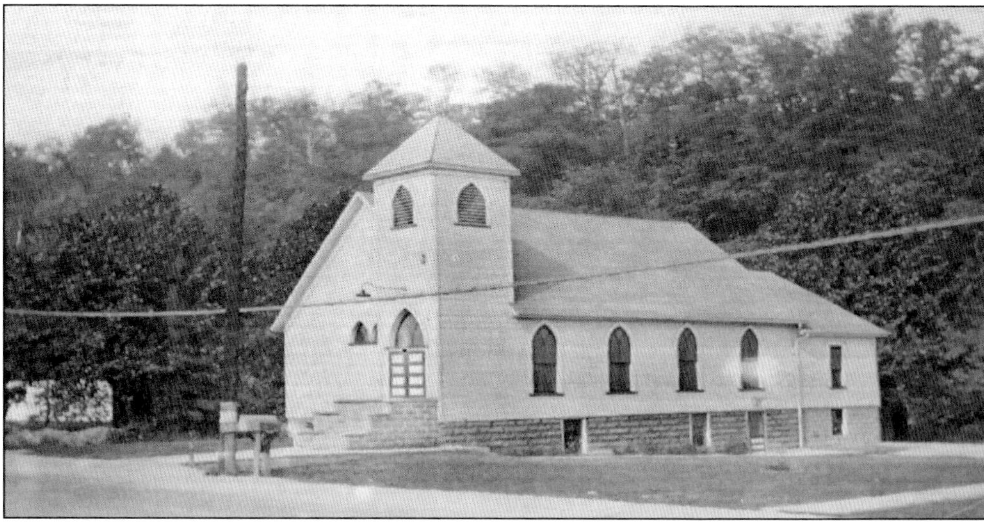

Harmony Methodist Church. This congregation, organized in 1909 in the Deandale-Georges Run area, opened its building on June 10, 1910, at a cost of $2,800. Its first pastor was the Reverend D. B. Cope. In 1959, the building was razed in the highway expansion of Ohio Route 7 and a new building was constructed. Early lay leaders included Urith Gillie, Grace Ingler, Emma McKin, Hattie McCain, Mary Gerke, Mary Ellen Hopkins, May Huden, Corrine Goodrich, and Mr. and Mrs. Ray Miller. Seen below is the new Harmony Methodist Church, located on 2119 South Commercial Street. (Above, courtesy Kathleen Dagenkolp; below, courtesy Virginia Howell.)

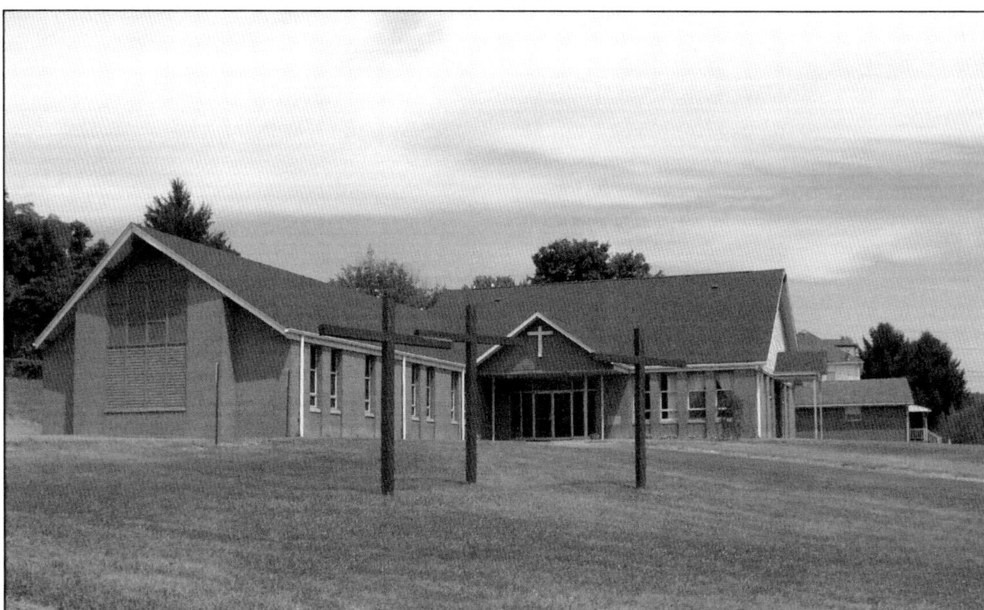

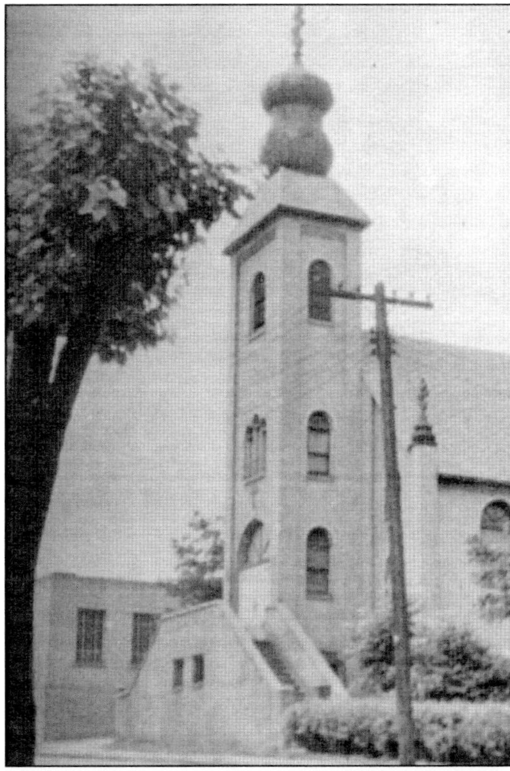

St. John the Baptist Byzantine Catholic Church. This church at the base of Standard Avenue was built in 1927 following 10 years of the congregation meeting in members' homes and at a small chapel on McLister Avenue. The first pastor was Rev. John Sokol. The Reverend Charles Kofile became the first resident priest. (Courtesy Darlene Hoff, originally published in *Bicentennial History of Mingo Junction, Ohio.*)

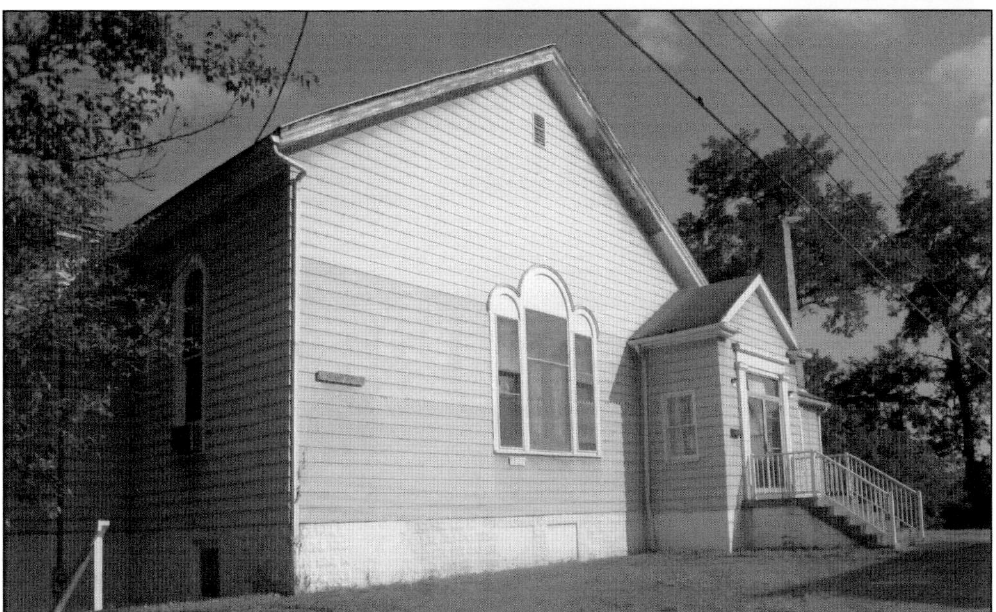

First Baptist Church. This church began in 1923 with meetings on the corner of State Street and Cleveland Avenue in the Mingo Bottoms. In 1929, S. J. Bridges became the pastor and served for 32 years. In 1945, because of mill expansion, they met at 428 State Street. In 1965, under the leadership of Rev. Roosevelt Suggs, they purchased the former Potter Memorial Church on Schoolway Avenue as their new church.

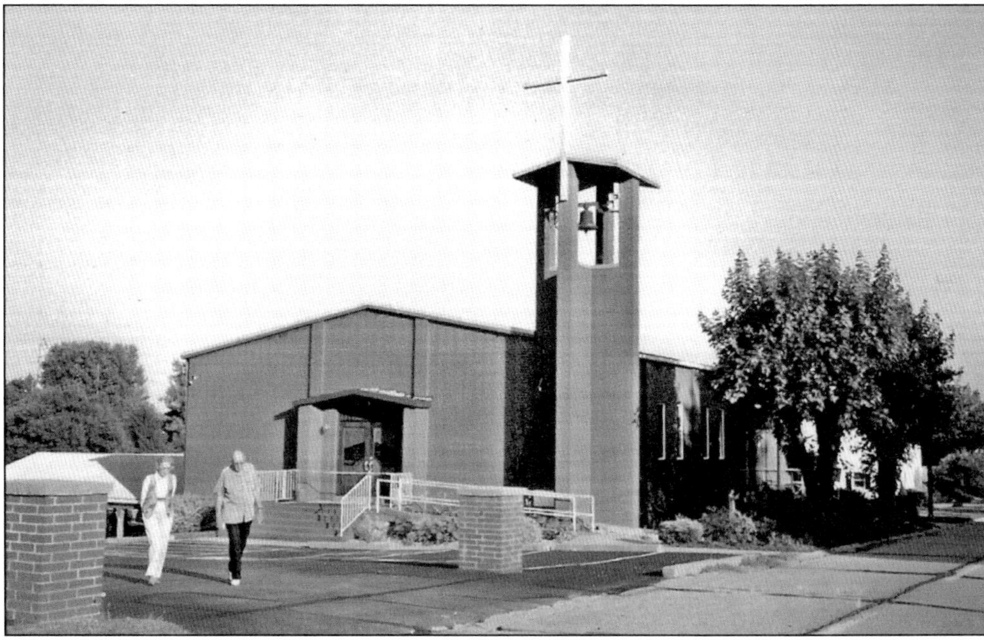

Annunciation Roman Catholic Church. Established in 1950, Annunciation's church building was soon constructed on the Hillsboro site. This brick structure was built in 1960; in 1998, the parish was closed by the diocese. In this photograph are Ed and Peg Bell coming from a meeting to save the church. Another small church, St. Bernadette Roman Catholic Church in the Deandale area, was also closed. (Courtesy Eileen [Hagerty] Moody.)

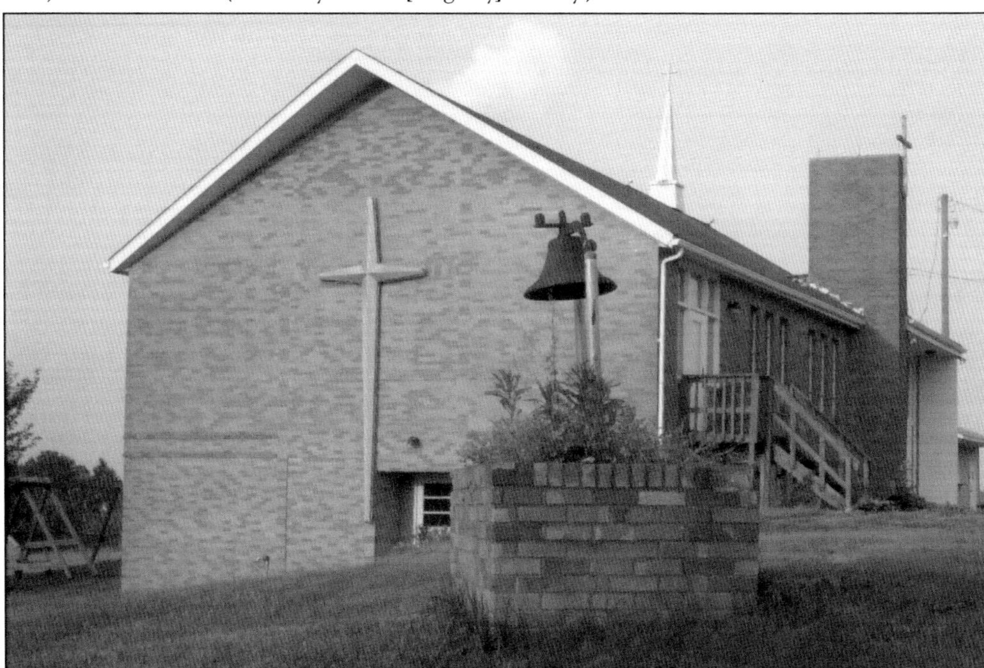

Raynes Methodist Church. Named after its founder, Rev. Ernest Raynes, this brick church was built in 1961, partly to accommodate the population growth in the Hillsboro area.

Three

Schools, Bands, Sports

Most communities look to their schools for signs of progress, success, and excellence for their children. This was especially true in Mingo, perhaps because it quickly became a diverse community with its large influx of hard-working immigrants. Arriving from many different ethnic and religious backgrounds, they saw America as their promised land, and they were willing to do whatever was necessary to ensure better lives and opportunities for their children. Mingo fathers typically worked long, hard, underpaid days—sometimes in unsafe environments. Their wives worked equally hard at cooking, mending, garden tending, water hauling, and laundering, often under primitive and difficult conditions.

Though acceptance of new immigrants who "talk funny" never happens overnight, Mingo was a forerunner in tolerance. Diverse ethnic groups were required to work side by side in the mills, on the railroads, in the coal mines, and in the oil fields, and this commonality of purpose quickly helped to break down cultural and linguistic barriers. Also contributing to this sense of community was the fact that class differences did not divide the town. Mingo has never had big mansions, and this speaks volumes about the town's egalitarian values and sense of unity.

This communal heritage lies at the roots of Mingo's school system; one thing that Mingo residents have always agreed upon is that their children deserve the very best schools and teachers possible. Accordingly, Mingo residents have always provided for school facilities and excellent teachers and principals through taxes and levies. Over the town's 100-year history, Mingo schools have produced multitudes of successful graduates, and Mingo voters have never once turned down a school levy.

The following pages offer a pictorial history of Mingo's schools—the sites, sports, students, teachers, fads, and fun that draw alumni back to town for reunions, year after year.

For much of the research in this section, the authors are deeply indebted to the work of Martha Sisler and Deb Stanley.

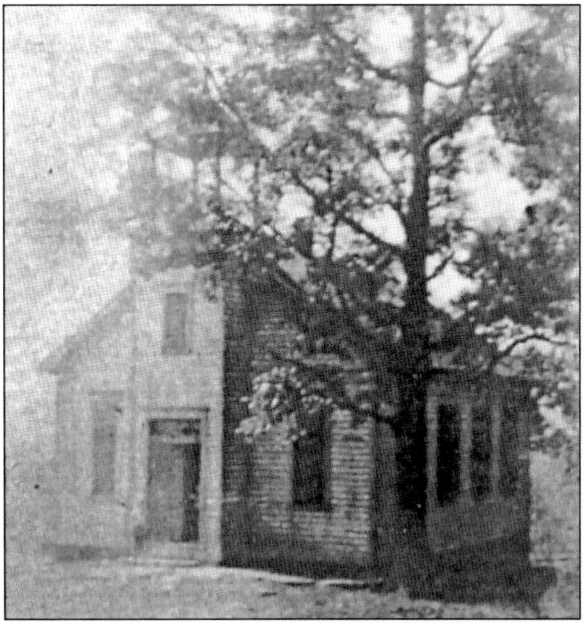

First Schools. One of Mingo's first schools was located west of town in what would become the Hillsboro area on Montgomery Lane, a one-room schoolhouse built on the Hill family farm. The Oak Grove Schoolhouse was later built on the triangle of land where Wilson Avenue and Montgomery Lane meet. In 1897, an enlarged two-room school was built on the same site. The original school structure became a barn on the Malletts' farm. (Courtesy Darlene Hoff, originally published in *Bicentennial History of Mingo Junction, Ohio.*)

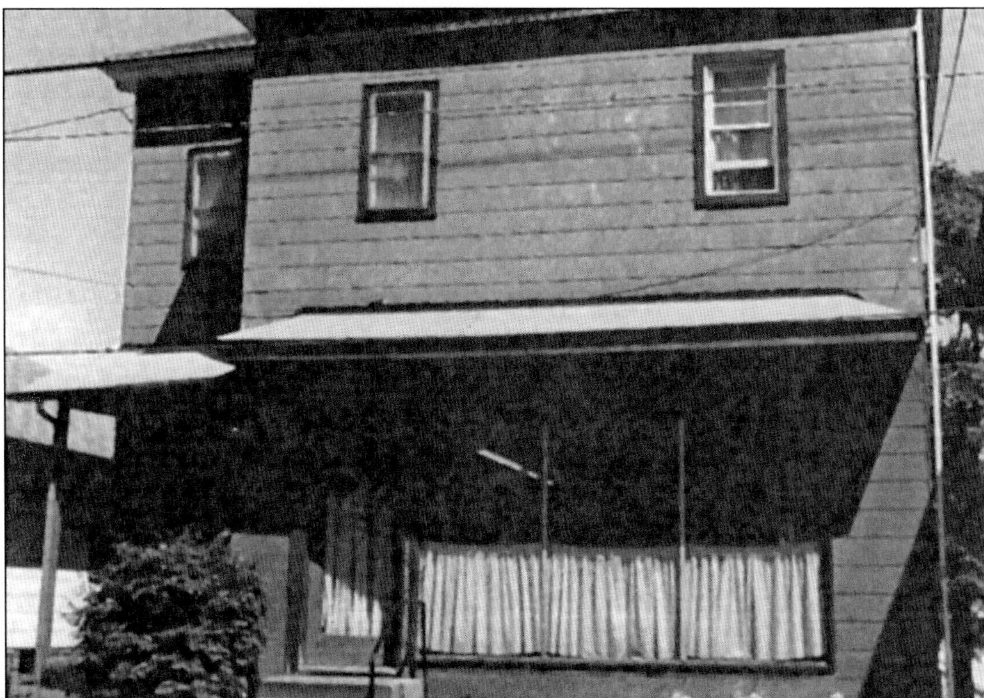

Old Harmony School. In 1856, the first school building in Georges Run was constructed on the Parr Farm and was thus called the Parr School. It was a traditional one-room schoolhouse with classes taught by one teacher. Forty years later, after enrollment grew and a second teacher was hired to restore "harmony" in the classroom, this two-story, four-room structure was built. It was located south of the Parr School and later moved to 2512 Commercial Street, where it was still standing in 2010. (Courtesy Darlene Hoff, originally published in *Bicentennial History of Mingo Junction, Ohio.*)

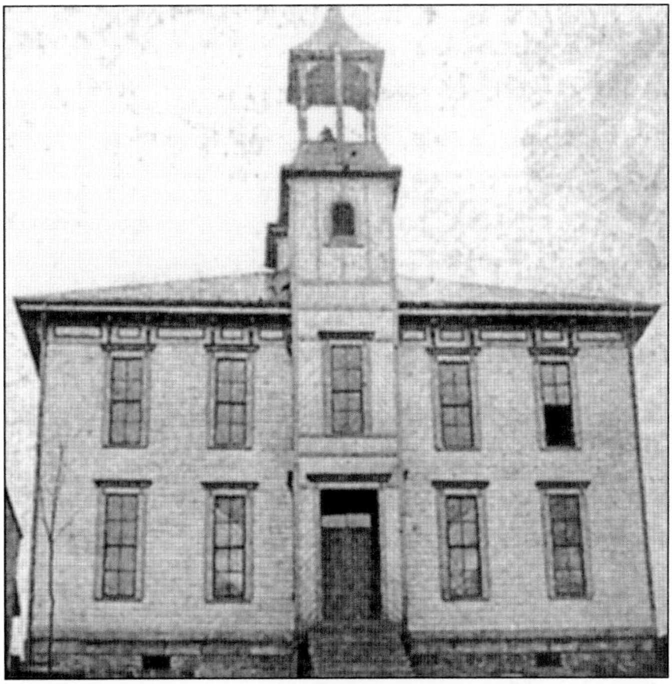

First Town School, 1873. Chestnut Ridge School was built on the grounds of the later Central building facing Commercial Street and the steel mill. It was a frame building of two large rooms—one upstairs and one down. It earned its name from the chestnut trees that ran along the ridge but later was christened Franklin School. Eventually four more rooms were added, and on May 25, 1894, the first five students graduated from high school. To make room for a new structure in 1907, part of the structure was sold and moved to the Order of the Odd Fellows site facing Ravine Street.

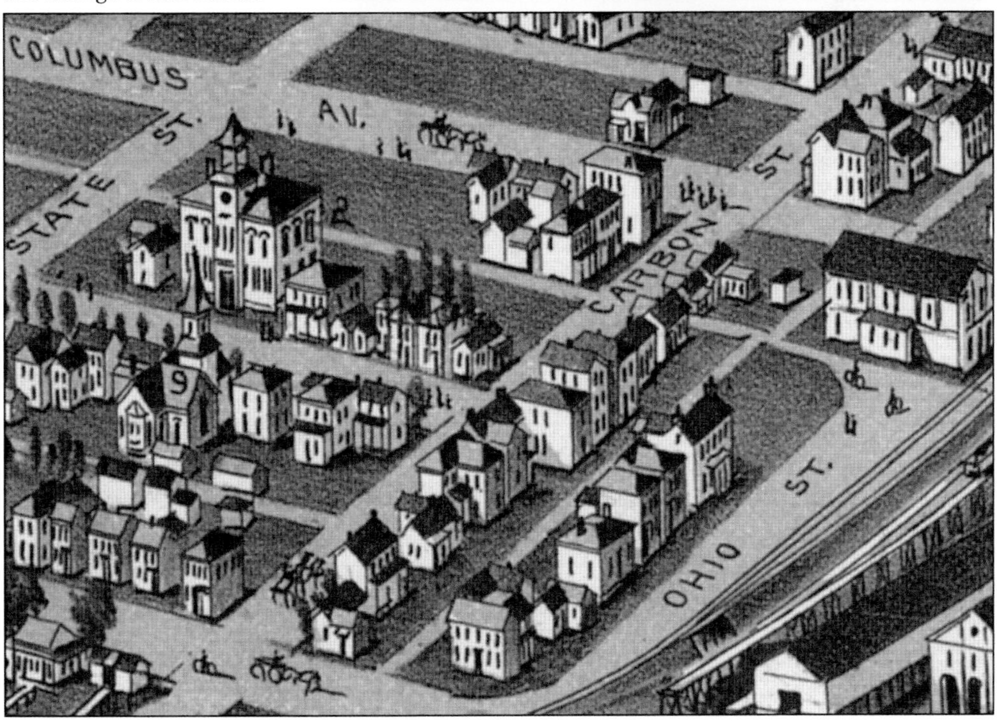

Second Town School, 1886. Logan School, located on the East Side or Mingo Bottoms, was built in part to handle an overflow of students. This 1899 map of Mingo provides a close replica. The building on Wheeling Avenue and State Street was later used for storage, then sold to the Wheeling Steel Company. A vital part of the Bottoms community, when the school was taken down in 1936, children from the Bottoms gathered up and sold remembrance bricks.

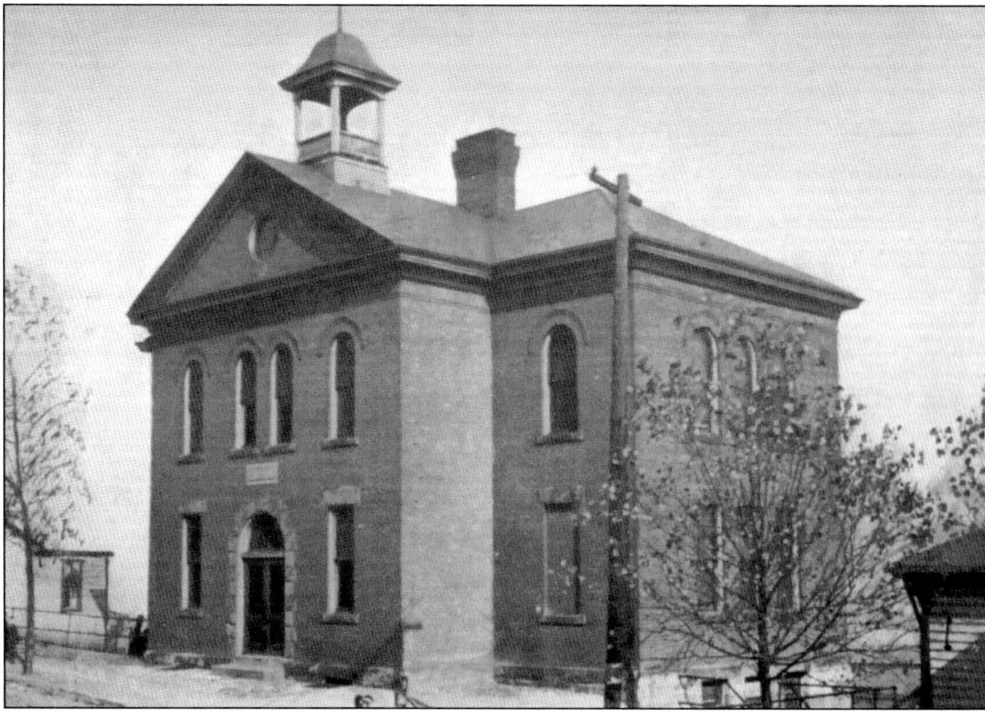

THE LINCOLN SCHOOL, 1893. The children of the North Hill area welcomed this building on its original 36-acre lot along Logan Street in 1893. The four rooms of the two-story were later expanded to eight; a playground encircled the building, which sat on a rise overlooking Commercial Street and the steel mill. The building sat closed for many years before it was demolished in 1962. Effie Farmer was the school's first principal, followed by Alice Edmonds and Emily Diday. (Courtesy Sondra [White] Hyde.)

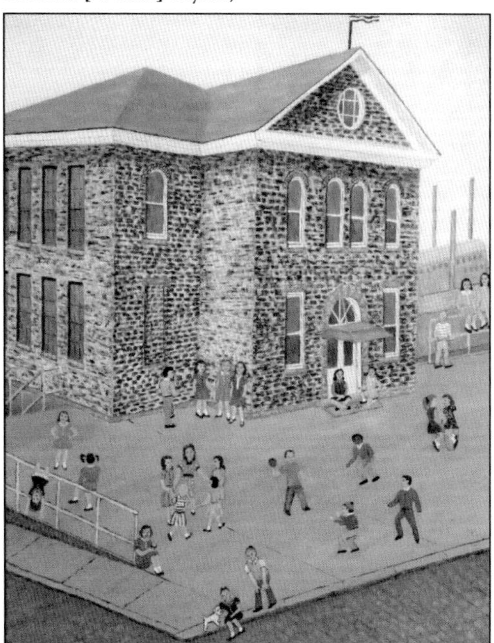

THE LINCOLN SCHOOL DRAWING. This painting by Sharon (White) Farmer depicts one of the most common sights in this small town: children at play on the school playground. The building is Lincoln Elementary School on North Hill, where the White family children attended—along with many decades of others. (Courtesy Sondra [White] Hyde.)

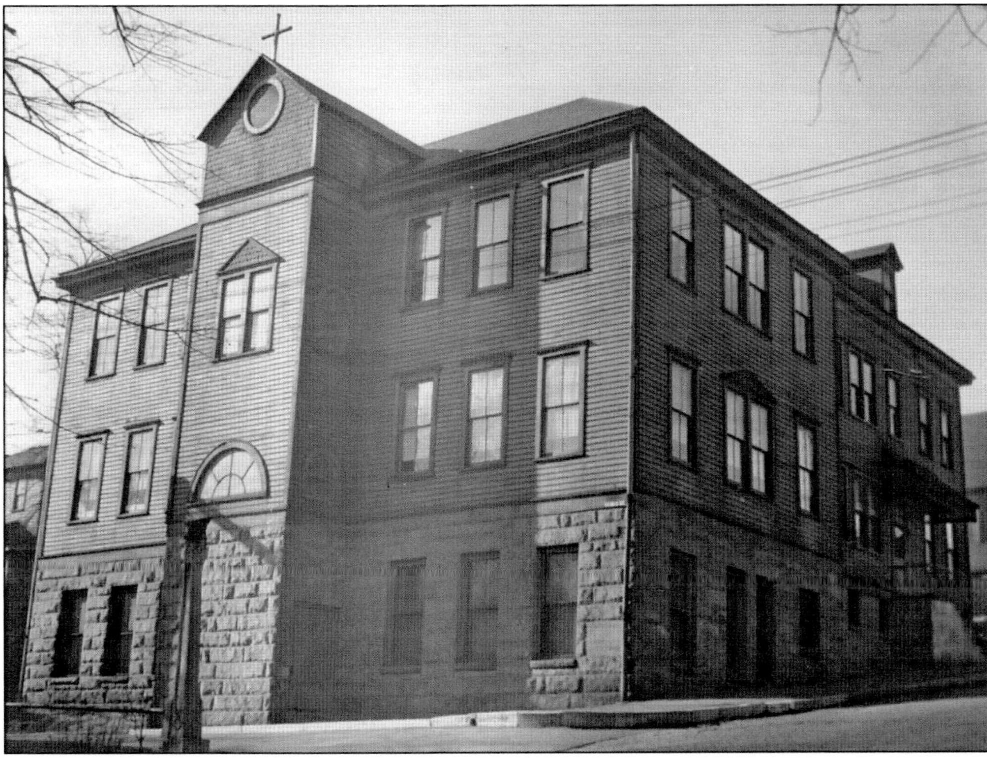

St. Agnes Catholic School, 1898. This parochial school of stone and wood-frame construction on St. Clair Avenue and Steuben Street opened its doors to classes in 1898 with instruction at first by the Sisters of Charity from Nazareth, Kentucky, and then in 1903 by the Franciscan Sisters of Charity. The 1911 photograph below shows the Franciscan nuns in front of the school building where grades 1–12 were taught. A new brick building on Murdock Street was opened in 1955; classes were held there for grades one through eight. (Above, courtesy Florence [Grantonic] Hirkala; below, courtesy Eileen [Hagerty] Moody.)

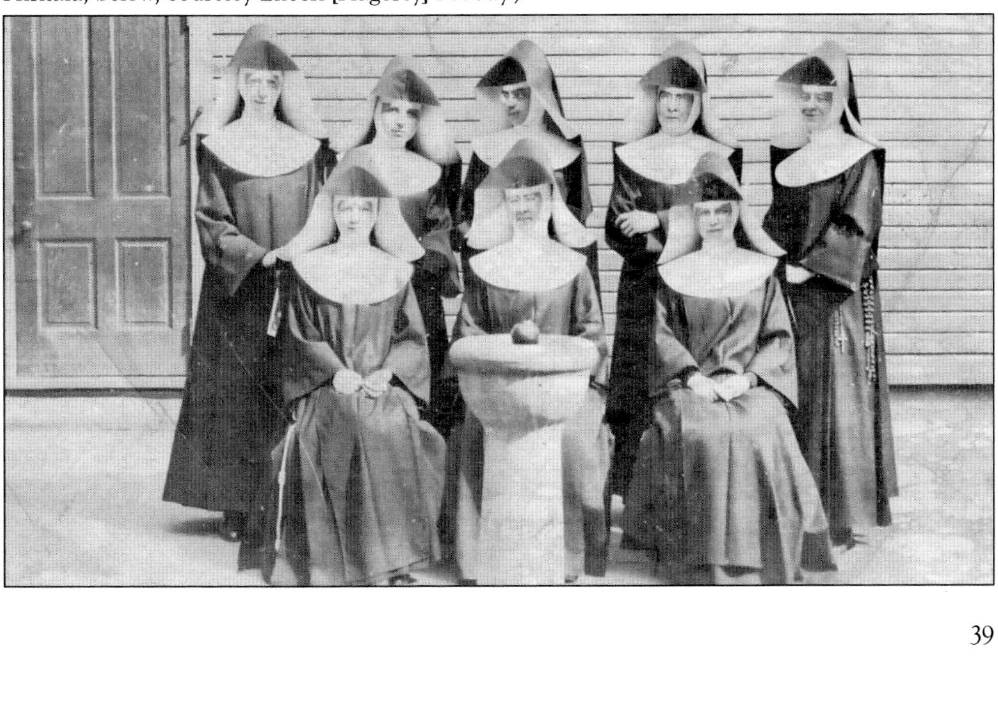

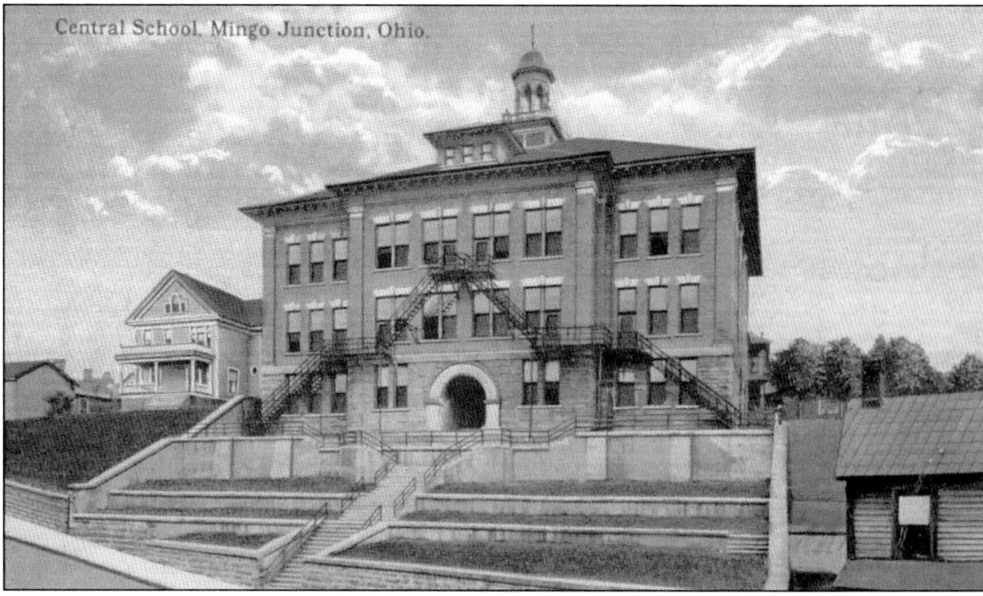

CENTRAL SCHOOL BUILDING NO. 1, 1907. This grand structure, a source of local pride, was constructed on the site of the former Franklin School facing Commercial Street, and it eventually housed grades 1–12. On December 10, 1817, a raging fire destroyed the entire building, and for over a year, classes were held in the Odd Fellows Hall and the basement of the Methodist church. (Courtesy Madeline [Brinskey] Campbell.)

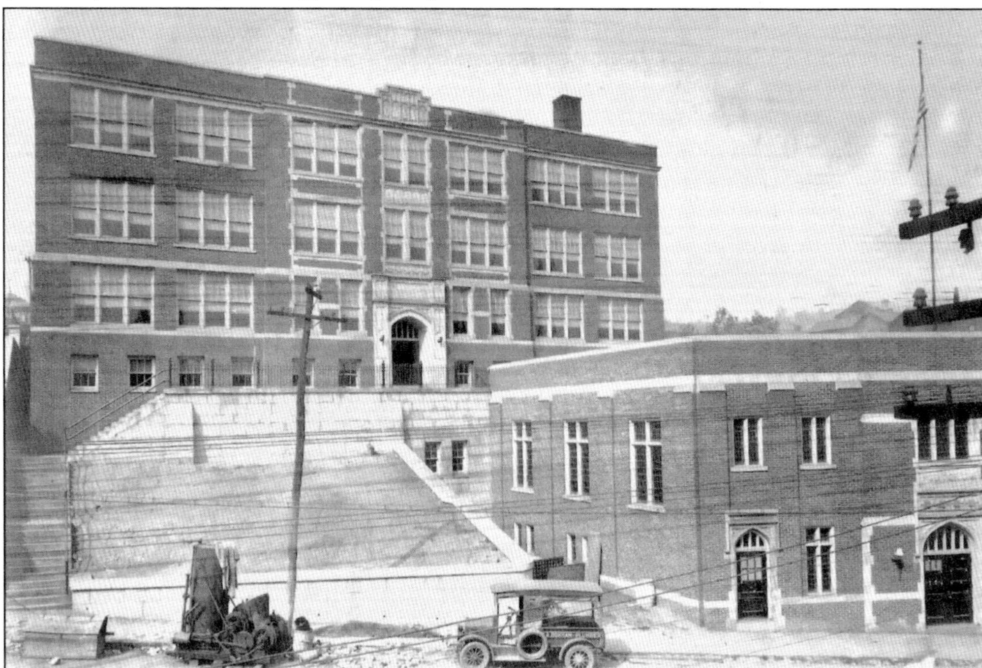

CENTRAL SCHOOL BUILDING NO. 2, 1920. This new complex housing grades 1–12 in four floors included a gymnasium, nurse's office, and board of education and superintendent's offices. The attached auditorium, which seated 565, served both the school and the town as a cultural center. (Courtesy Sophie [Dojonovic] Schoolcraft.)

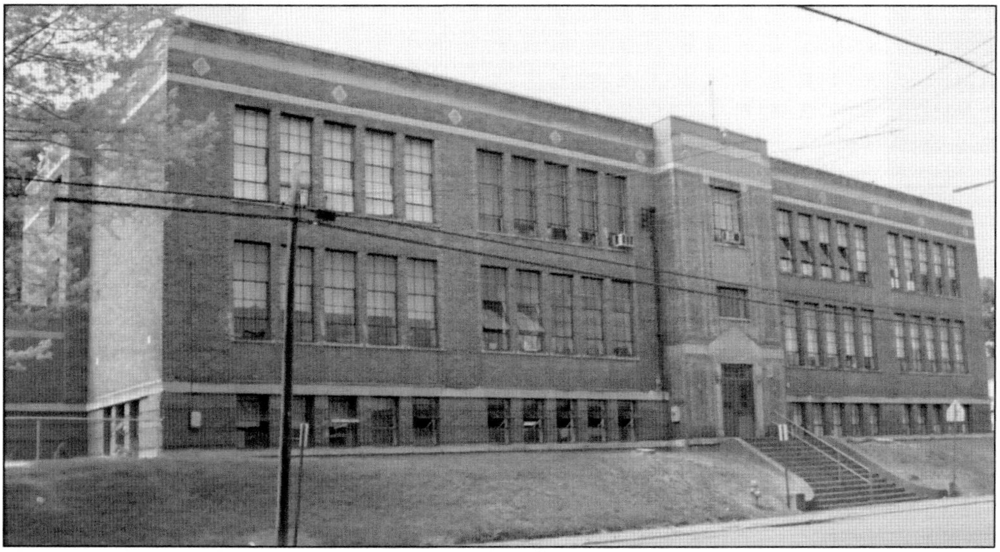

HARMONY SCHOOL BUILDING NO. 3, 1926. This three-story brick structure housed two floors of classrooms, a gymnasium, cafeteria, and included grades one through eight; in the 1960s, it housed grades one through six only. Early principals were Wilbert Brown (25 years) and Michael Ondayko. In 1986, declining enrollments and rising costs forced its closure, and it has since served as Jefferson County Christian School. (Courtesy Guy Mason II.)

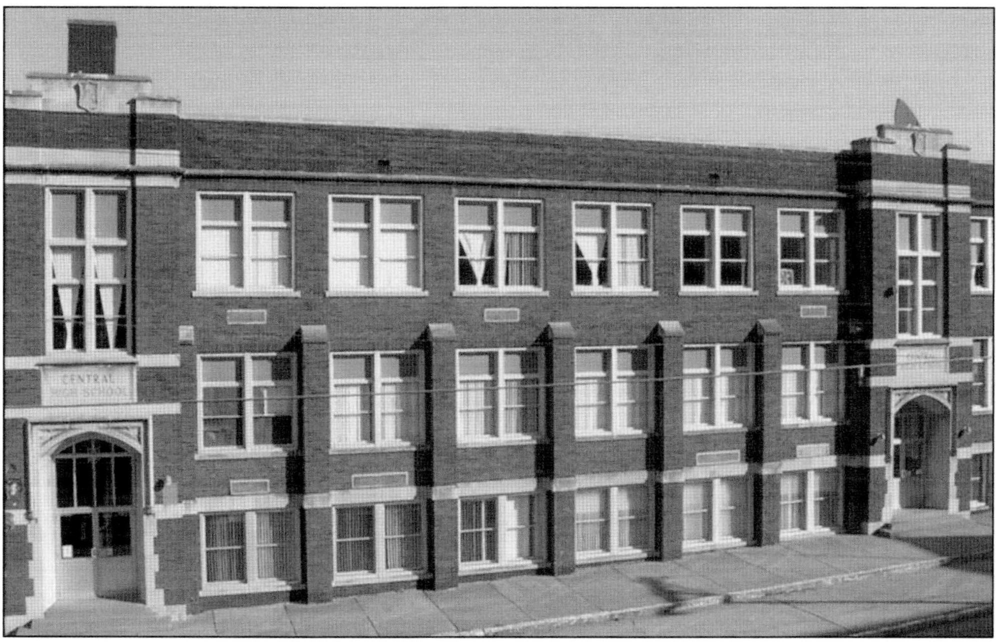

MINGO HIGH SCHOOL, 1929. Following a $200,000 bond issue in 1928, work began on a new high school to house grades 9–12. A wood shop and home economics section were included along with chemistry and biology laboratories. In March 1930, the new building was officially opened. Even after consolidation with Wintersville and Bloomingdale districts in 1966, MHS continued to graduate high school students until 1993–1994, when the building became the Indian Creek Middle School. High school students were afterwards bused to high school in Wintersville. (Courtesy John "Wiz" Fabian.)

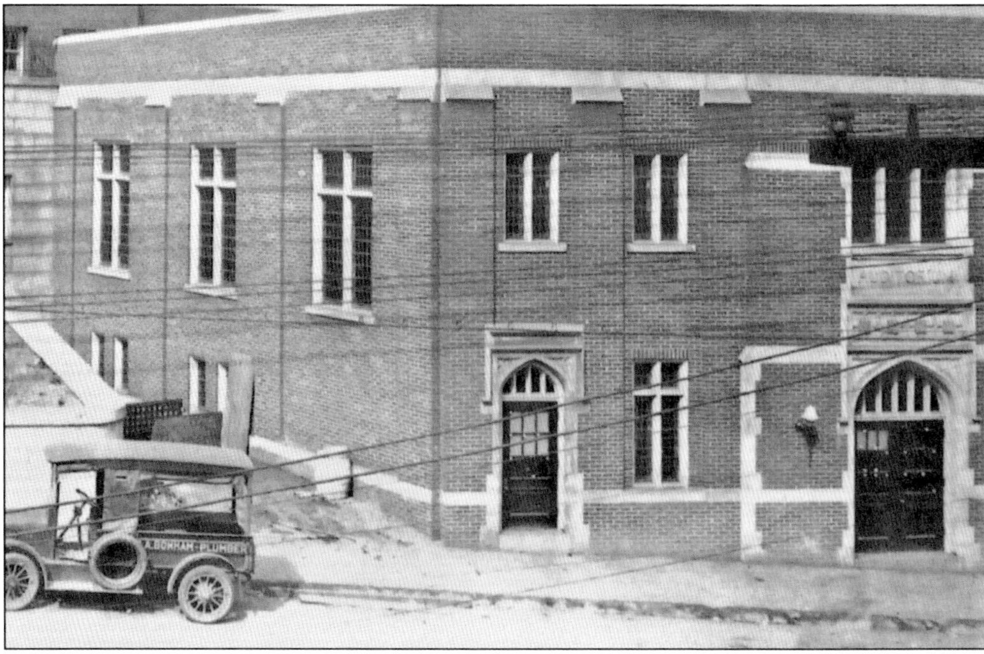

MINGO AUDITORIUM. The auditorium, shown here when it opened in 1920, served both the school and the larger community as a venue for concerts, traveling minstrel shows, school plays, graduations, and other programs. The ornate stage often used the backdrop seen in the photograph below for its various plays and programs, and many children stood before its colorful panorama. (Above, courtesy Sophie [Dojonovic] Schoolcraft; below, courtesy Sondra [White] Hyde.)

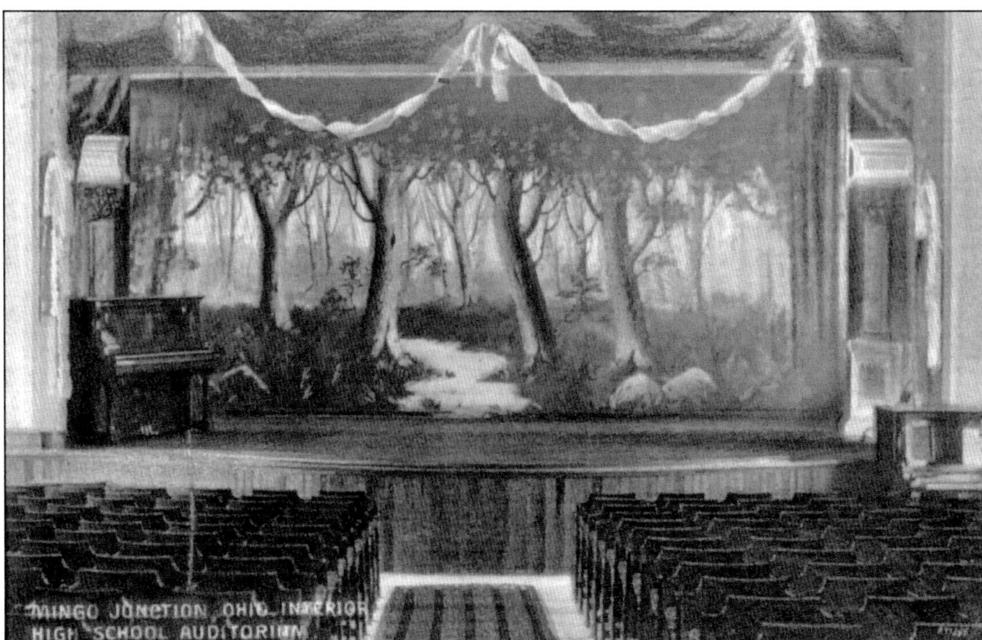

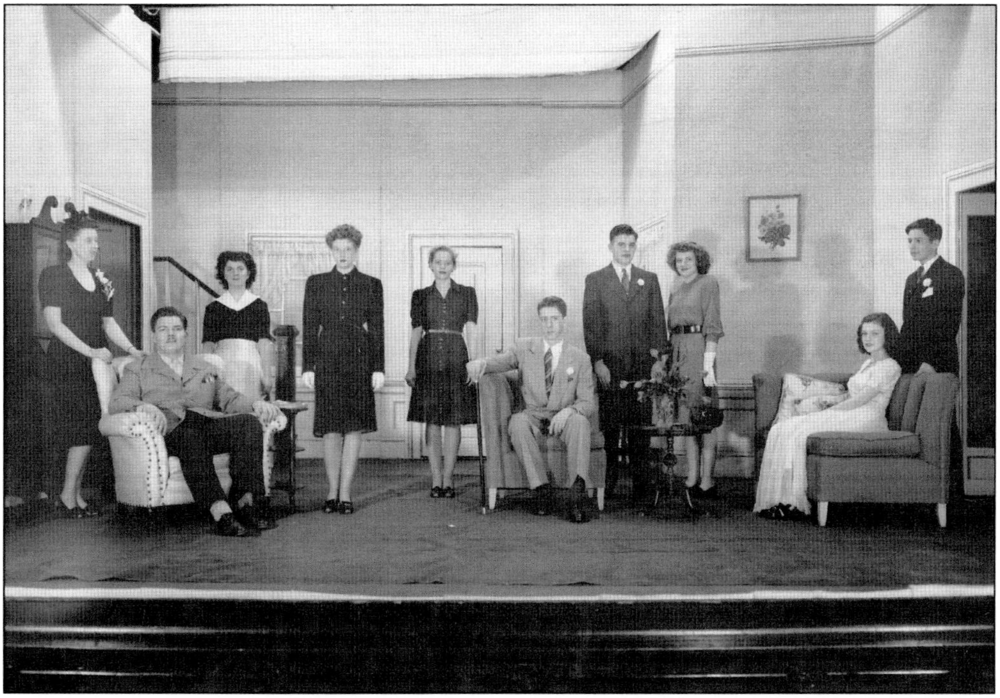

The Stage. In the 1948 play pictured above, young students could get a taste of acting as well as theater production. Joanne (Peeler) Sogan is seated at right. The plays were typically performed for school audiences as well as the townspeople. Elementary, middle, and high school students performed here. The photograph below shows the class of 1959 on graduation day in the auditorium. Before the use of the large gymnasium in the 1970s, graduating classes would walk across the auditorium stage to receive their diplomas. (Above, courtesy Joanne [Peeler] Sogan; below, courtesy Darlene Hoff.)

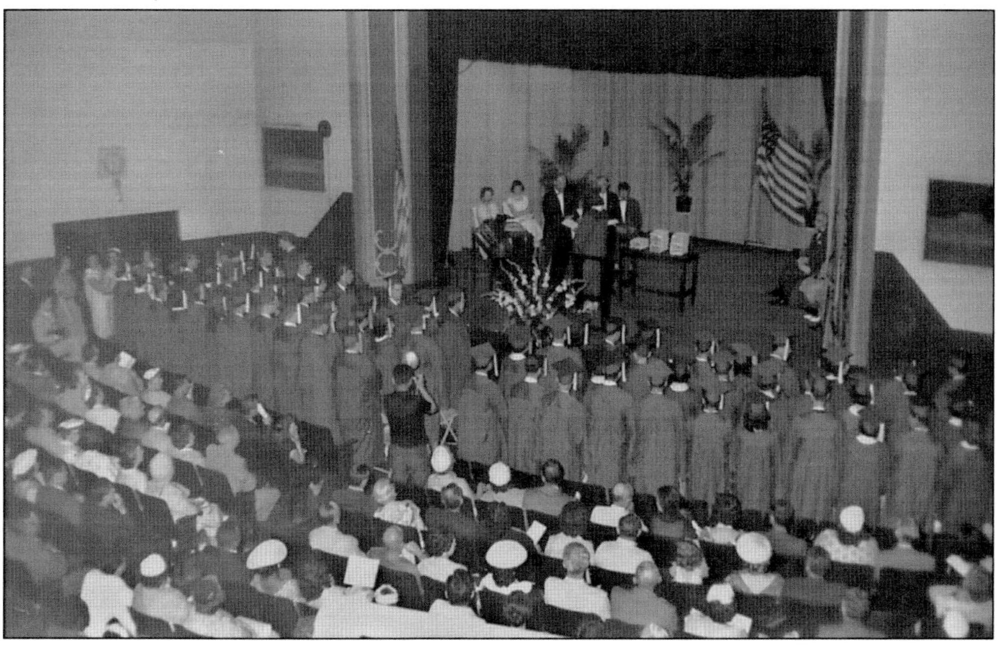

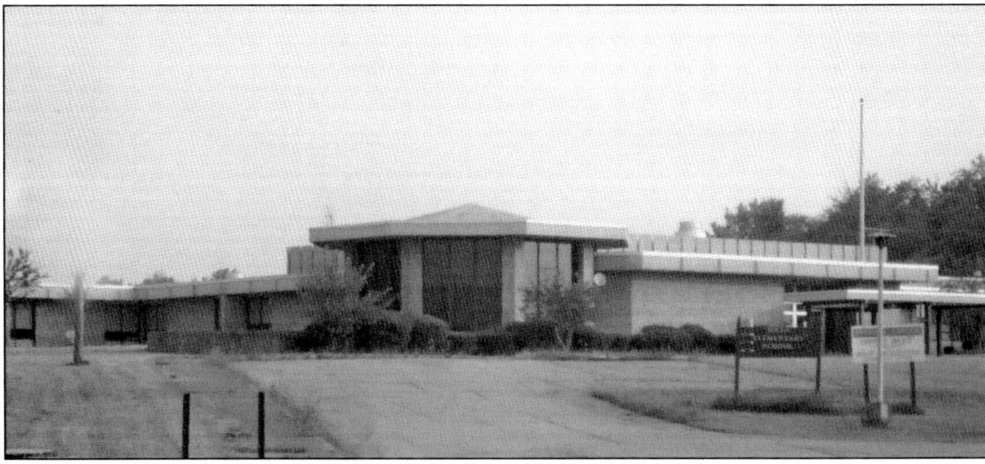

New Hills School. Following the consolidation of schools into the Indian Creek School District in 1966, this new building opened in 1968. Mingo residents resisted consolidation, taking legal action at the state level, but the consolidation went into effect in 1966. Beatrice Francis had been principal in the older building for 25 years. Today this Hills School features two wings, a cafeteria, and a library and serves grades one through six. The John Muth Baseball Complex, which includes a playing field, stands, and track, was added in 2008. Construction of a new middle school on adjoining property began in 2009.

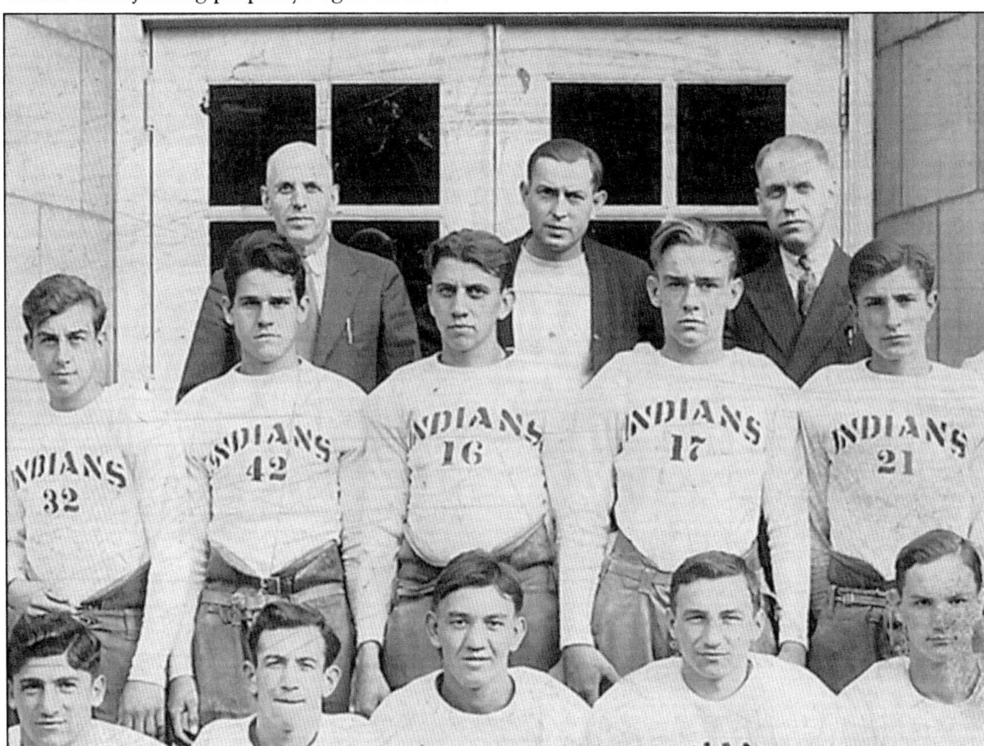

School Support Staff. Pictured from left to right behind the 1934 MHS football team are school administrator Claude Brunner, coach and principal John Muth, and superintendent Merril Dennis. The Mingo High School stadium would eventually be renamed the John Muth Stadium. (Courtesy Riney Roberts.)

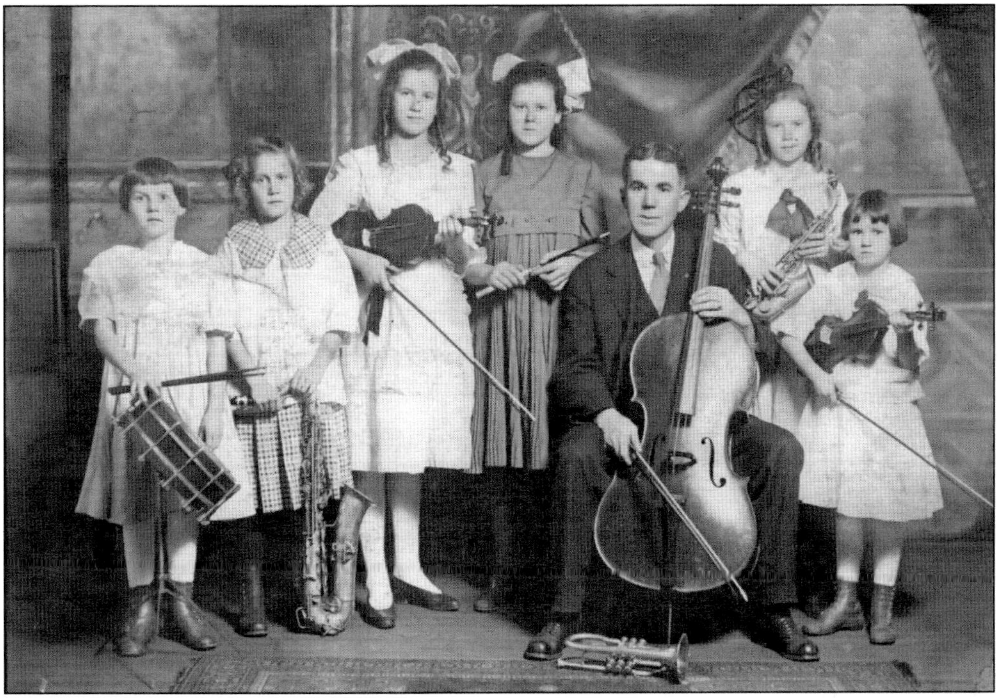

Mingo Family Band, 1919. Here is the Godfrey Family Orchestra, a string and instrument group that played at most town events. All of the girls were students at St. Agnes Catholic School. Seen here from left to right are Ruth, Gertrude, Elizabeth, Catherine, Mary, and Alice. Their father, Joseph (seated), gave music lessons. (Courtesy Eileen [Hagerty] Moody.)

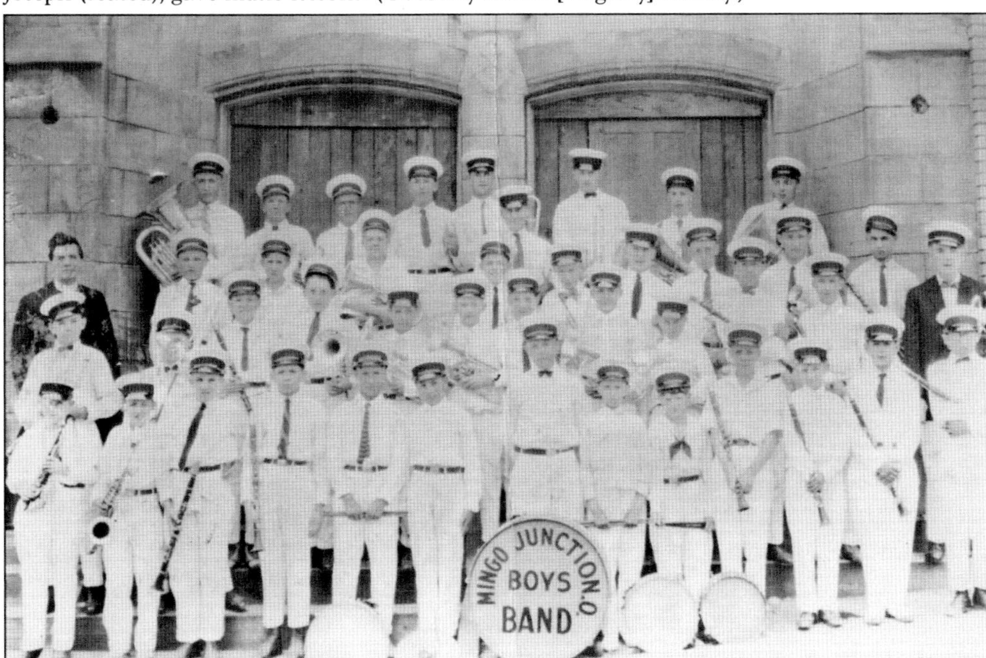

Mingo Boys Band. Assembled here in 1922 on the footsteps of St. Agnes Catholic Church with Fr. Joseph Dooley (far left) is the award-winning Boys Band. (Courtesy Eileen [Hagerty] Moody.)

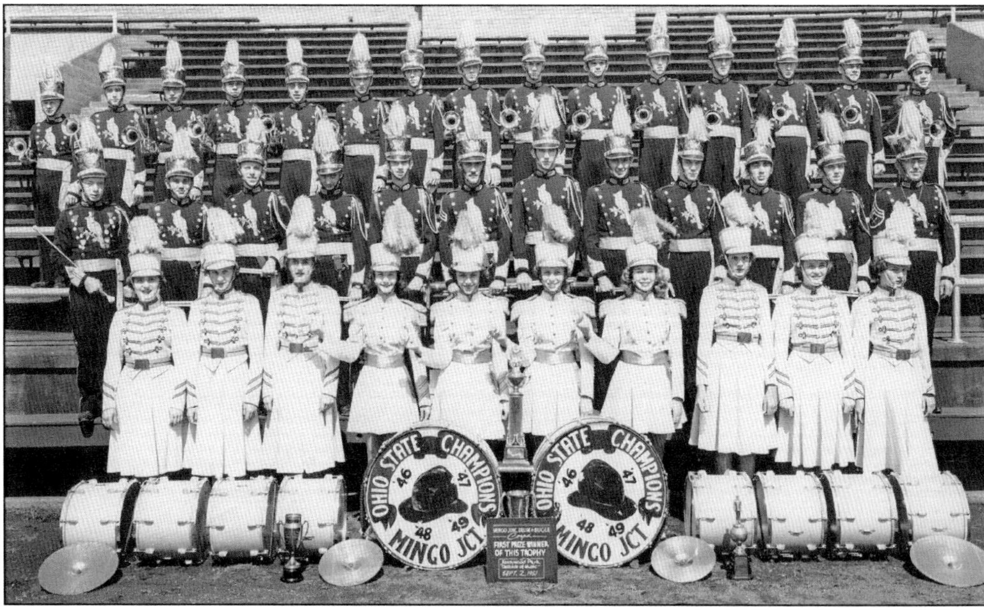

Drum and Bugle Corps. Marching bands enjoy a long history in Mingo Junction. Pictured here is the Mingo Volunteer Drum and Bugle Corps, state champions from 1946 to 1949. The organization was supported by the Volunteer Firemen of Mingo Junction and was led for years by Joe Grantonic. (Courtesy John Grantonic.)

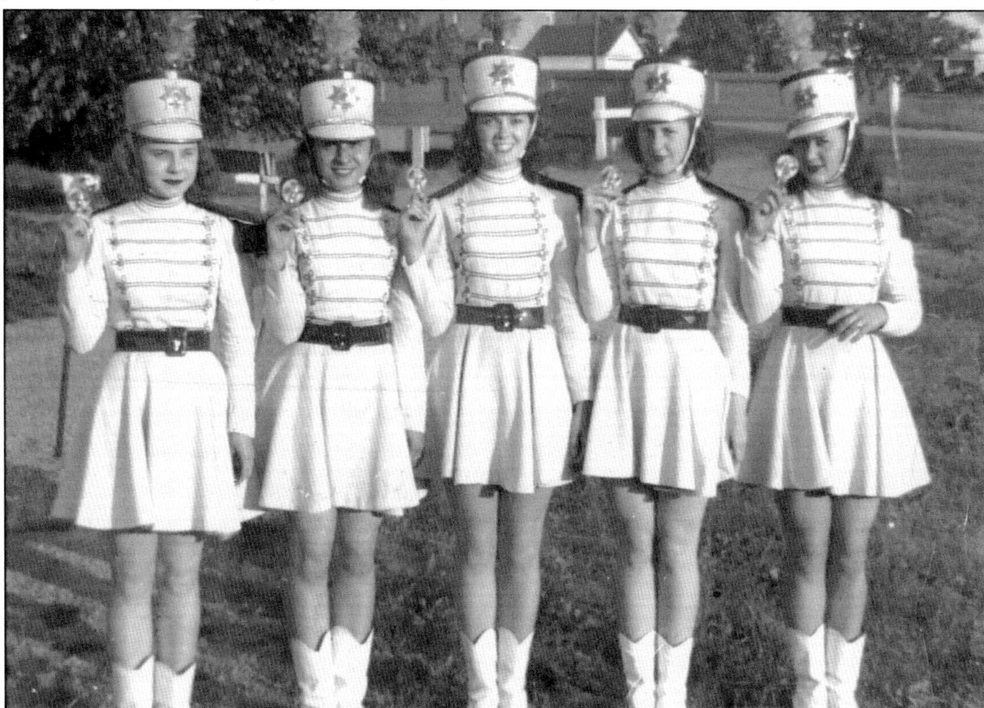

Drum and Bugle Majorettes, 1947. Pictured below in the traditional drum majorette uniforms of the Mingo Volunteer Drum and Bugle Corps are, from left to right, Mary Margaret Heath, Martha Vasich, Pat Tracy, Heddy Young, and Anna Chuma. (Courtesy Martha [Vasich] Trombetta.)

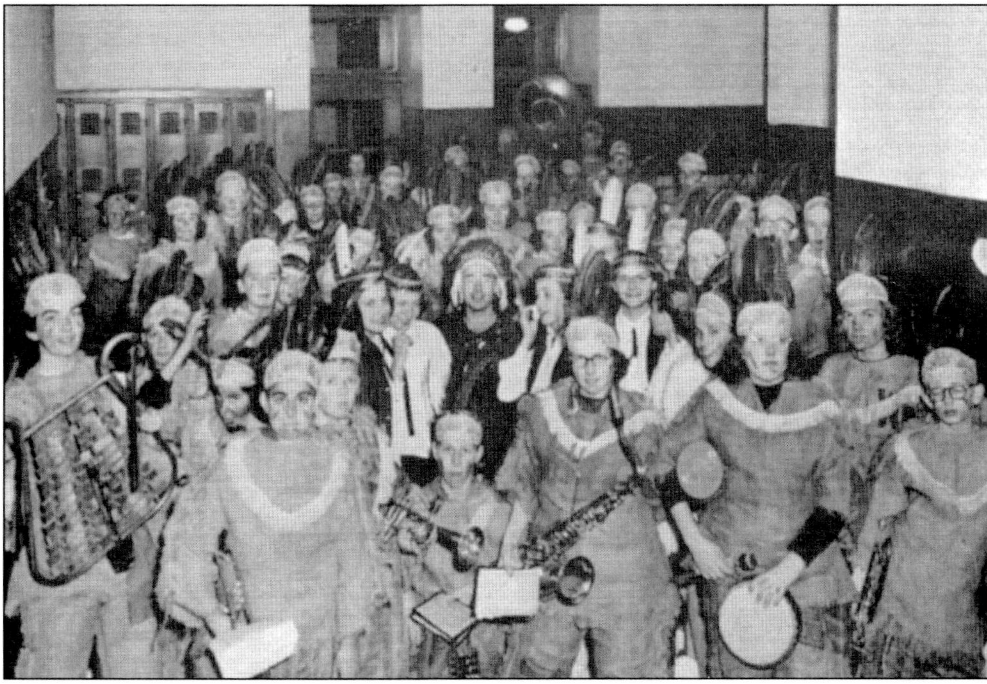

Mingo High School Marching Band, 1956. One of the traditions of the MHS marching band was to adopt the costume of the Mingo Indians. Here they wear their occasional dress for a pep rally—a garb made of burlap sacks and feathers. (Courtesy Darlene Hoff, originally published in *Bicentennial History of Mingo Junction, Ohio.*)

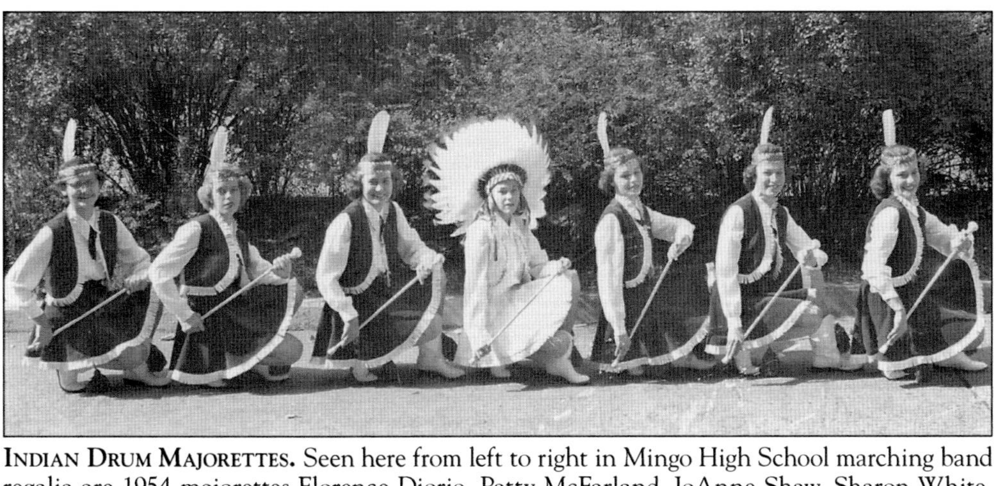

Indian Drum Majorettes. Seen here from left to right in Mingo High School marching band regalia are 1954 majorettes Florence Diorio, Patty McFarland, JoAnne Shaw, Sharon White, Shirley Menzel, Barbara Blankenship, and Lola Haislet. (Courtesy Bea [Petroskey] Daily.)

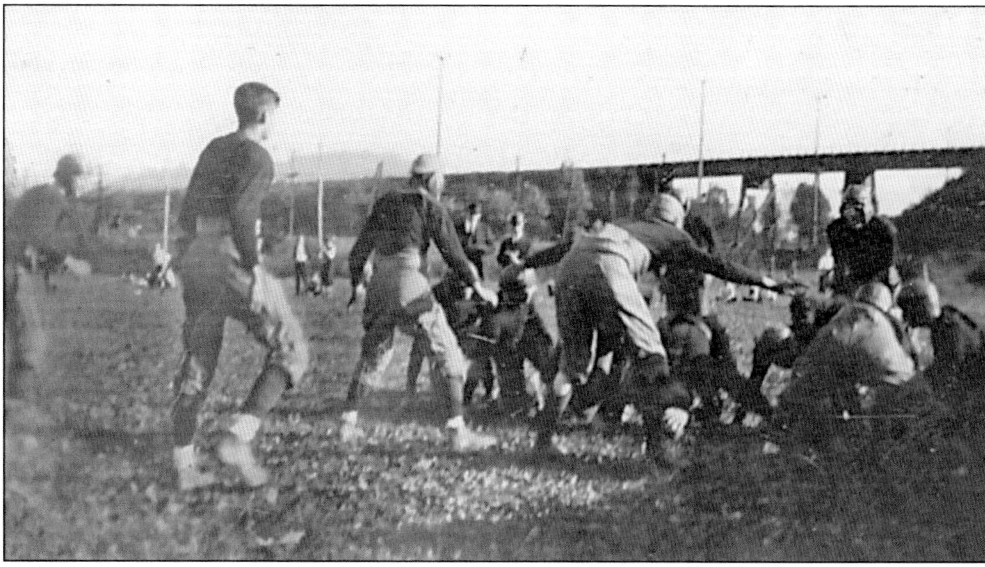

MINGO FOOTBALL GAME, EARLY 1900S. The old Wabash Field was used before the Mingo Stadium was built in 1936. One of the players is not wearing a helmet. The back of the photograph reads, "Steubenville and Mingo 1918." Though the teams cannot be verified, there is no doubt that the location is under the railroad trestle leading into the Deandale and Georges Run area. (Courtesy Eileen [Hagerty] Moody.)

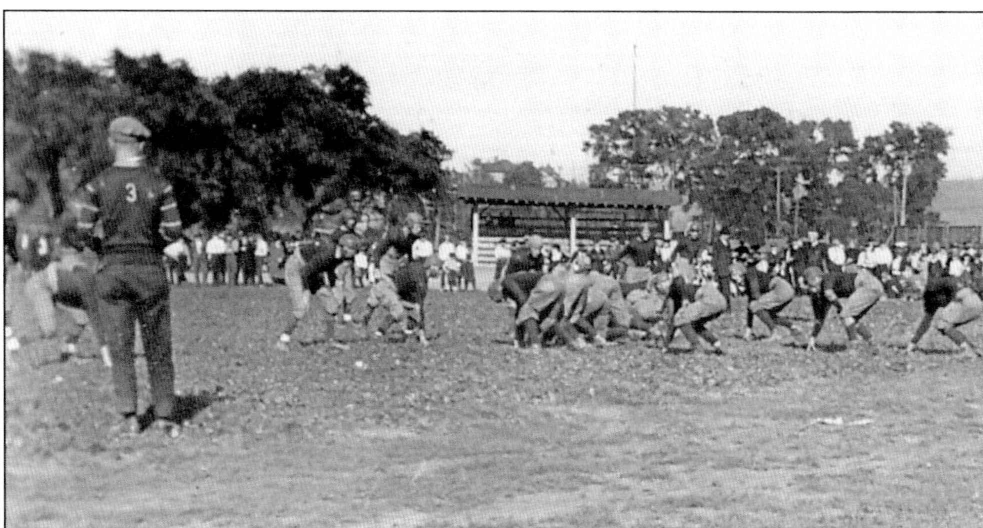

DOUBLE WING FORMATION. This may possibly be the same Mingo football game as photographed above but from a different angle. A nice crowd of people is on hand for the game. The backfield is typical of the time "Double wing" (variation of the Single wing) formation. Notice the player off to the left of the referee who seems to be the same helmetless player above. These amazing photographs of the old Wabash Field document Mingo sports history. (Courtesy Eileen [Hagerty] Moody.)

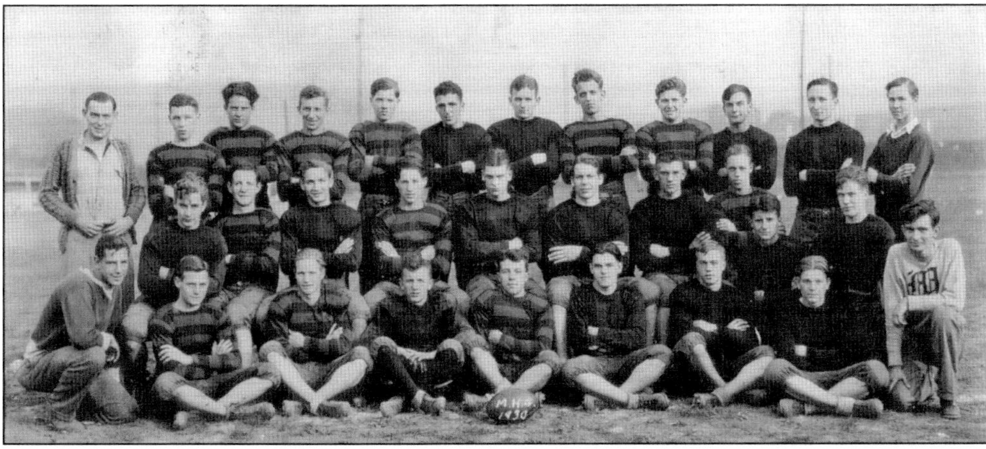

1930 Mingo Football Team. This team had two future Pittsburgh Pirates (today's Steelers) on the squad: Arthur "Jake" Strutt is in the second row, sixth from left; and George "Bunco" Kakasic is in the third row, fifth from left. Also in the picture are future Mingo mayor Benny Leone (first row, center) and coach John Muth (third row, left). (Courtesy Gabe Frieling and Mingo Downtown Pizza Shop.)

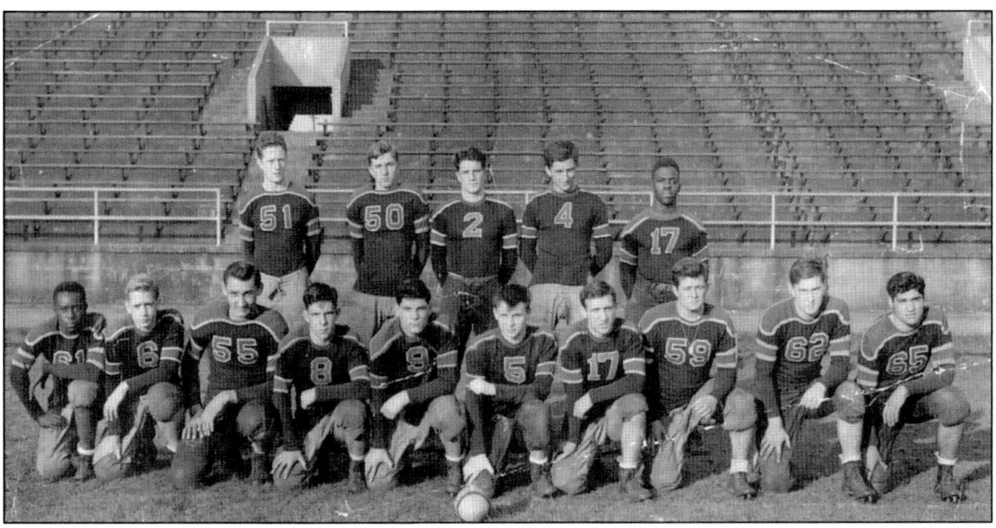

An Impressive Group. The class of 1945 senior football players seen here in the first row include Aldo Diorio, no. 55 (third from left) and Delmo Trombetta, no. 9 (fifth from left). In the second row are James McKenna, no. 51 (far left) and Clyde "Duck" Marshall, no. 17 (far right). Duck was one of Mingo's finest running backs and received a scholarship to Ohio State University, where he earned a letter for the Buckeyes. Eight members of this senior class received college scholarships. (Courtesy Martha [Vasich] Trombetta.)

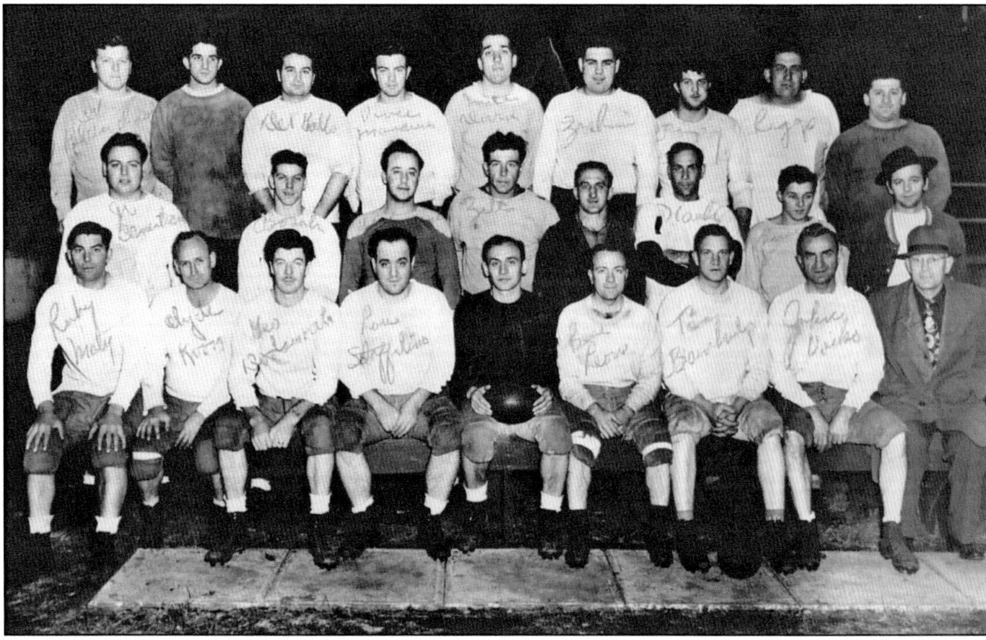

The Old Mingo Indians, 1949. Apocryphal or not, the story as related claims that after the Mingo High School had a team cancel a game, leaving a gap in their schedule, these Mingo graduates volunteered to play the varsity. Supposedly, the alumni won the game 12-7. Did the MHS varsity team ease up on the old guys? Note Paul Sogan (in black) beside Mayor Benny Leone. (Courtesy Benita Leone.)

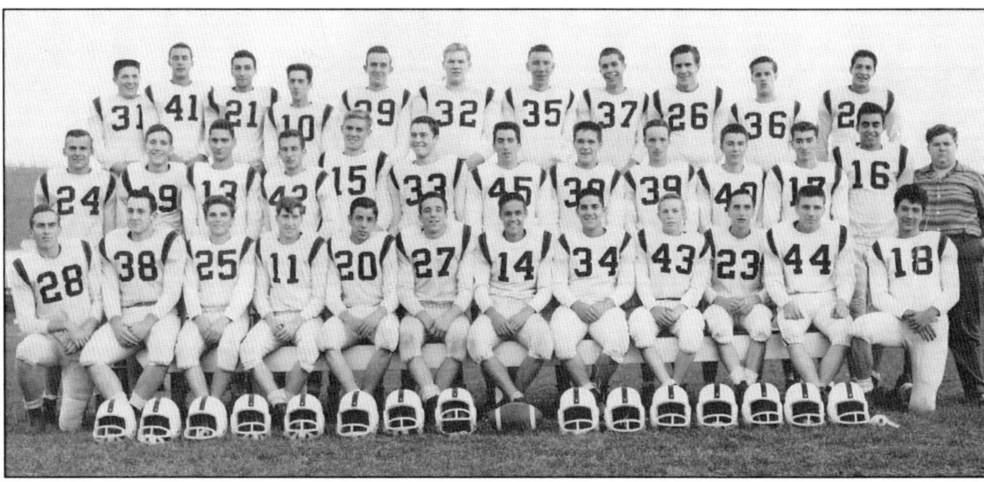

The Mingo High School Indians, 1959. The team looks forward to a successful season under head coach George Zatezalo. From left to right are (first row) Jim Ritter, Bill Criss, Guy Mason, John Hannen, R. Mazik, Carl Fisher, Tom Knutson, Rich Angelica, Larry Buckalew, Allen Merzi, Gene Richards, and "Cuz" Balzano; (second row) Jerry Mazik, Ben Shriver, Jay Bellopatrick, Tim Bainbridge, Greg Schilling, Jim Urdzik, David McKee, John Dagan, Mike Boka, Jim Cuccarese, Nick Drzayich, Abbie Santangelo, and George Tate (manager); (third row) Phil Pergi, Homer Keller, Frank Fuscardo, Howard Mallett, Larry Starr, David E. Smith, Archie Wolford, David R. Smith, George Milak, Wayne Morris, and Jim D'Alesio. (Courtesy Jim D'Alesio.)

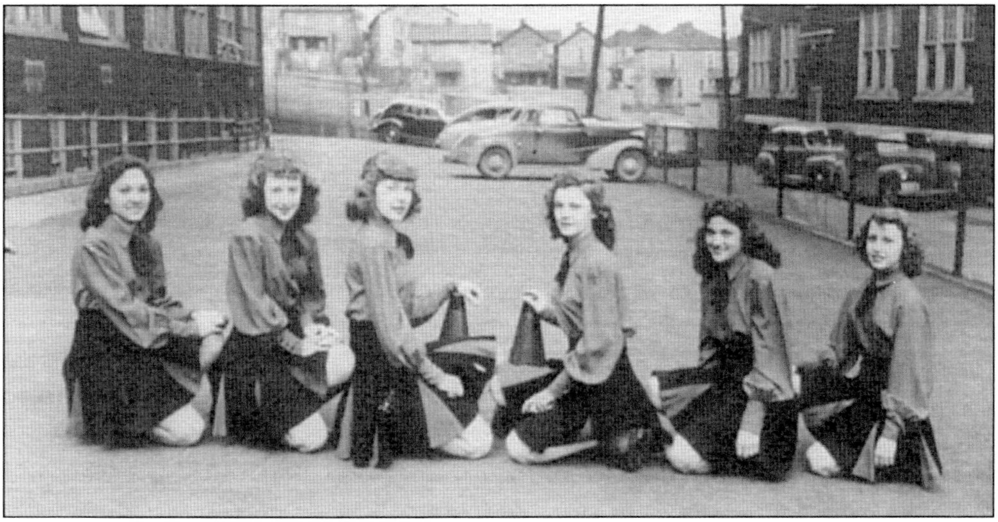

Mingo High Cheerleaders, 1947. This team is posing in the parking lot between the high school and the Central grade school buildings (which have since been torn down). They are, from left to right, Grace Gulino, Betsy Koon, Ann Louise Parks, JoAnn Peeler, Nina Gulino, and Janet Hudson. Mingo cheerleaders were always lively and well prepared and were much appreciated by the team and fans. Coach George Bosley's old 1942 Ford is in the background. (Courtesy Joanne [Peeler] Sogan.)

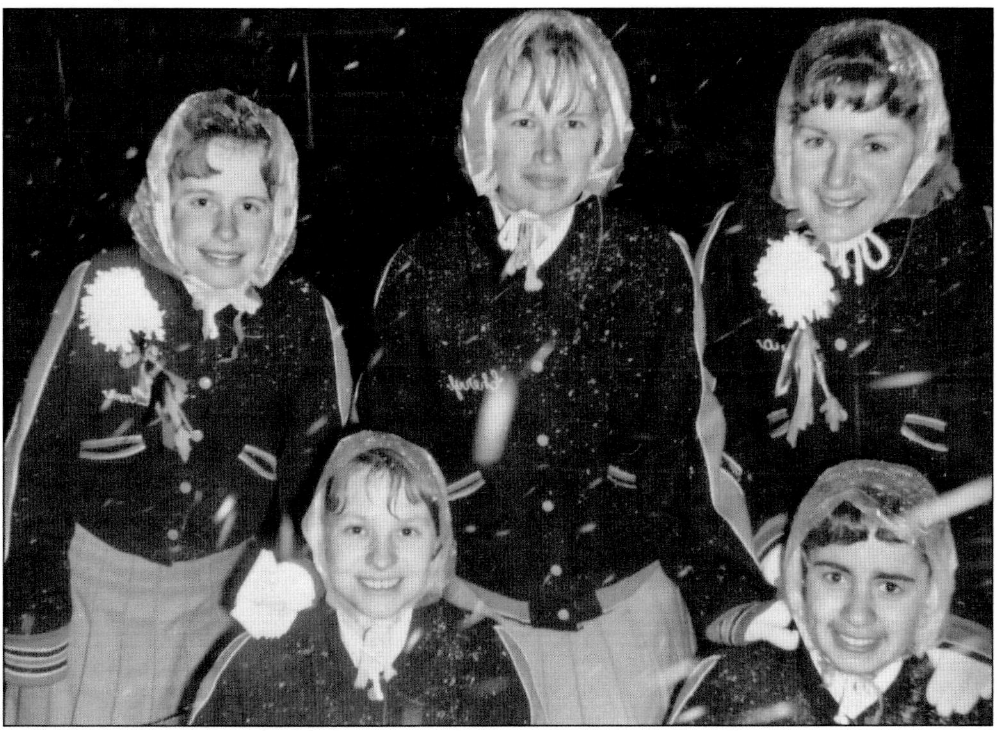

Mingo Cheerleaders, 1963. Despite an icy wind and a mix of sleet and snow, Mingo cheerleaders do their best to urge on the Indians to victory against Dillonvale (and stay warm) on Father's Night, 1963. Seen here from left to right are (first row) Mary Ann Vasich and Michelle Bellardine; (second row) Thelma Yount, Cheryl Westlake, and Ina Petrick. (Courtesy Mary Ann [Vasich] Mason.)

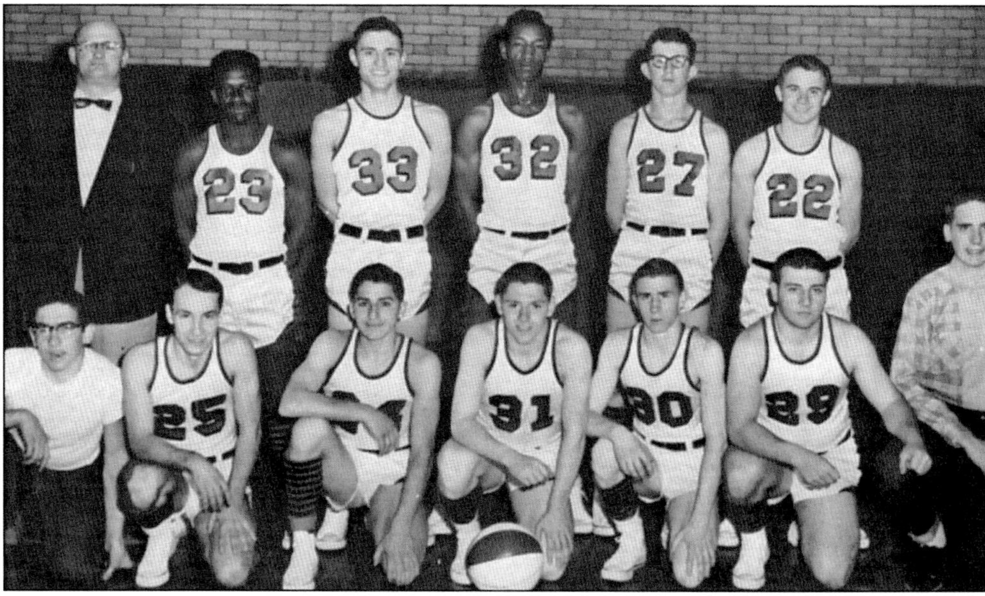

1955–1956 MINGO VARSITY BASKETBALL TEAM. As a small school, Mingo's sports teams often rivaled bigger school teams, as with this fine crew. From left to right are (first row) manager Louis Muscedere, Mario Petrella, Willie Rychlick, Larry Fellows, Bob Platt, Dan DiCenzo, and manager Jack Evans; (second row) coach Mike Rodak, Willie Edwards, Nick Bellopatrick, Ron Reynolds, Dave Valuska, and Oran Kamerer. (Courtesy of Bill Minch.)

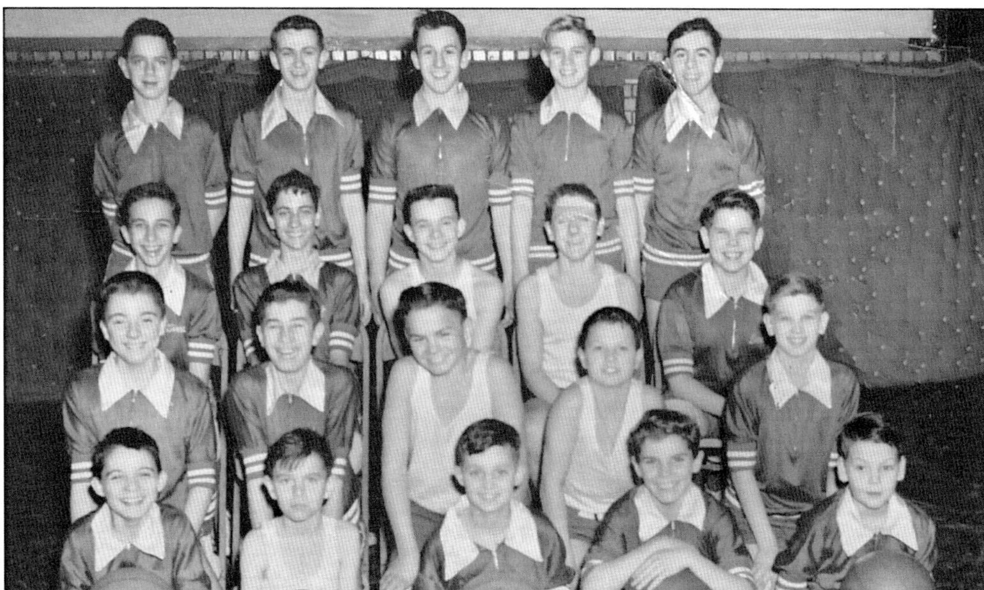

HARMONY GRADE SCHOOL, 1956. The basketball team wears their new uniforms. Seen here from left to right are (first row) Richard Ogden, Jim Frieling, Bob Kaufman, Guy Mason, and Roger Powell; (second row) Jim Cuccarese, Nick Drzayich, Bill Vasich, Chuck Antill, and Bob Takach; (third row) Tim Bainbridge, Jay Bellopatrick, Gibby Barcus, Richard Simmons, and David Humes; (fourth row) Jan Newman, David Bynum, Bill Criss, Greg Schilling, and Buddy Garrett. (Courtesy Jim Frieling.)

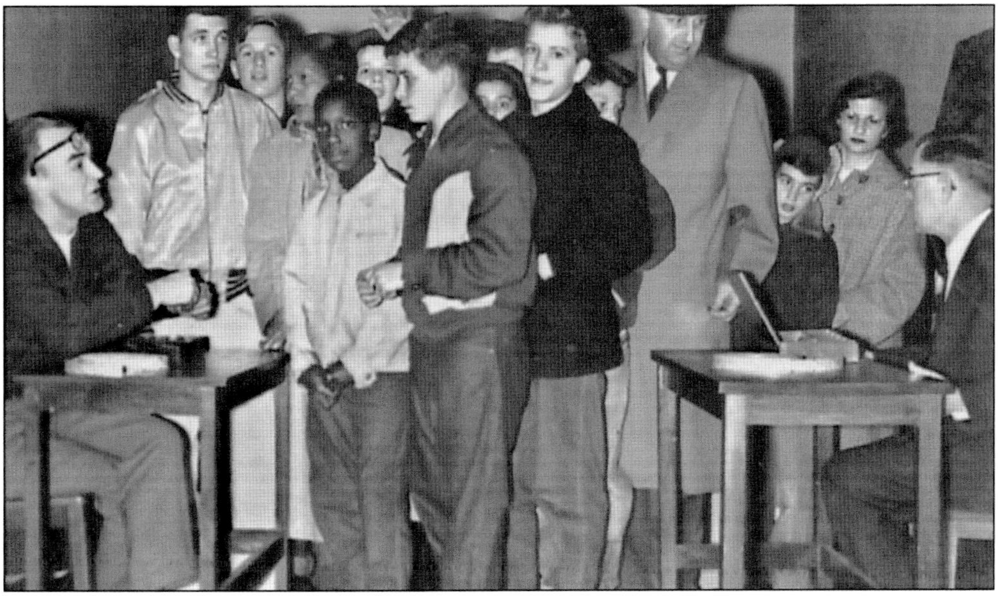

Taking Tickets. It is a basketball night and probably a game against a big rival, as the students are rushing in to grab a good seat up front. Teacher Emory Hendon (left) and principal John Muth (right) sell tickets at the old Central "Snake Pit" Gym, around 1949. From left to right, the fans seen here include (first row) Wayne Coffman, Bill Murtland, Luella Lewis, and Robert Lewis; (second row) David Petroskey, ? Panetta, Jimmy Lane, ? Howard, ? Cutri, and Carmel Cutri. (Courtesy Bea [Petroskey] Daily.)

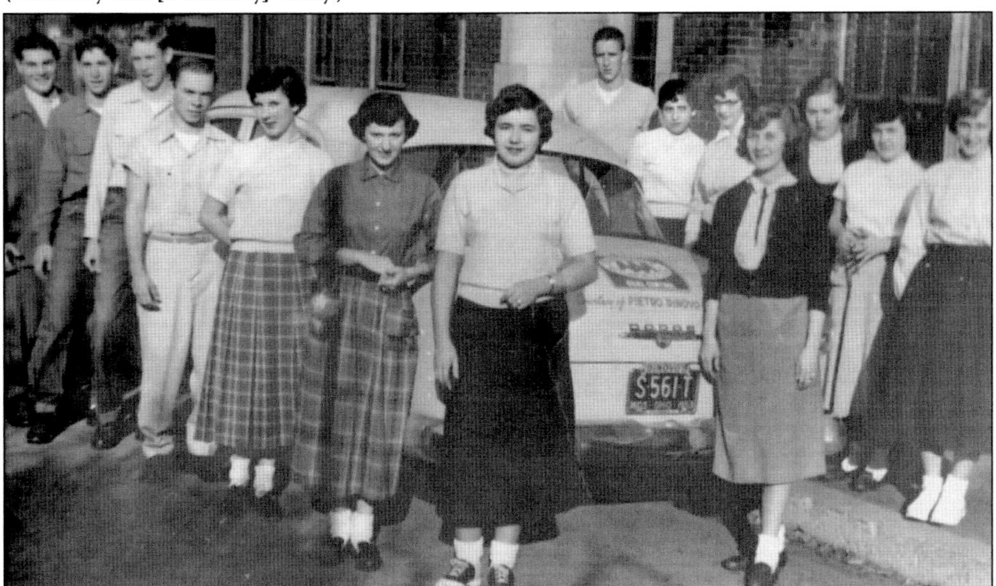

First Drivers Education Class, 1959. Coach and teacher Delmo Trombetta (far left) stands with the students of the first Drivers Education class at Mingo High School. From left to right are (first row) Delmo Trombetta, Alex Trombetta, Dalton Hobson, Riggie Petrella, Pat Vengrin, Margie Russciolli, and JoAnne Biggio; (second row) Arden Keller, LaPeta Patina, Nadine Farmer, Pat Snyder, Martha Hope, Phyllis Lockart, and Irene Verba. Although not pictured, Bea (Petroskey) Daily was also in the class. (Courtesy Bea [Petroskey] Daily.)

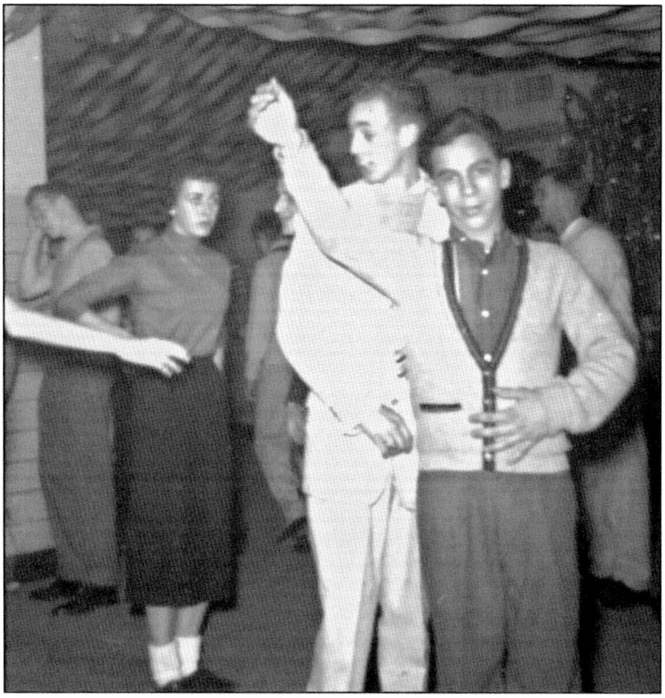

WIG WAM HOLIDAY SEASON, 1958. Always a great place for the gang to meet up, dance, or just support the walls and act cool, the youth center at the Mingo City Building provided good times for all, especially after a weekend's victorious sports game. This is a typical 1950s scene and dress. From left to right are Ken Looman (at pillar); Gloria Persutti (hand on hip); unidentified; future mayor Dominic "Noony" Chappano (forefront with right arm up), who appears to be having a very good time, perhaps leading a conga line; and Homer Keller (far right in front of Christmas tree). (Courtesy Homer Keller.)

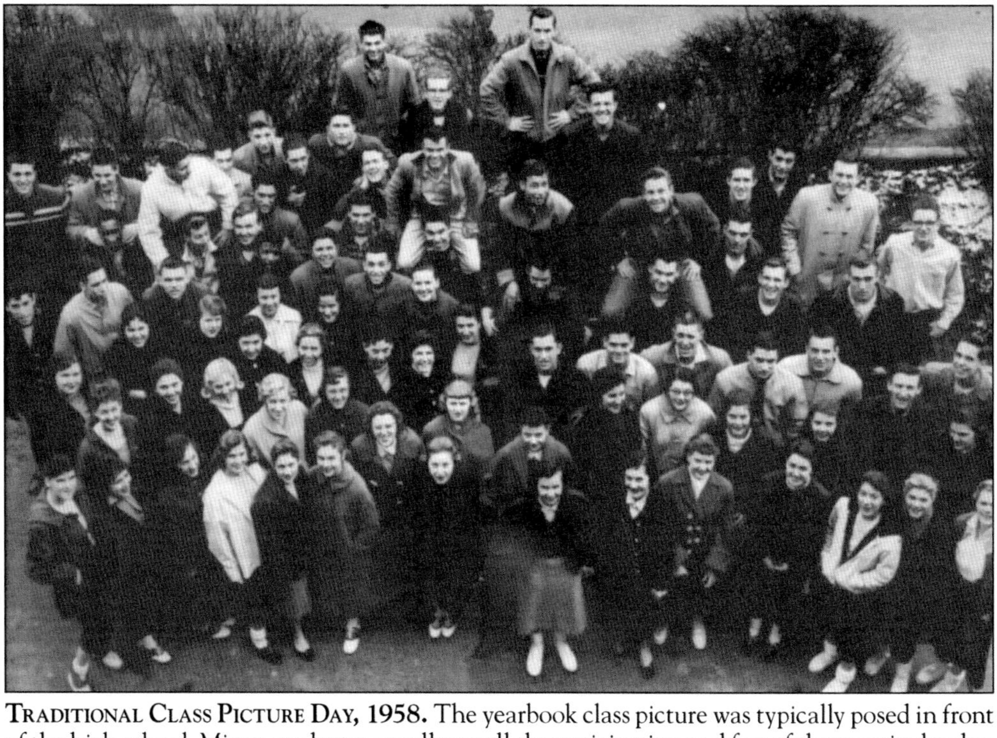

TRADITIONAL CLASS PICTURE DAY, 1958. The yearbook class picture was typically posed in front of the high school. Mingo graduates usually recall the anticipation and fun of that particular day. Proud seniors now had finally made it. Only later did they realize that those carefree, fun days were forever gone. Most still have their Mingo Indians memories in their yearbooks, golden and untarnished. (Courtesy Lewis and Sandy Leone.)

Four

A Town along a River

One cannot describe the town of Mingo Junction without including the productive, beautiful, and sometimes-destructive Ohio River. Over the years, the river has provided for the Mingo Indians, frontiersmen, settlers, farmers, and laborers. Mingo and the Ohio River are one, for the river provided the means to transport the ore, coal, and coke for its steel mills. In the early days, it also made an easy route for the merchants' wares and for goods to stock their stores. It allowed a relatively safe and easy means of travel from Pittsburgh south to southern Ohio and all the way to New Orleans. Unquestionably, however, the Ohio River could also deliver destructive might in the form of floods to towns along its path. The town has survived, and its residents have coped with these annual disasters while still enjoying the river's calmness and beauty.

Mingo, like many other small towns, has its share of landmarks, special buildings, parks, and cemeteries. Mingo residents are proud of their ball fields and give thanks to the volunteers through the years who maintained those fields and coached the young boys and girls. Aracoma City Park is second to none in its size and natural beauty. The Olympic-size swimming pool, the tennis and basketball courts, and the play areas are important to the youth here as well as shelter sites for family and class reunions. Mingo fathers and mothers have provided their children with fine recreation areas.

The present city building (seen on the cover), constructed in 1954–1956 after citizens passed a levy, has withstood the test of nearly 60 years. Most Mingo youth have fond memories of the dances and activities in the building's youth center, the "Wig Wam." The streets and avenues have been well maintained, and they offer a place to gather in neighborhoods or stroll to downtown. They have been the scene of many parades as well as the Community Days events of past years. Mingo's fire and police departments have been serving the town for over 200 years, providing a sense of peace to us all.

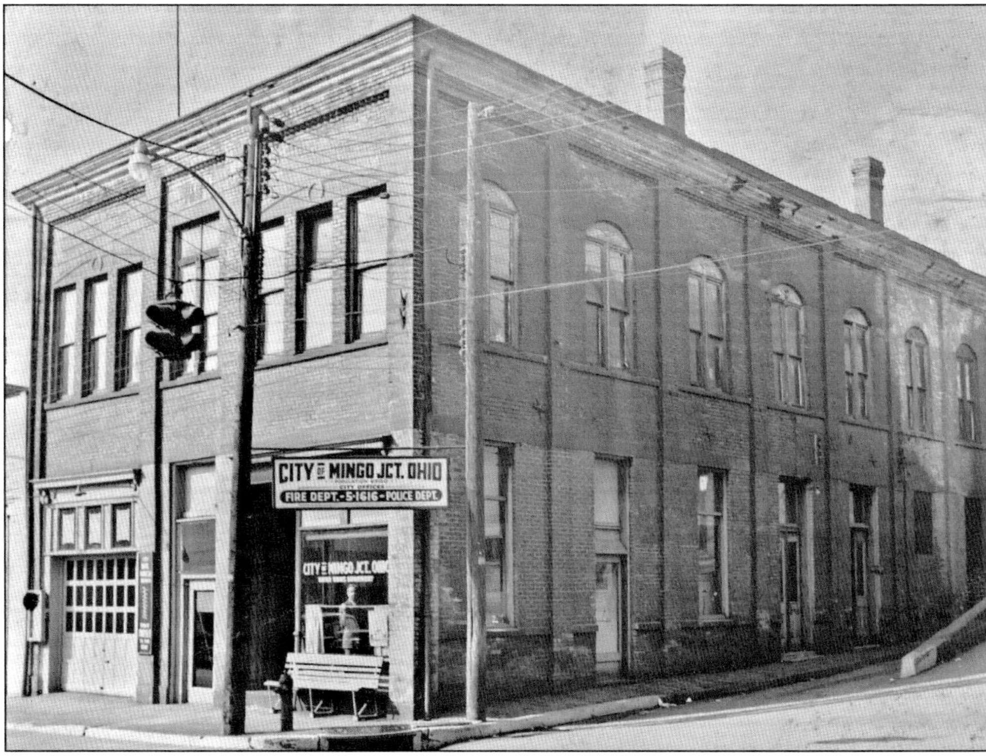

Old Mingo City Building. Located at Potter and Commercial Streets, this two-story brick building was constructed in 1888. It remained a busy and well-used landmark that served the town well for over 65 years. The building contained all of the village's offices, including the fire and police departments. It also housed the town jail with two basement cells that usually served as "sleep it off" tanks. (Courtesy Lewis and Sandy Leone.)

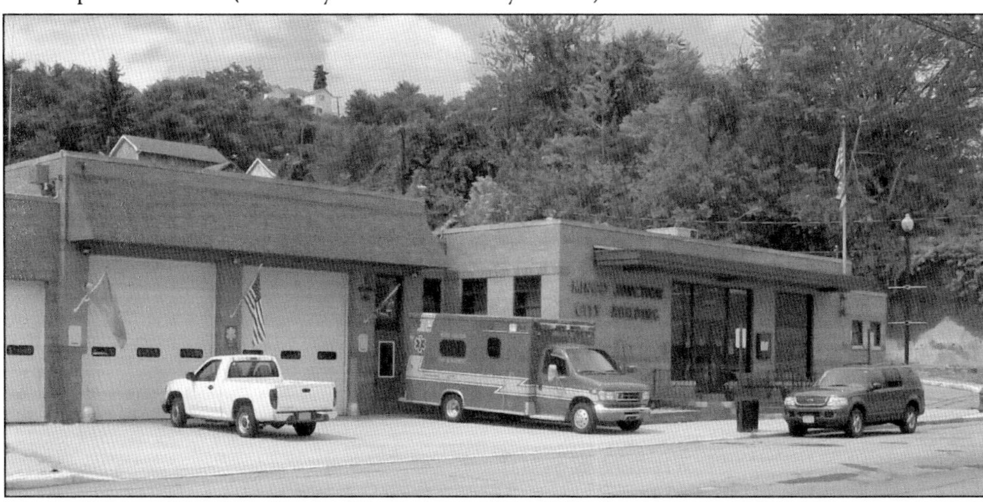

Present Mingo City Building. Built in the same location as the old city hall, this building was dedicated on January 15, 1956. The one-story city building contains offices for all the city departments, including police and fire. The lower floor houses the youth center, later named the Wig Wam. Most Mingo youths carry fond memories of their teenaged Wig Wam weekends. (Courtesy Steve Roby.)

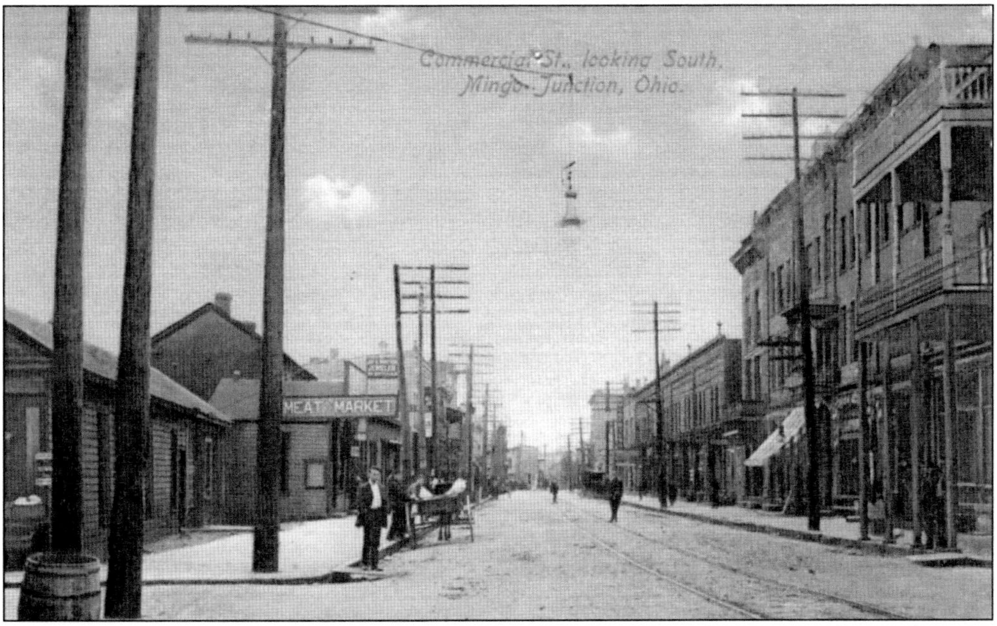

LOOKING SOUTH ON COMMERCIAL STREET. In this vintage postcard is a view of an early-1900s Mingo Junction. Trolleys were the main means of transportation in this era, along with the horse and buggy. Trolley tracks can be seen along with a horse and delivery wagon at the curb. The Hotel McDevitt is off to the right at the corner of McLister Avenue and Commercial Street and stands to this day—though without its beautiful portico. (Courtesy Madeline [Brinskey] Campbell.)

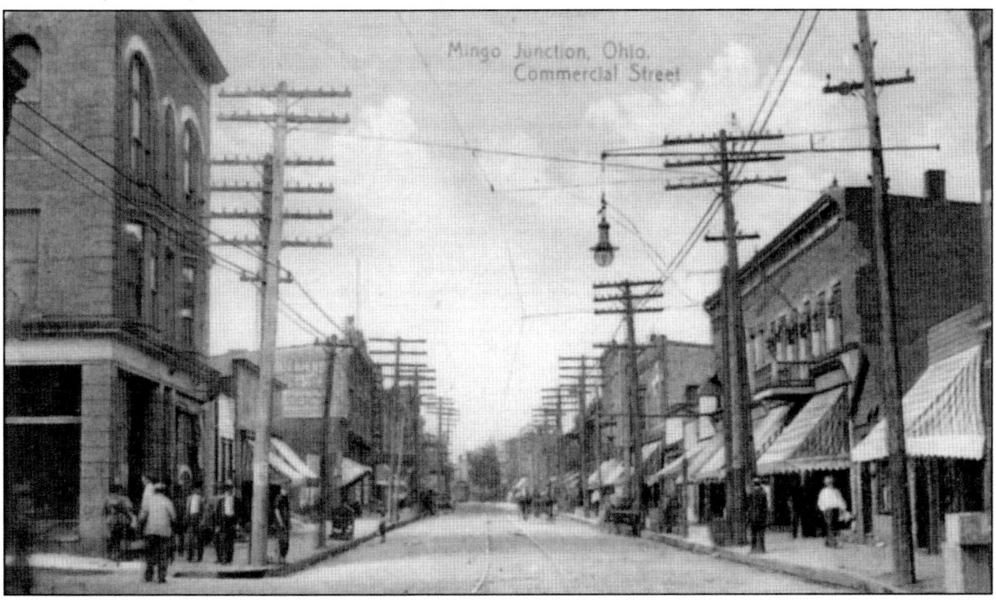

LOOKING NORTH ON COMMERCIAL STREET. This rare glimpse of 1900 Mingo Junction reveals a very young and fast-growing town where Ravine Street (left) converges with Commercial Street. Trolley tracks are readily apparent, as is the Edison incandescent hanging streetlight. Three horses and buggies can be seen along with the Goodfriend's sign. Many merchants of that era had wonderfully colorful awnings, which were cranked up every night. (Courtesy Madeline [Brinskey] Campbell.)

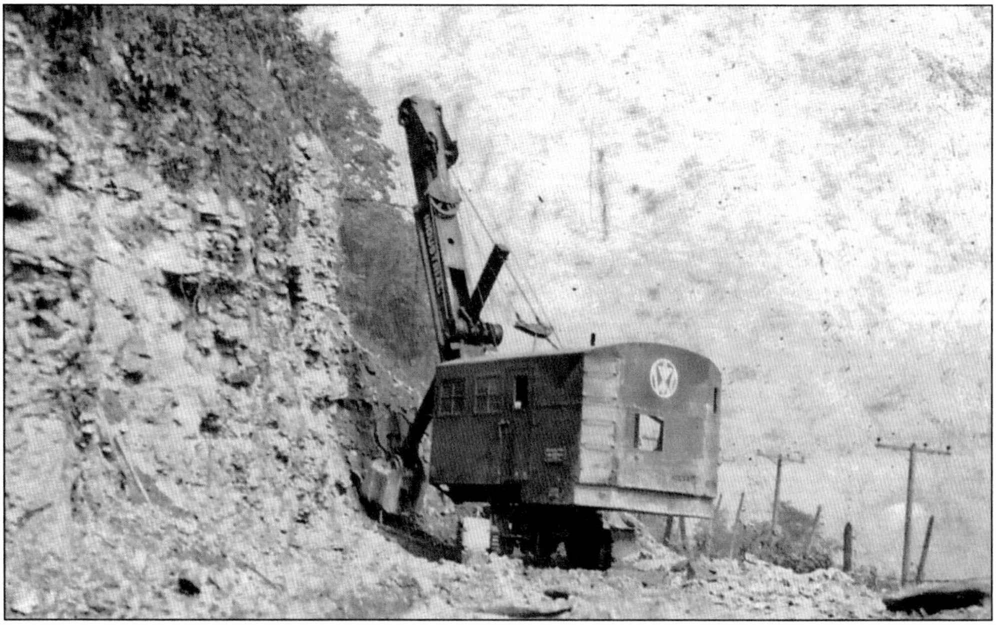

THREE-QUARTER YARD BAY CITY GAS SHOVEL, EARLY 1920S. This shovel is carving the original Route 7 out of the steep, sloping valley inclines between Steubenville and Mingo Junction. The new era of the automobile had dawned, and trolleys were on the way out. The trolley routes were too steep and too impractical to maintain their profitability. Roads needed to be built because Americans quickly fell in love with their cars—unruly crank handles and muddy roads be damned. In 1956, the town would again undergo a major destruction and construction stage when the new Route 7 made its path through the very heart of the town. (Courtesy Schiappa Library.)

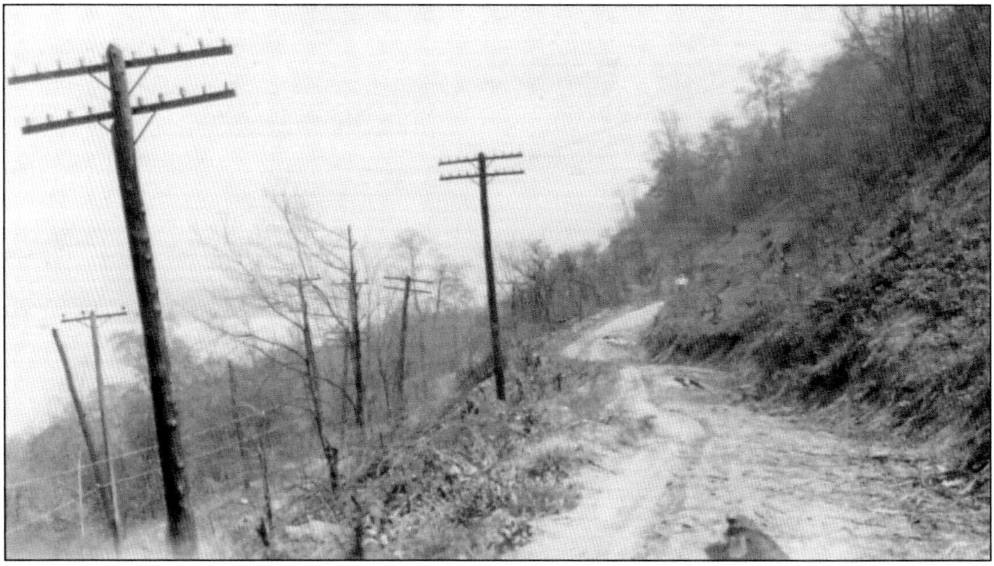

ROUTE 7 PLOWS THROUGH. All dug out and drivable? This early 1920s scene was viewed by many a motorist—and still the occasional buggy driver—heading south toward Mingo Junction from Steubenville. After a few days of heavy rain, roads would not be passable. Power lines have been strung here, and the railroad tracks are located just over the hill to the left along the river flats. (Courtesy Schiappa Library.)

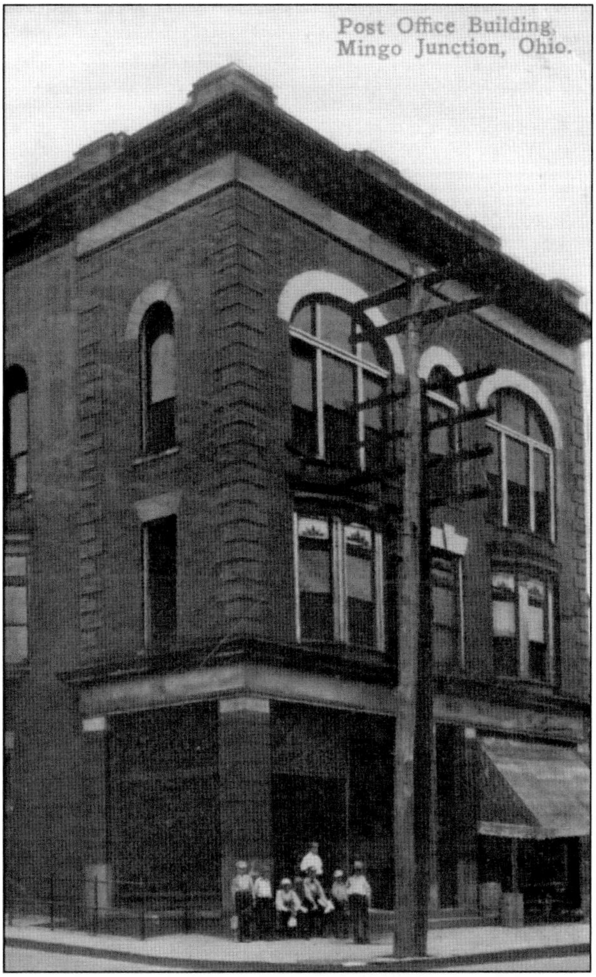

Old Post Office. Workers are waiting at the trolley car stop outside the "old" post office building on the corner of Ravine and Commercial Streets. They appear to be carrying their lunch bags to work, perhaps at the Carnegie Steubenville works. Trolley was the carrier of choice in the early 1900s. The rise of affordable cars was still a decade off. (Courtesy Sondra [White] Hyde.)

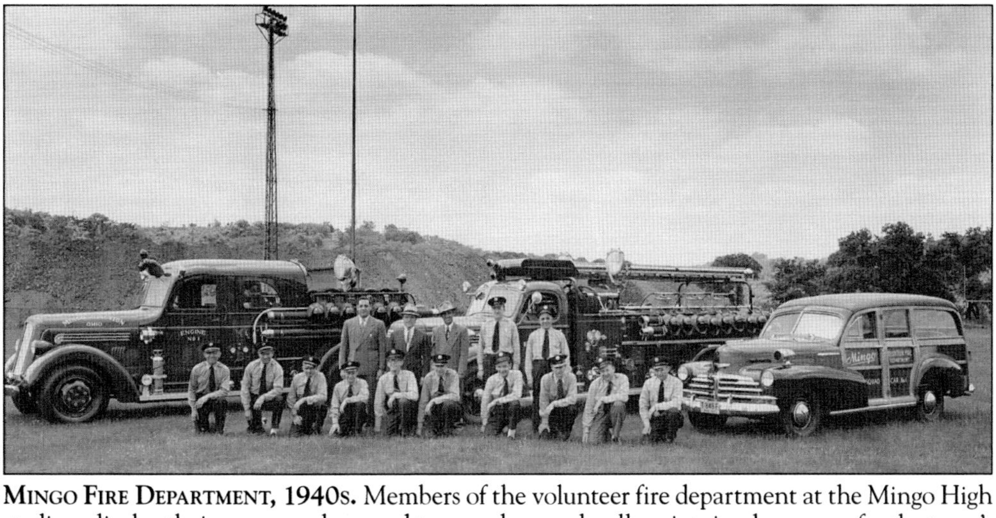

Mingo Fire Department, 1940s. Members of the volunteer fire department at the Mingo High stadium display their new squad car and two modern and well-maintained pumpers for the town's citizens. (Courtesy Paul Yates.)

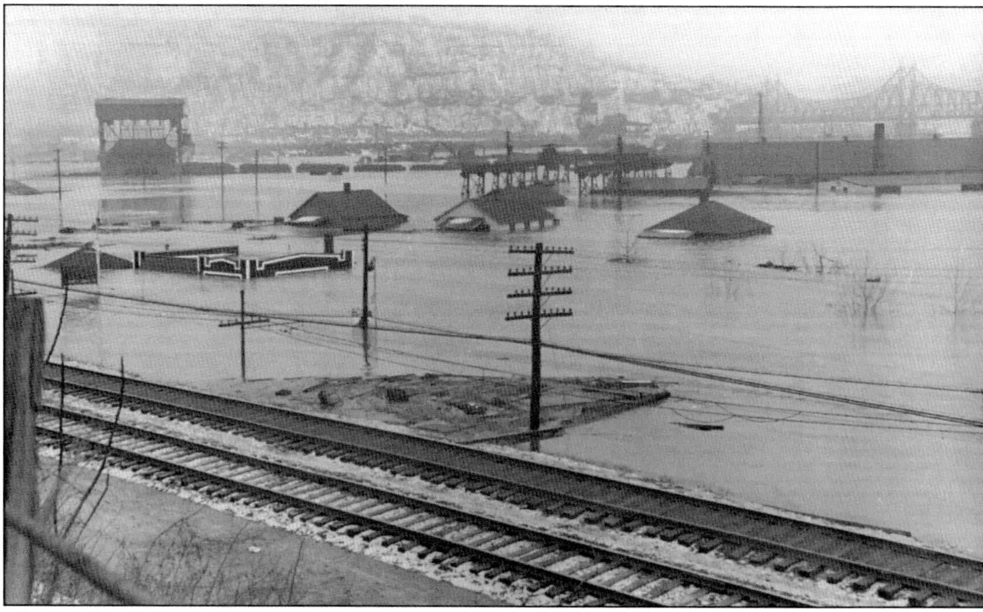

The Big Flood. The 1936–1937 flood was the flood of the century. It started raining during the last two weeks of December 1936 and continued nonstop into the first two weeks of January 1937. This rain, along with the flash snow melt-off, led to perfect flood conditions. Homes and garages were nearly submerged, and the water nearly rose level with the railroad tracks. Folks in the Bottoms area would first move furniture up a flight of stairs, then ultimately have to abandon all and escape in rowboats. (Courtesy Louise "Aunt Weezie" [Shannon] Kestner.)

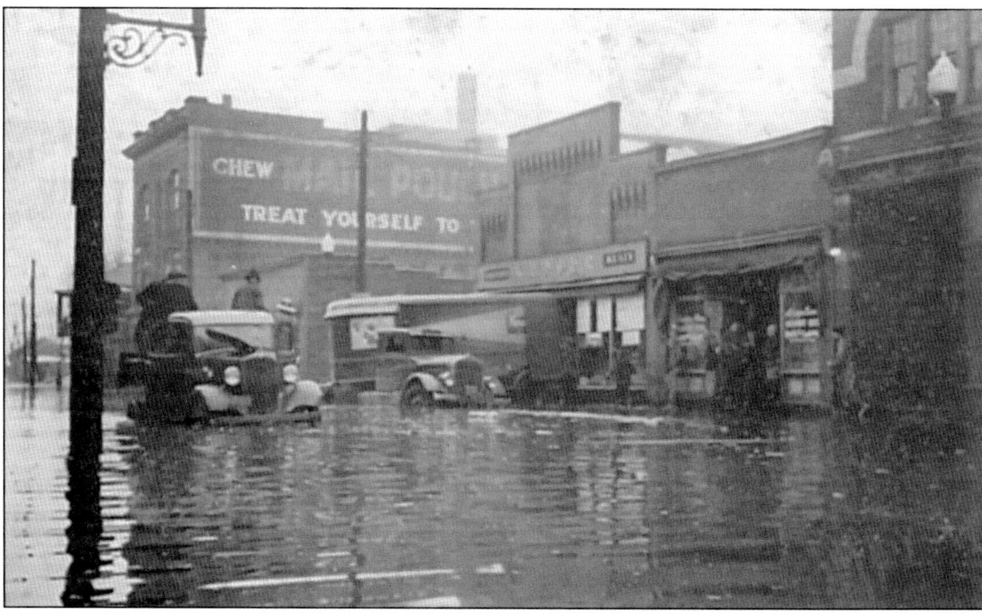

Downtown Mingo Underwater. The only time in recent history that the Ohio River and Cross Creek floodwaters would extend virtually all the length of Commercial Street was the flood of 1937. The city building was nearly surrounded by water, yet two trucks here made it onto Commercial Street. The two men in the truck bed are returning from an aborted attempt to make emergency deliveries. (Courtesy Eileen [Hagerty] Moody.)

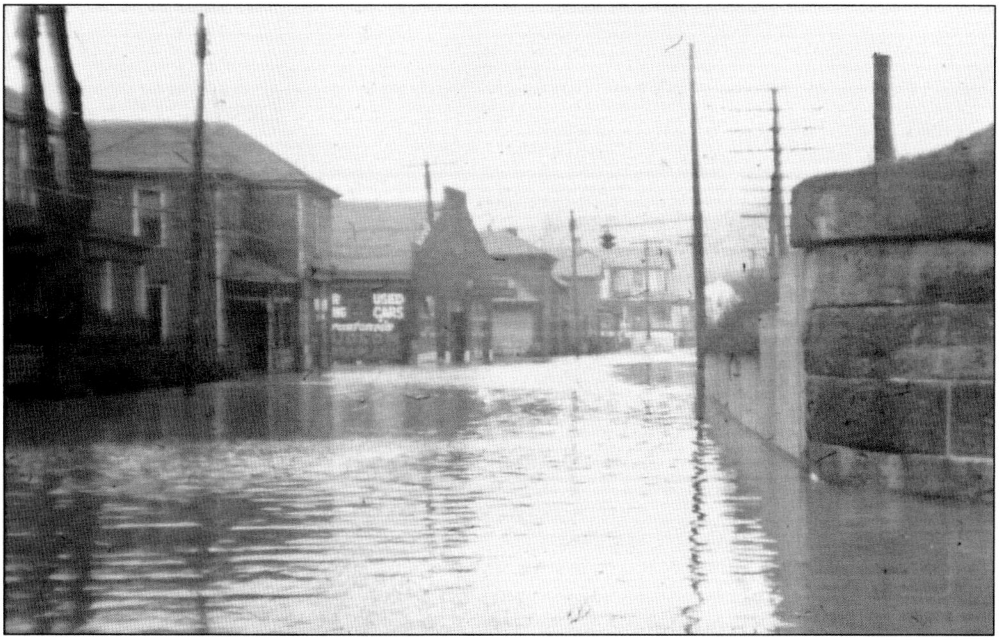

1940 A Normal Flood. This was the high-water mark of the flooding in April 1940. Looking south on Commercial Street just below the underpass, one can compare the difference in the water height on the Grantonic Terraplane-Hudson Car garage and dealership. Later it became the long-lived Weldon's Trucking garage. Floods from the Ohio came about every two years until dams were built in the late 1950s. (Courtesy John Grantonic.)

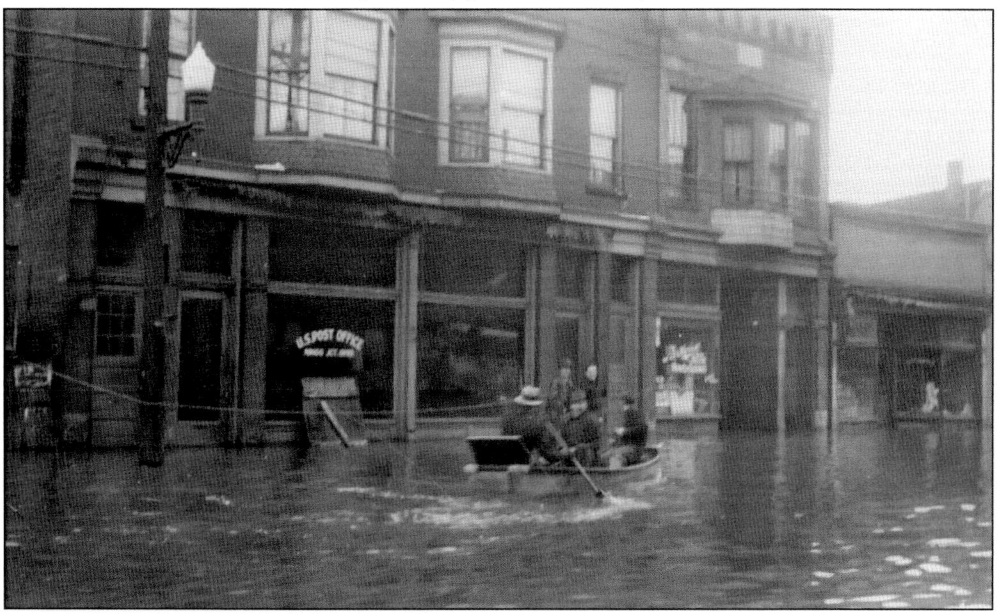

Rowboats on Commercial Street, 1937. The rowboat is across from the Mingo Post Office at 656 Commercial Street. The post office had been relocated from its 685 Commercial Street location. This was originally the Sharp Building (1902), which housed the Sharp furniture store. Later in the 1970s, the building was occupied by the Mingo Pharmacy, with proprietors and pharmacists Tom Indovina and Justin Scarpone. (Courtesy Barbara [Cook] Pesta.)

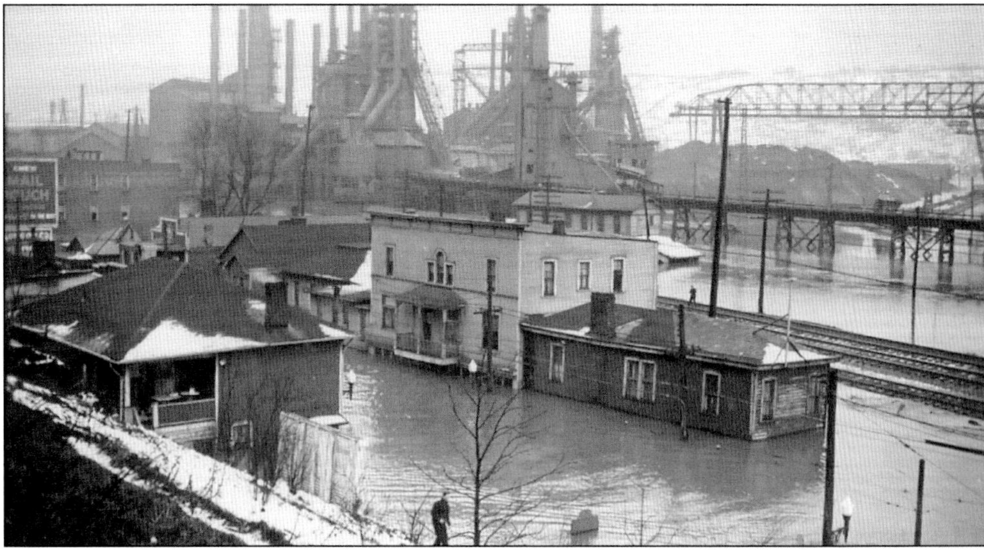

Town and Mills Submerged. A view of the 1937 flood shows the Carnegie Steel mill's blast furnaces, huge mountains of iron ore, a train trestle, and the massive ore-bridge crane acting as a stark backdrop. The George Washington sign at lower right is nearly totally underwater. Some of the snow still remains on rooftops and the ground where the melt-off added to the heavy rainwater volume, which led to the record water levels. (Courtesy Bessie [Priest] Quinn.)

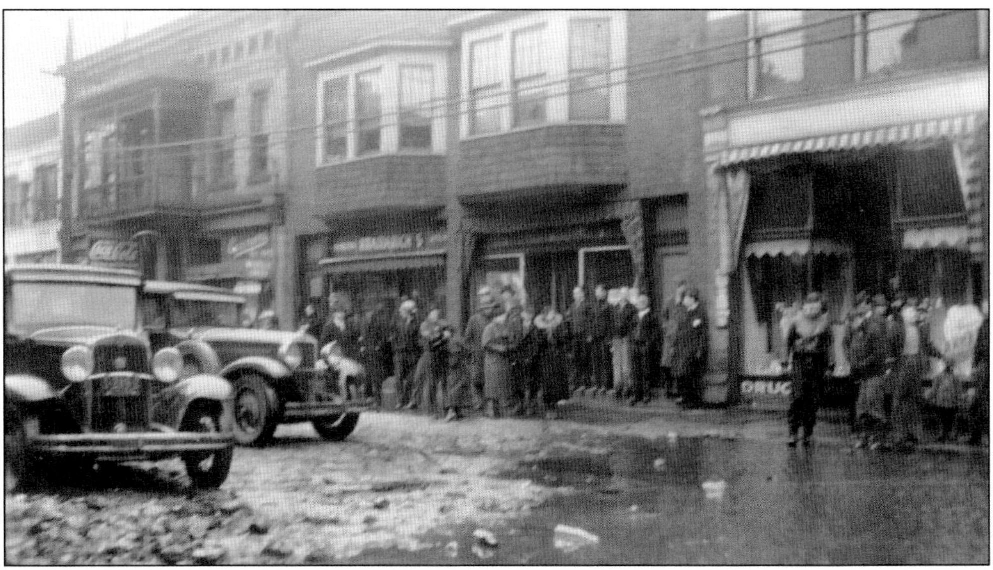

Flood Aftermath. The 1937 floodwaters slowly begin to recede. Stunned Mingo residents on Commercial Street gather, seeking words of solace or hope. It is time for the monumental cleanup job to begin. People keep to the sidewalks as they ascertain the damage and plan for an uncertain future. (Courtesy Barbara [Cook] Pesta.)

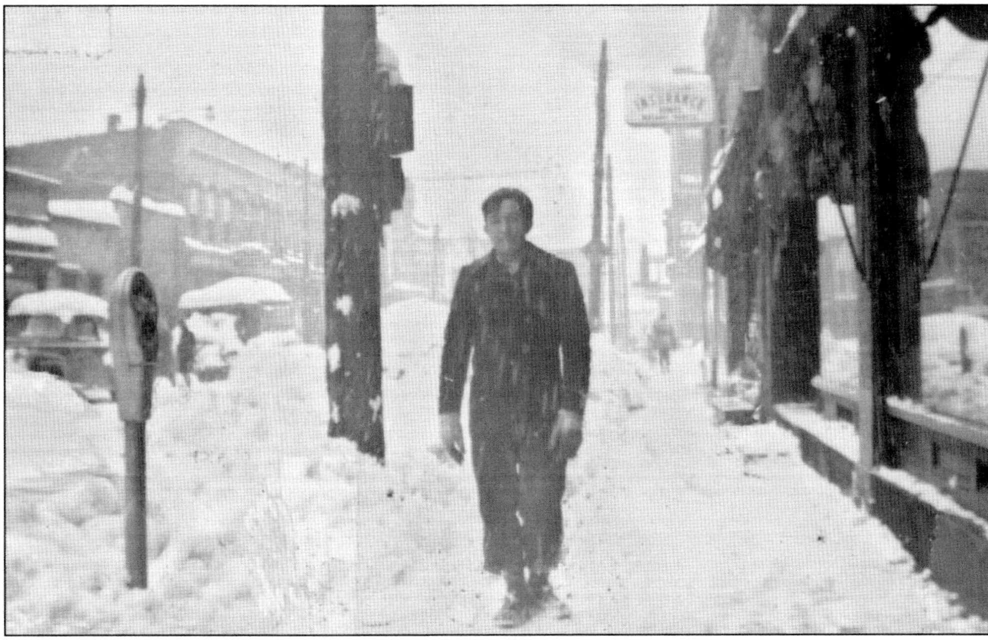

THE SNOW STORM, 1950. This was the record monster of a snowstorm at 41 inches, and it raged without respite from November 24 to November 27, 1950. Here is one of the few people brave enough to venture out, walking down Commercial Street as the snow continues to come down. Reports of roof collapses circled around the valley, and roof trusses quite literally groaned under the weight of the snow. (Courtesy Babe [Karas] Ardito.)

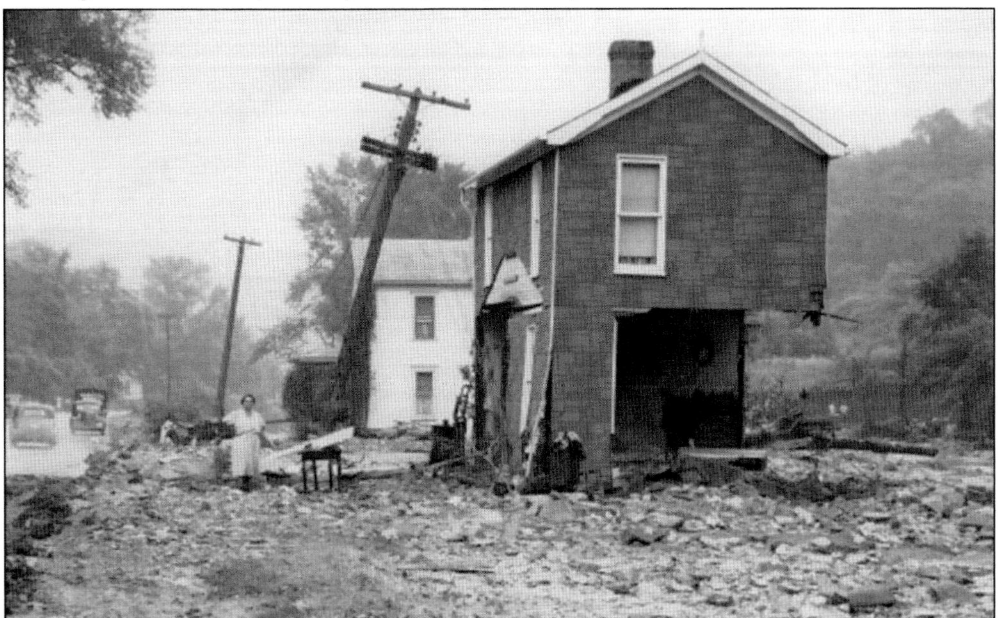

FLOOD "UP THE RUN." In this photograph from the 1950s, a teenage Carole O'Connor stands outside of her family's devastated home "up the run" in the Deandale-Georges Run area. Flood images were all too common in the early years of Mingo Junction and often personally costly, though the town recovered again and again. (Courtesy of Curtis O'Connor.)

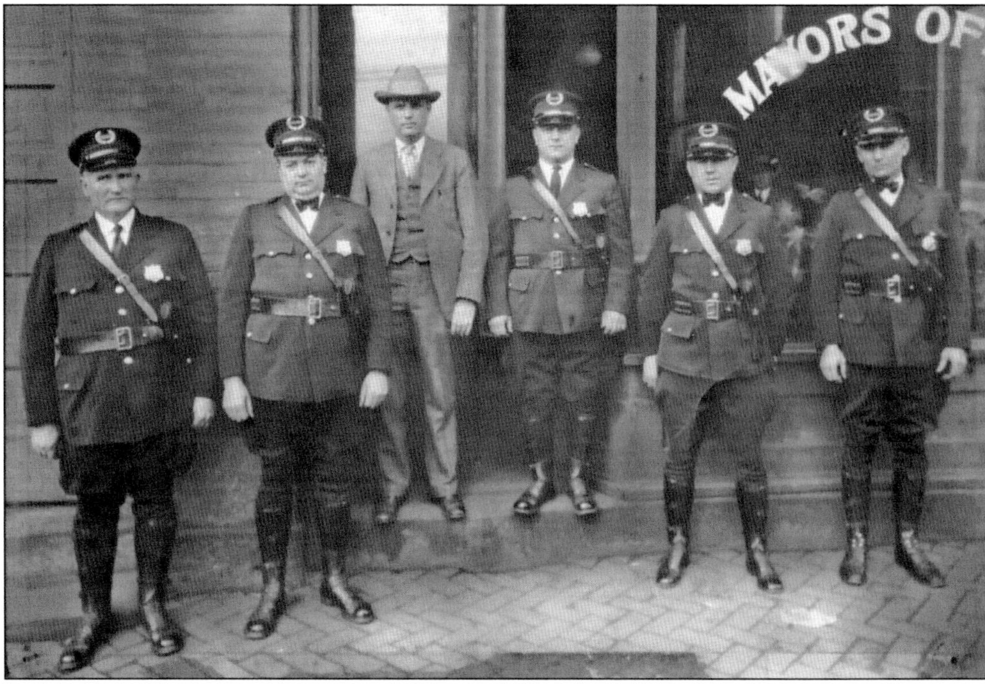

1928 Mingo Chief and Police Force. Mingo's protectors are seen here posed outside the old city building. Notice the high boots and pants—they were both the uniform of the day and practical. The police department did not have a cruiser and used a Harley Davidson motorcycle with a sidecar for bringing in offenders. Seen here from left to right are Tom Eckard, Ed Bell Sr., police chief Nick Carter, Albert Kakasick, Basil Defranco, and Mike Colley. (Courtesy Ed Bell.)

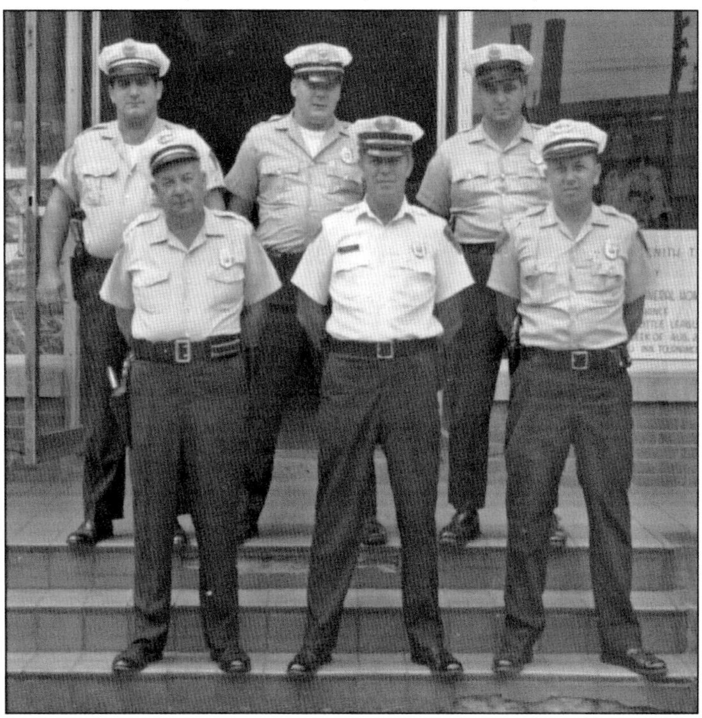

Mingo Police Force, 1968. Here are some of the town's efficient and friendly peace officers. From left to right, they are (first row) Ed Bell, Chief George Dodsworth, and Michael Maguschak; (second row) Joe Molinaro, Mike Meatris, and Dan Pizzerferrato. (Courtesy Chief Steve Maguschak, Mingo Police Department.)

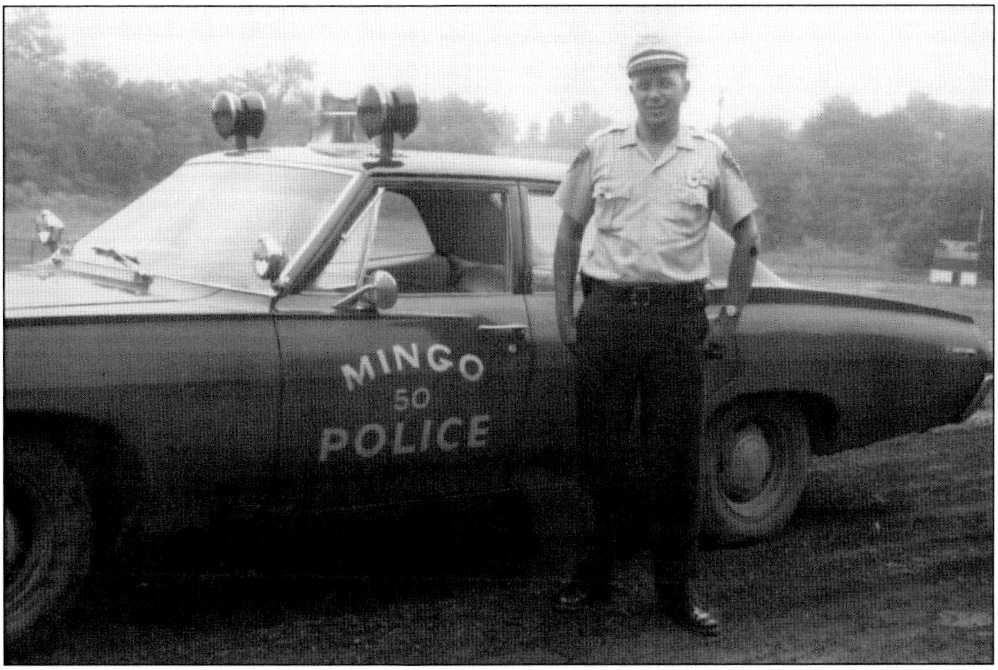

Lt. Mike Maguschak Down. Felled by gunfire, an excellent police officer and individual gave his life in the line of duty on Wednesday, December 30, 1970. Lieutenant Maguschak was one of two Mingo police officers that made the ultimate sacrifice. Two of his sons, Mike and Steve, became police officers, and both of them later became Mingo's chief of police. (Courtesy Chief Steve Maguschak.)

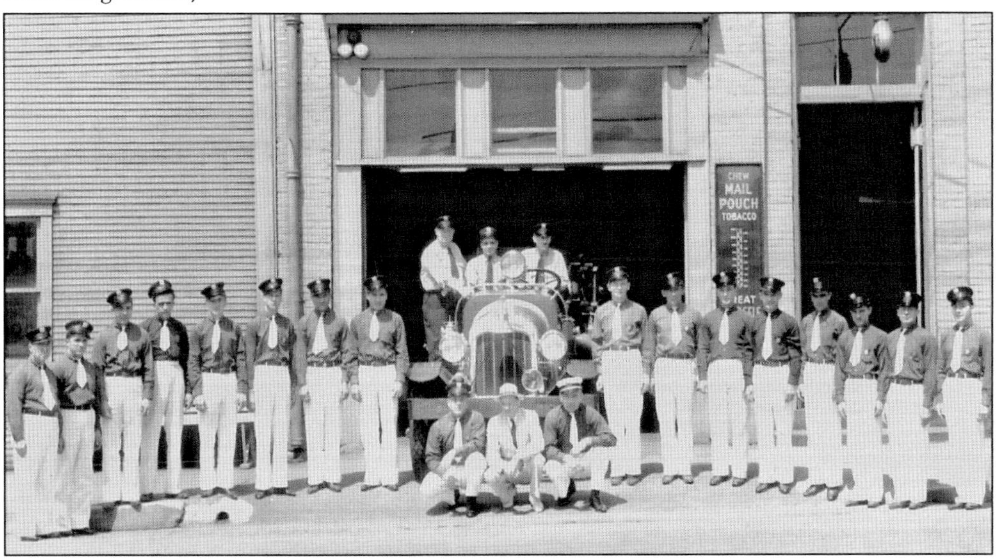

Mingo Fire Department, 1937–1938. Seen here from left to right are (first row) assistant fire chief Paul Brandt, safety director Ira Dalrymple, and fire chief Joe Grantonic; (second row) Edriss Jackson, Fred O'Reilly, Frank Morrocco, Eli Lalich, Albert Green, Willard Pry, Orin Diomidi, Mike Dicarlo, Earl Fithen, Nick Ross, Mont McLuan, Joseph Tokar, John Slivka, Albert Trombetta, George Grantonic, Sam Zatezlo, J. Carducci, Dom Figlio, and Tal Scott. (Courtesy Rick Blair and the Hillsboro Tavern.)

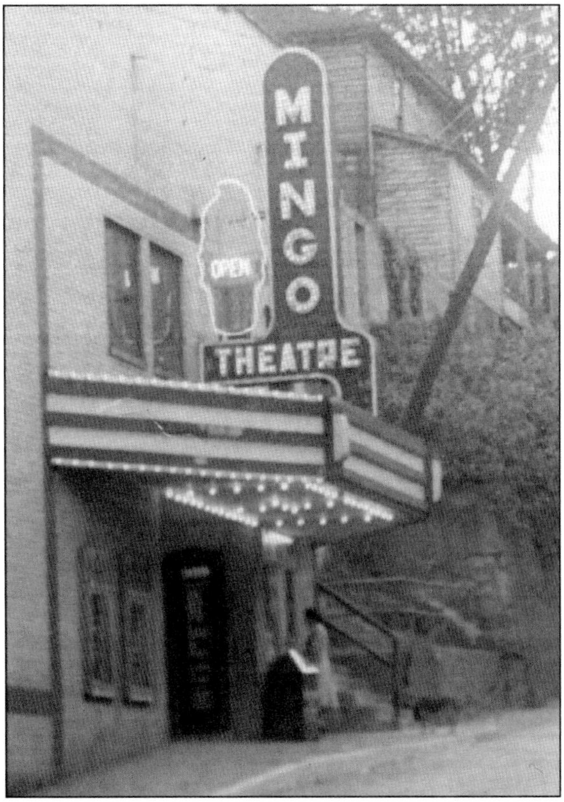

"LET'S GO TO THE SHOW." The image of the Mingo Show on Ravine Street usually invokes fond memories. For kids in a working-class town, it was a way to see the world outside the valley—and at times, to have their own world projected onto a large screen. The show was run well by Mike Kendrach. Eagerly awaited matinee weekends of youth were always just ahead. The building is gone now, torn down decades ago and replaced by the multiscreen cinema complexes of today. (Courtesy Paula [Kendrach] Kopcha.)

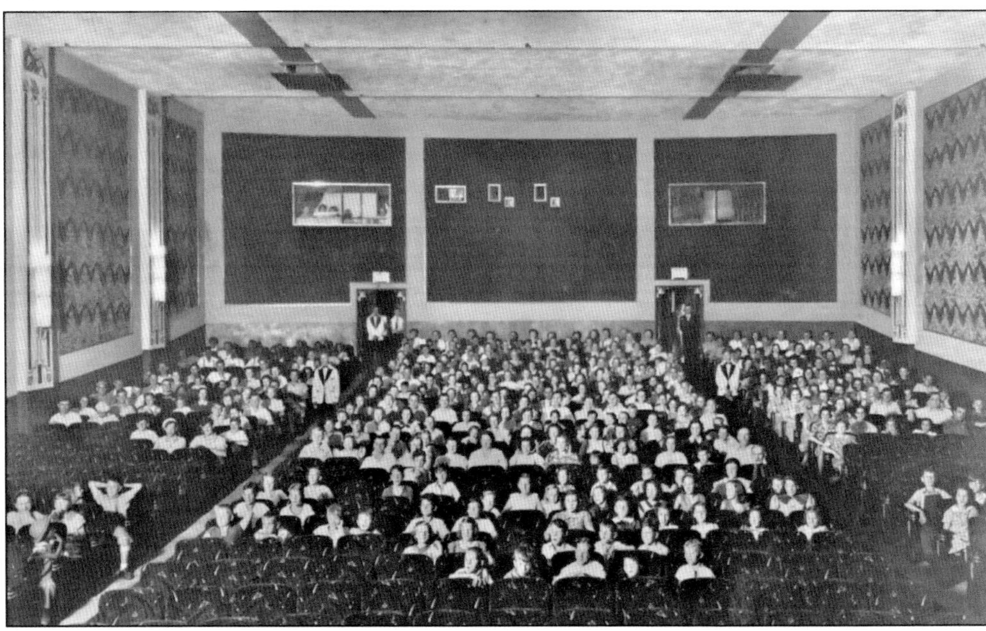

MINGO SHOW INTERIOR. In small, one-screen towns like Mingo, most of the shows had a certain ambiance and were rich with the anticipation of coming attractions. New films would debut on Sundays, Wednesdays, and Fridays. Note the tuxedos on the young ushers. As the lights came down, the children would cheer in anticipation. (Courtesy Paula [Kendrach] Kopcha.)

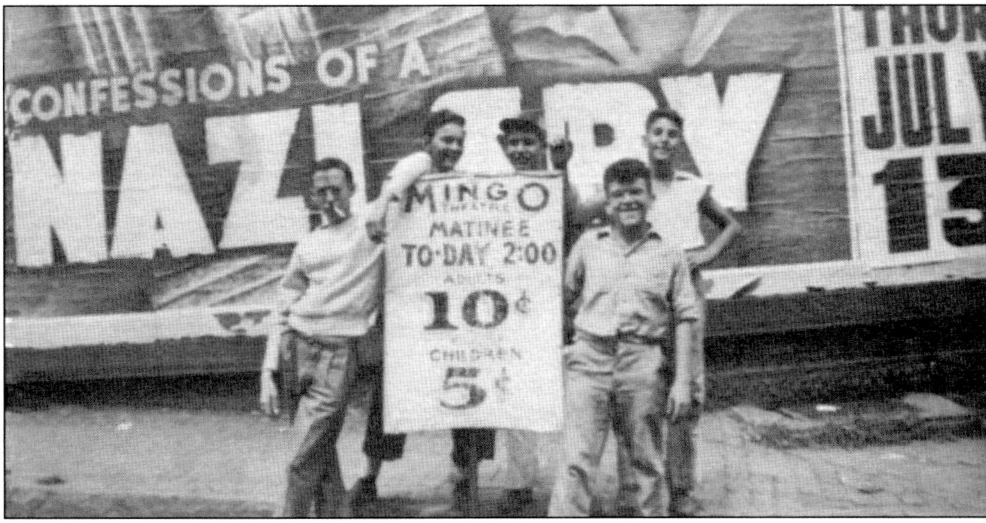

Coming Attractions. This was Mingo in the 1930s, with the tradition of posting the Mingo Show's weekly coming attractions on the wall of the building on the corner of Commercial Street and McLister Avenue. That building housed the Corner Café and Benny Leone's Hardware store. The building has been replaced by a small rest area and a beautiful, large four-sided clock. (Courtesy Darlene Hoff, originally published in *Bicentennial History of Mingo Junction, Ohio.*)

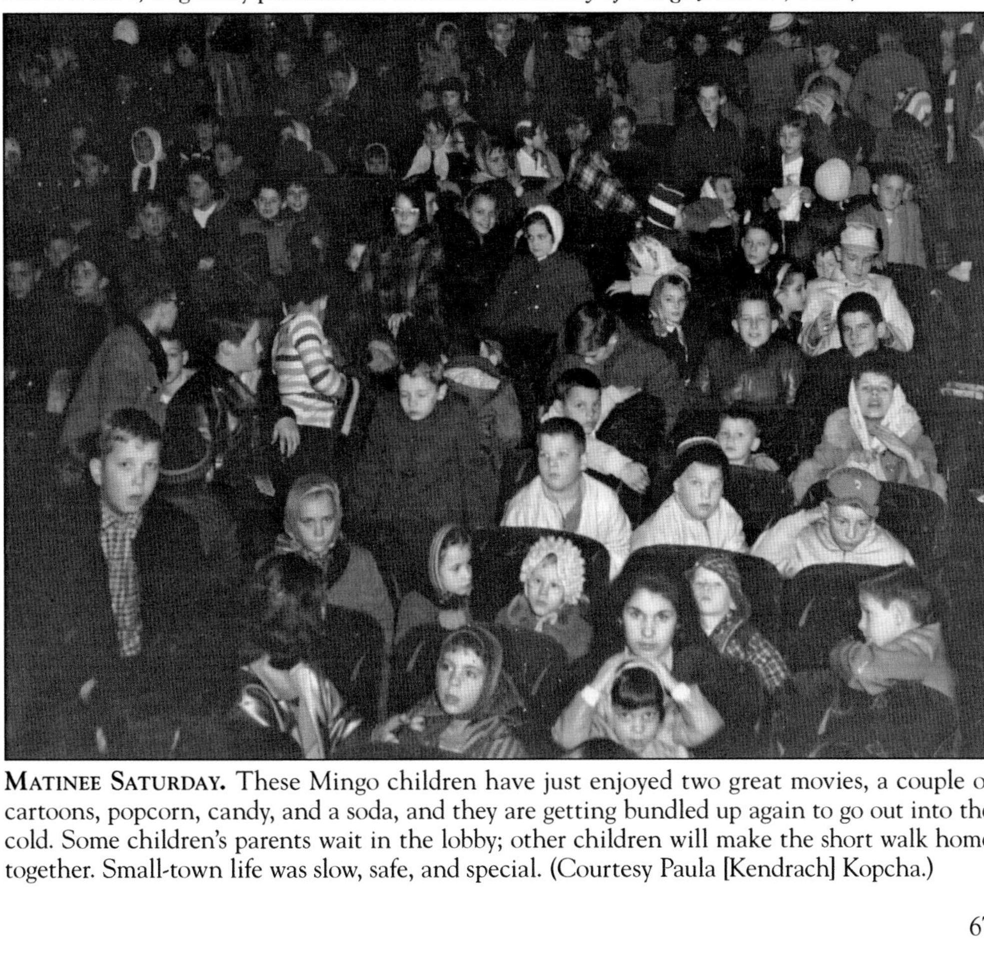

Matinee Saturday. These Mingo children have just enjoyed two great movies, a couple of cartoons, popcorn, candy, and a soda, and they are getting bundled up again to go out into the cold. Some children's parents wait in the lobby; other children will make the short walk home together. Small-town life was slow, safe, and special. (Courtesy Paula [Kendrach] Kopcha.)

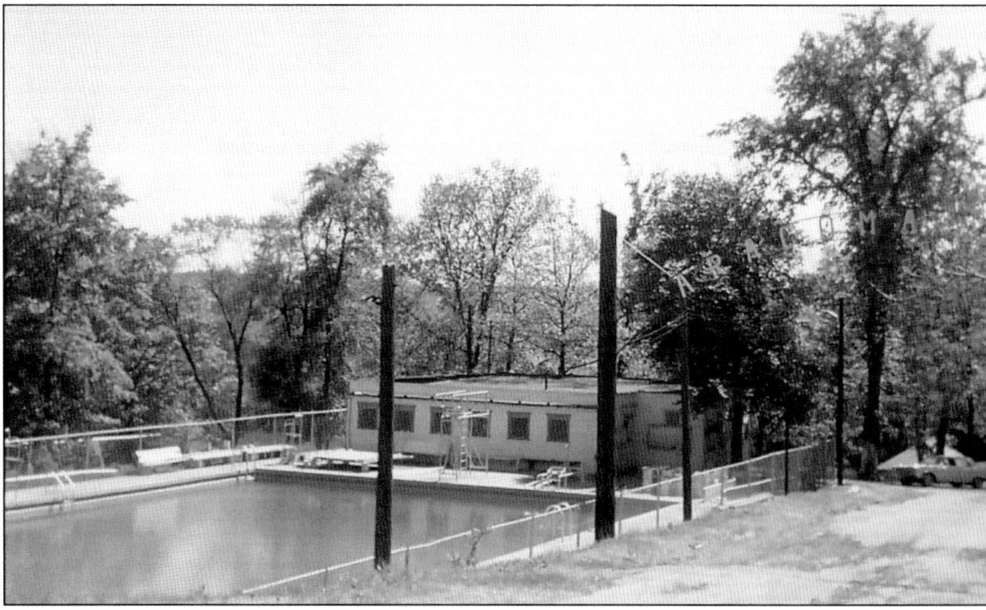

"Old" Swimming Pool. This pool served the village well for years, but eventually a new pool needed to be built. The pool area was filled in and blacktopped and is used today for parking. The bathhouse was torn down and is now the site of a shelter house for recreational outings. Many a car cruised beneath the Aracoma sign with its top down, its radio just a bit loud, and its driver and passengers busily "checking out the action."

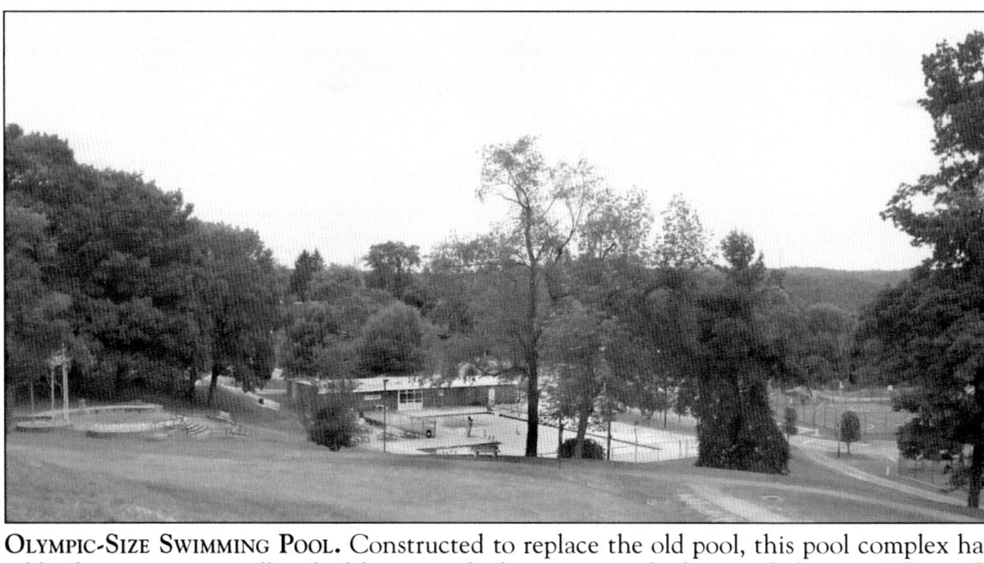

Olympic-Size Swimming Pool. Constructed to replace the old pool, this pool complex has tables for eating, an excellent bathhouse, and a large grass sunbathing and play area. This truly beautiful facility located in the wonderful Aracoma Park instills a sense of pride in the community. (Courtesy Mayor Dominic "Noony" Chappano.)

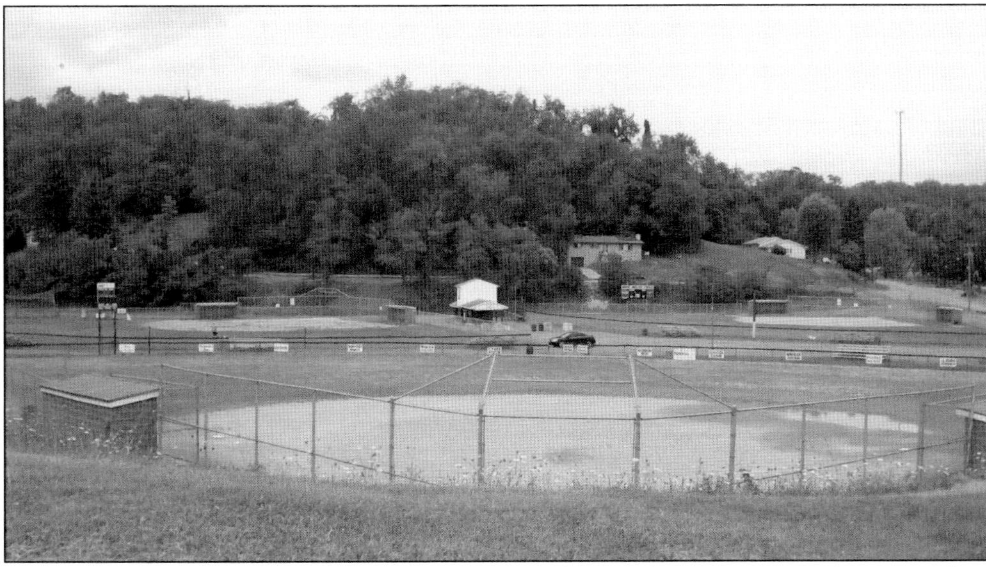

Youth Baseball-Softball Complex. This three-field complex is an outstanding example of Mingo's long-term and long-standing commitment to the youth of the community. The goal is to provide the finest and safest athletic facilities possible. The hard work and long hours of literally hundreds of volunteer coaches and helpers over the past 50-plus years says much about Mingo and its residents. (Courtesy Guy Mason II.)

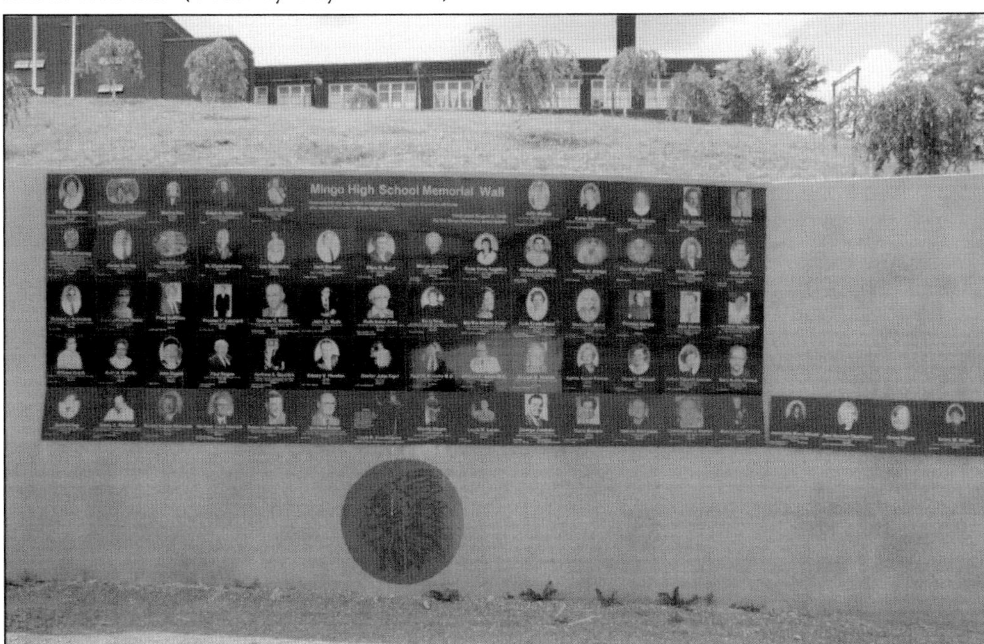

Cherry Blossom Memorial Park. Constructed and dedicated in 2008, the wall showcases the Mingo commitment to excellence and its appreciation for its past educators and school staff. The memorial wall was the concept of Jimmy Frieling and was ultimately funded and completed due to the hard work of countless volunteers, the Village of Mingo, the Mingo Business Association, and hundreds of past Mingo graduates and families willing to sponsor teachers and staff who were instrumental in their lives.

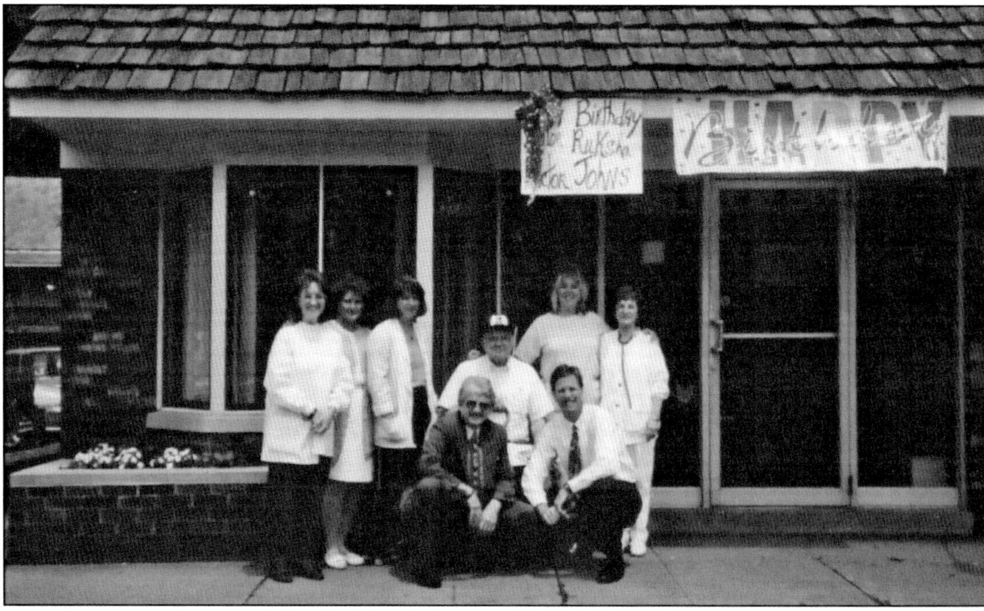

Town Doctors. Dr. William Johns is shown here in front with the late Dr. Paul and Penn Kurtz. In 1977, Johns associated with Ruksha, who began his Mingo practice in 1957. Pictured here from left to right are (first row) Dr. William Johns, Dr. Paul Ruksha, and Penn Kurtz; (second row) Joann Johns, Julie Boso, Val Buaghman, unidentified, and Carol Fisher. Earlier physicians in the town included Drs. Fred Riney, Jason Albaugh, Jasper Cava, Stephanus Abraham, and Samuel Justice. (Courtesy William and Joann Johns.)

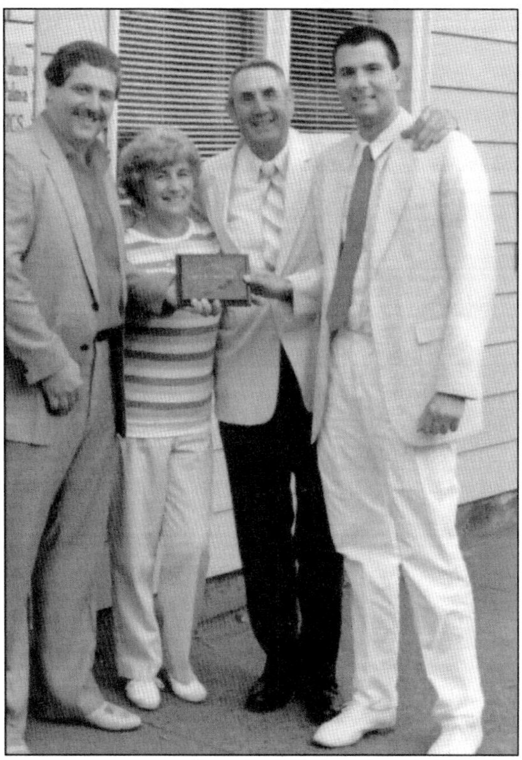

Town Dentists. Here are former mayor John Corrigan (left), Marie Palma, and Bernie Palma with Dr. Pat Palma (right) at the 1989 opening recognition for his new dental office in Mingo. Other town dentists included John Novotny, C. E. Rasor, Dr. Sweet, Ross Reed, James Brettell, and this book's coauthor, Guy Mason. (Courtesy Dr. Pat Palma.)

Community Days in Mingo. Residents looked forward to the parades, ethnic food booths, diverse entertainment, and fireworks. No one enjoyed it more than Mac Timcho and his family. Here is Mac enjoying himself behind the wheel of his vintage car. Community Days have been canceled for the past several years due to the economy, but they may revive. (Courtesy Mac Timcho.)

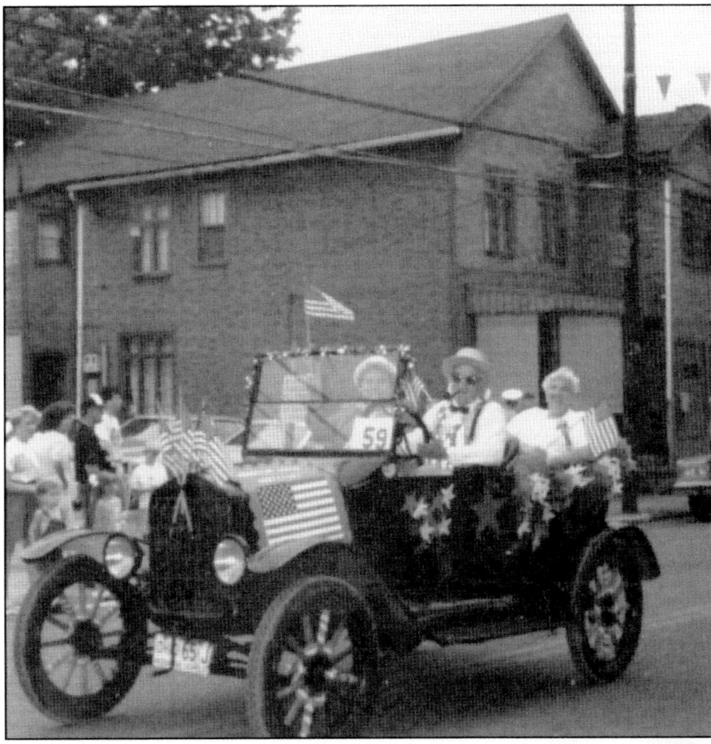

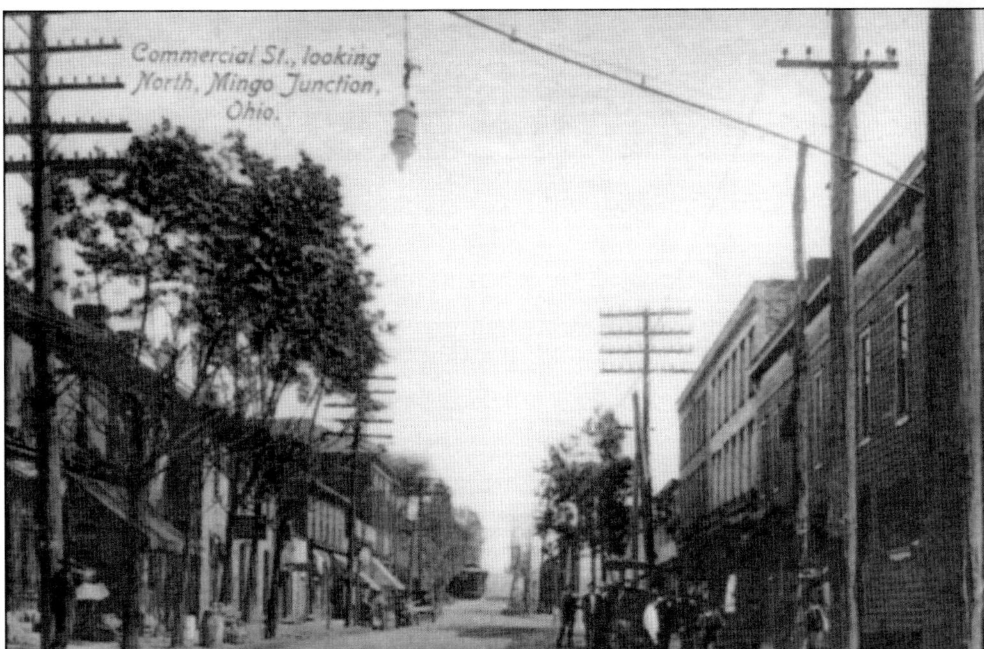

Unique Retro Look Back. This early 1900s postcard depicts a close approximation as to where Mac Timcho (above) would actually be with his vintage car in the parade heading north on Commercial Street. A trolley can be seen on the rise, which in the future will lead to Route 7. The two-story city building, built in 1888, stands way off to the left, just in front of the trolley. (Courtesy Sondra [White] Hyde.)

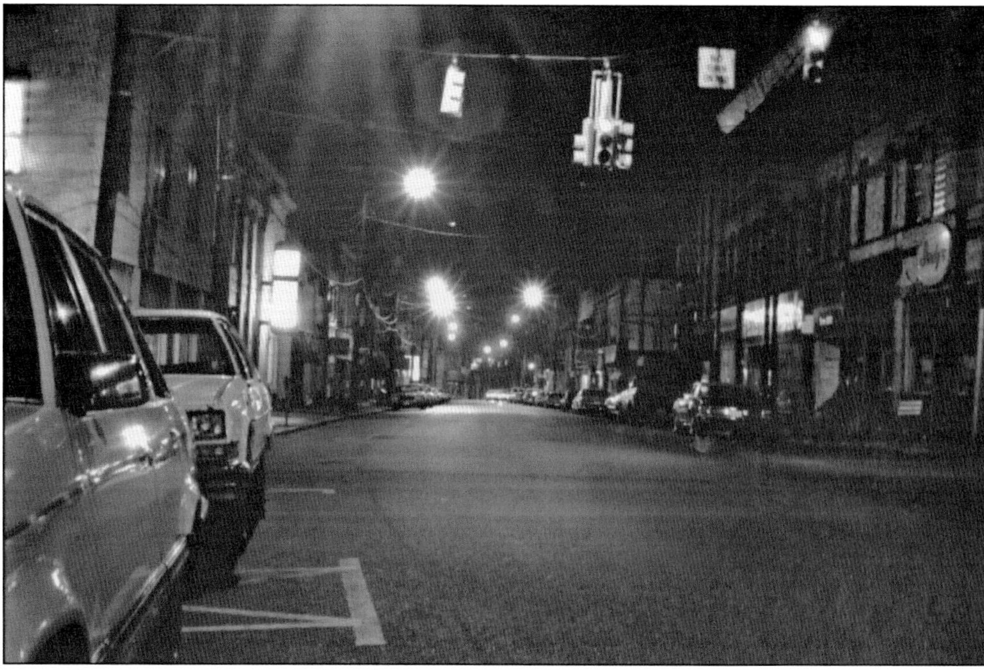

Late-Night Mingo, 1970s. This photograph captures a sight familiar to many Mingo natives. The Mingo Bank, Weisberger's, and Isaly's have closed since this picture was taken, and the clock and signs are gone as well. (Courtesy Ed "Spuds" Fithen, Parkview Inn.)

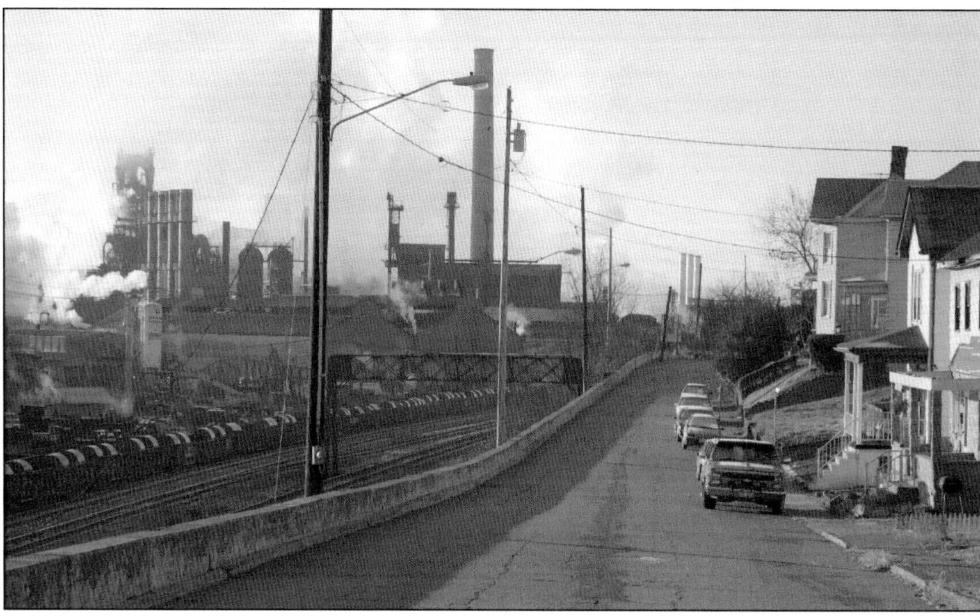

Looking Back Now. This familiar scene depicts better times for the mill. Shown are the blast furnaces, railroad tracks, signal tower, and railroad gondola cars laden with the freshly minted Wheeling-Pittsburgh steel coils ready for shipment. The steel process began from the mountains of raw iron ore and proceeded to the finished product in the fully integrated Mingo steel mill. The local steel heritage approaches 150 years but is faced with an uncertain future as the mill has remained idle and the town and mill seek new ways to persevere. (Courtesy Kevin Scanlon.)

Five

Daily Life

As a town is made up of its people, those people then create its sense of community. Mingo Junction was and is primarily a working-class town with a sprinkling of business owners, mill mangers, teachers, and a few lawyers and doctors. Though the melting pot metaphor has served us for over a century, perhaps the image of a salad bowl better suggests the rich individual flavors found in the town. Successive waves of immigration brought new color and character to Mingo. In Joseph Conroy's 1921 biography, *A Mill Town Pastor*, he borrows mill records for this list of worker nationalities: native-born "Americans" form the largest group, followed by Slovaks and Italians, then by Serbians, Englishmen, Irishmen, Austrians, Hungarians, African Americans, Germans, Scotts, Bulgarians, Polish, Russians, Croatians, Spanish, Romanians, Swedes, and Greeks.

Work, family, and—for many—church were the centers of life. "Where you working?" was the typical greeting question, meaning where in the mill and on what shift. Shift life affected families where work came first and all plans were made around it. With limited vacation time, working families made their own recreation along the river and in the parks, at family reunions, and at covered-dish suppers held at the school and church.

As the downtown grew alongside of its industry, they met at its clothing, grocery, butcher, and bakery stores and at its many bars and social clubs. They gathered at the Mingo Show for movies, the Auditorium for performances, at restaurants and bars for music and dancing, and at school sporting events in the gym and stadium. Social groups grew up, such as the Knights of Columbus, Knights of Pythias, Odd Fellows, and Women's Club, among others. Ownership of downtown stores seemed to rotate regularly, though some have lasted for almost a century now. Like most small towns, people watched each other and kept track of family relationships even as nationalities, religions, and races blended in marriage. Though "uptown" Steubenville was nearby via trolley, bus, or car, downtown Mingo was always home to its people.

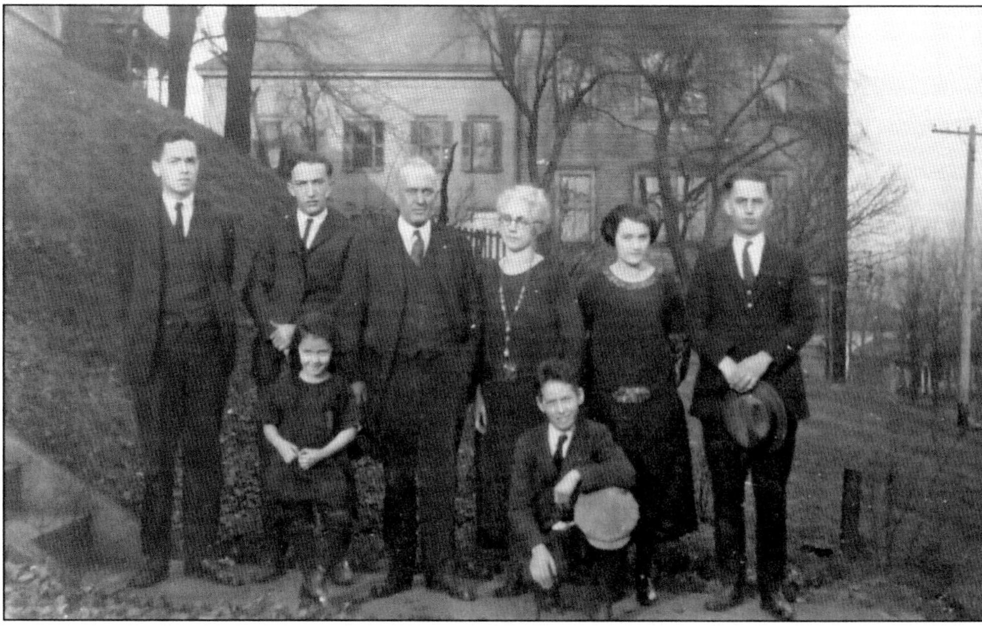

The Hagerty family, 1925. Pictured here is the Hagerty family in front of their home between Steuben and Churchway Streets. Included in the photograph are, from left to right, Andrew, James, Robert Sr. with wife Anna Sophia (Binder), Sophia, and Fred. In front are Anna and Robert Jr. Among other businesses, James owned and operated the Amoco Service Station on Route 7 between Mingo and Steubenville, then became a postmaster, and Andrew moved from being a blacksmith in the Carnegie Mill to being a Fuller Brush salesman. Note the image of St. Agnes School in the background. Seen in the photograph below is their home, which was built in 1880 and is still occupied by Amelia Frund, Andrew's widow. (Both courtesy Eileen [Hagerty] Moody.)

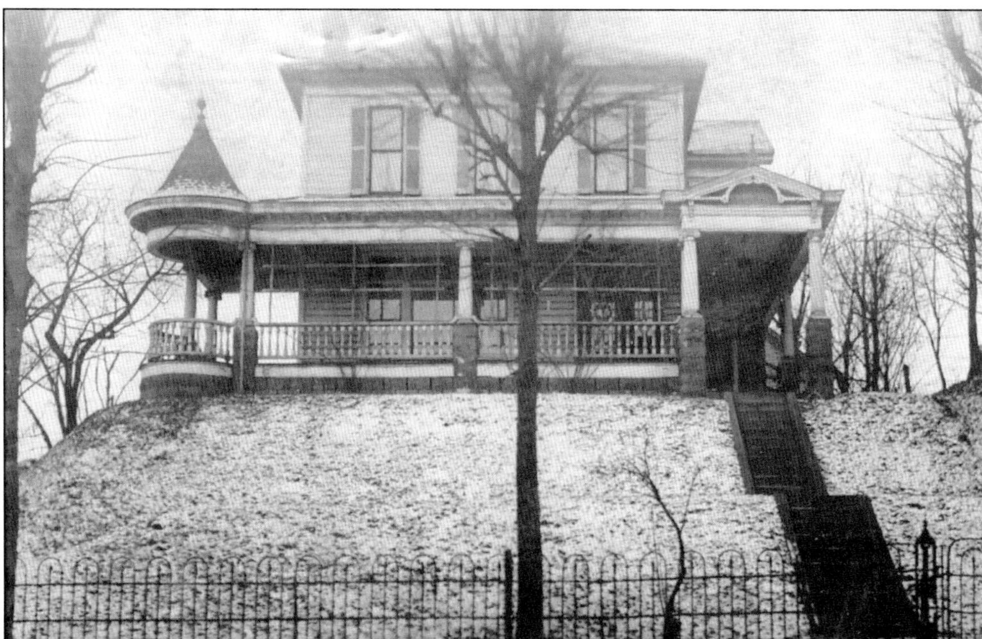

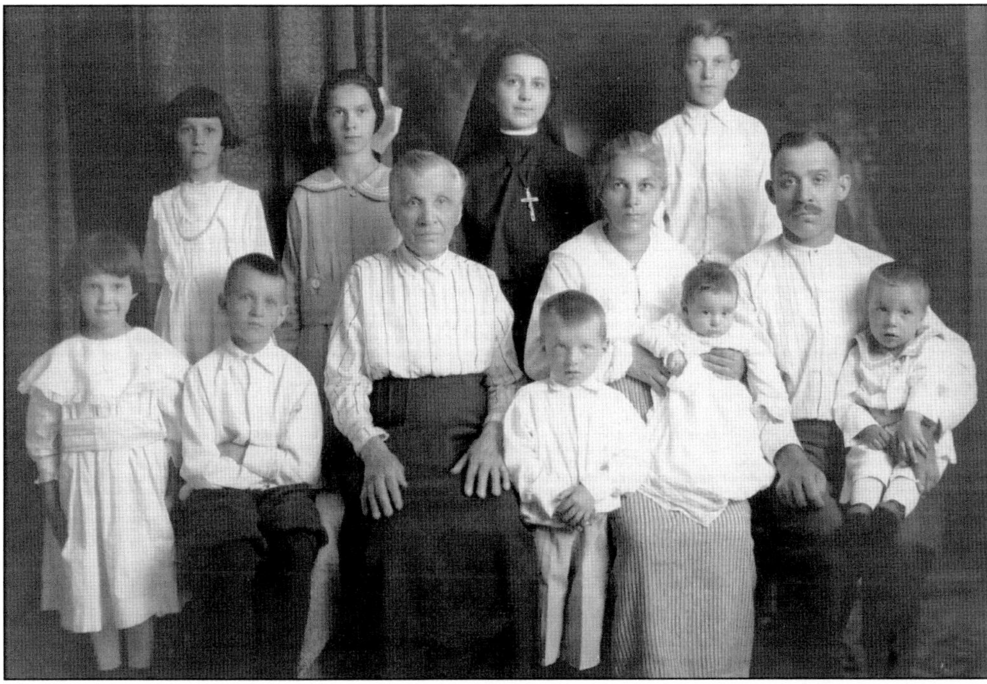

THE JOHN AND ANNA BUCHMELTER FAMILY. This photograph of a Hungarian-Austrian and Polish-Russian family includes, from left to right, (first row) Helen, Joseph, grandmother Maria (Buchmelter) Vincent, unidentified, mother Anna with baby Agnes, and father John with Edward; (second row) Anna, Mary, Sister Clementine, and John. The father, John Buchmelter, worked as a blacksmith in the steel mill, and the family lived on Lincoln Avenue on Reservoir Hill. (Courtesy Sommer Roach and Icey Hagedorn.)

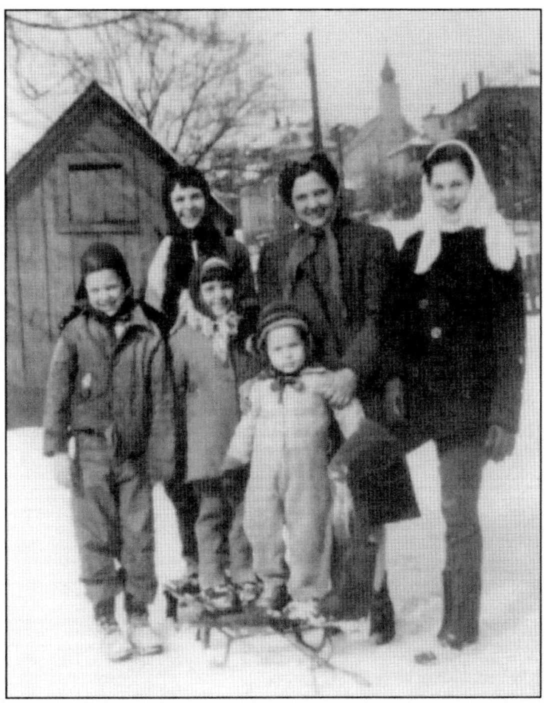

SNOWY DAY. Pictured on this snowy day in 1946 at the base of Reservoir Hill are the younger Buchmelter children. From left to right are (first row) John "Boom Boom" Buchmelter, Mary Kay Buchmelter, and Rita Buchmelter; (second row) Clementine (Buchmelter) Cacciarro, Mary Jarzabek Buchmelter, and Dolores (Buchmelter) Stewart. (Courtesy Sommer Roach and Icey Hagedorn.)

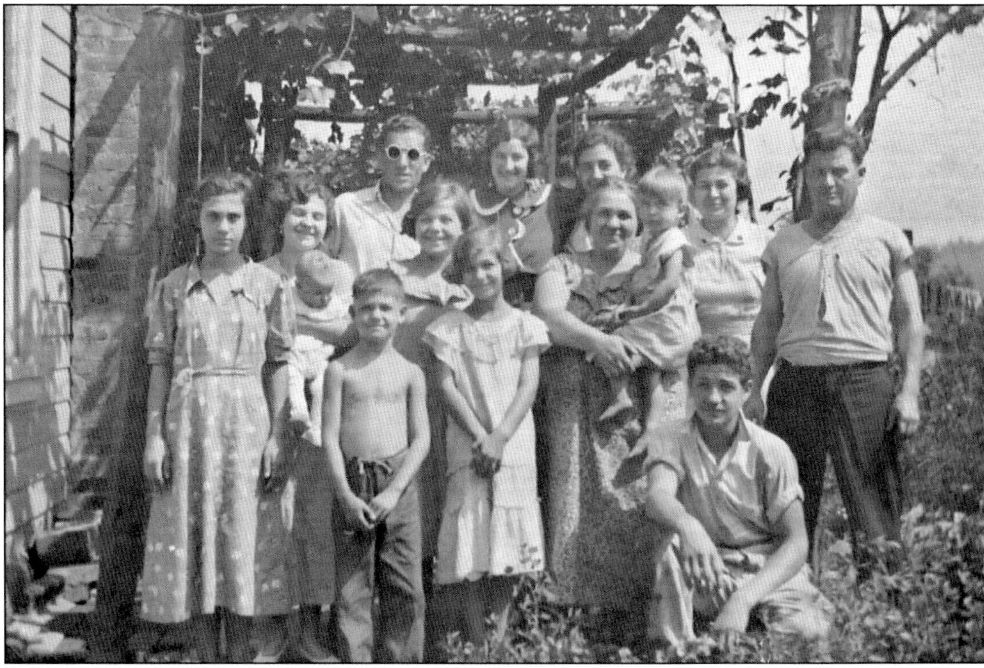

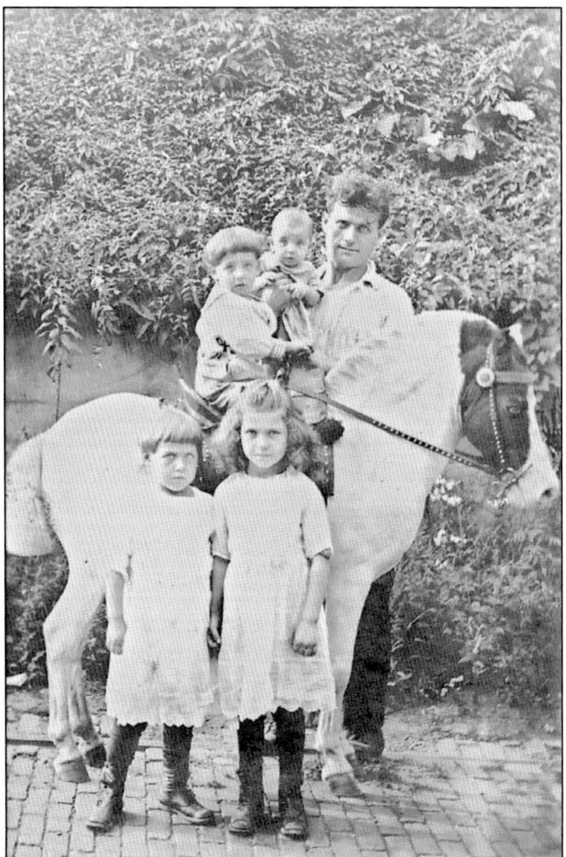

The Cesare and Amelia (Morrocco) Ferroni family. Pictured here in 1936 at their double home on South Commercial Street (shared with the Petrozzi family) are the Ferronis. From left to right, they are (first row) Mary, Assunta "Susan" (holding her sister Mary Alice), Alfonso "Al," Ann, Philomena "Fanny," mother Amelia, Charles, and Emedio "Sam"; (second row) Sam and Grace Ferroni (from Columbus), Adeline Petrozzi, Helen Ferroni, and her father, Cesare.

The Pony Photograph. A frequent visitor to town was the photographer who came with his pony. Pictured here around 1920 are Helen (left) and Susan in front and Sam (mounted) and Mary with father Cesare Ferroni. Cesare worked on the crane in the steel mill; they later moved to Clifton Avenue, then Peeler Street. (Courtesy Charles Ferroni.)

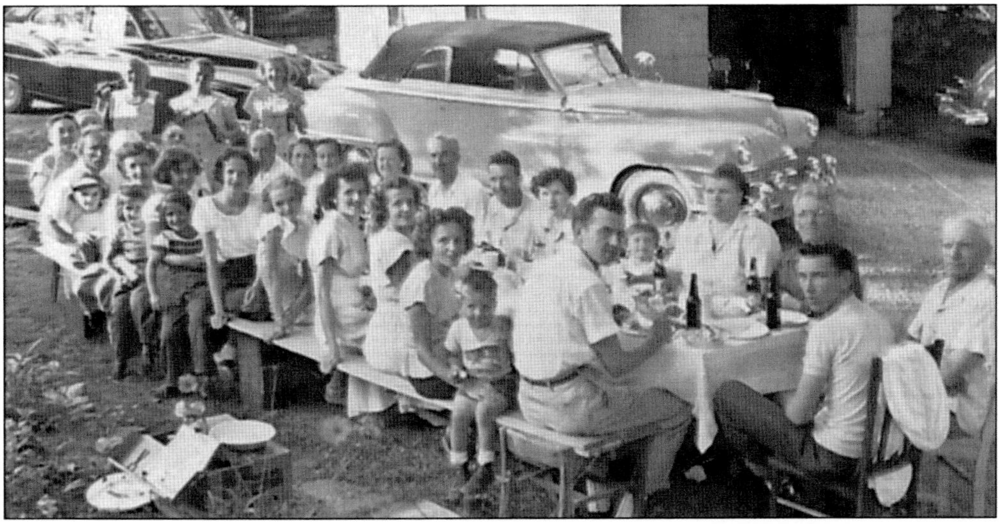

Behary-Malesick Reunion. Seen here from left to right are (first row) Mrs. Mike Malesick, Poker Smith with Geraldine Malesick on her lap, Margaret (Malesick) Smith with Nannette Carducci on her lap, JoAnne Biggio with Janette Carducci on her lap, Beatrice (Petroskey) Daily, Ruth Ann (Rogers) Graninger, Mary Alice (Petroskey) Trombetta, Betty Jane (Petroskey) Stinard, Mary (Malesick) Carducci, Johnny Carducci, Paul Malesick, and Joe Malesick; (second row) George Malesick, Steve Malesick, Mrs. Steve Malesick holding her granddaughter, Jeannette Malesick, John Malesick, Joe Petroskey, Mary Petroskey, David Petroskey, Susie (Malesick) Knowles, Bud Knowles, and Mike Malesick; (third row) Anne (Rogers) Malesick, Elizabeth Martin, and Anne Malesick. The men in the families shown here typically worked in coal mines and steel mills. (Courtesy Bea [Petroskey] Daily.)

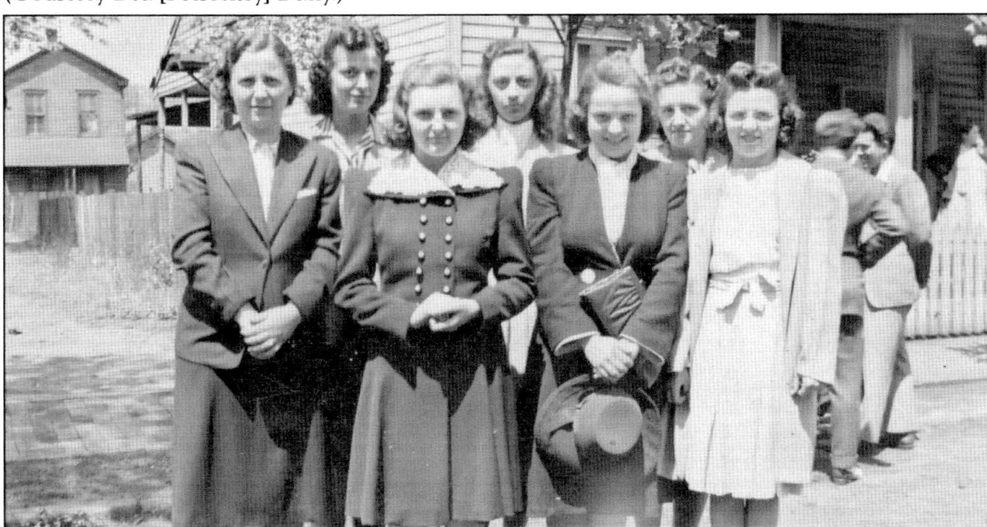

Our Friends as Family. Often in small towns like Mingo, neighbors and friends would become like family and remain so throughout their lives, as seen in this 1930s group of Serbian women standing near the Serbian Eastern Orthodox Resurrection Church in Mingo Bottoms. Shown here from left to right are Mildred Vokovich, Helen Bizich, Mary Vitas, Zori Mamula, Mary Visnic, Baba Zatezalo, Selma Dojonovic, and Mike Busic (background, right). (Courtesy Mary [Visnic] Drzayich.)

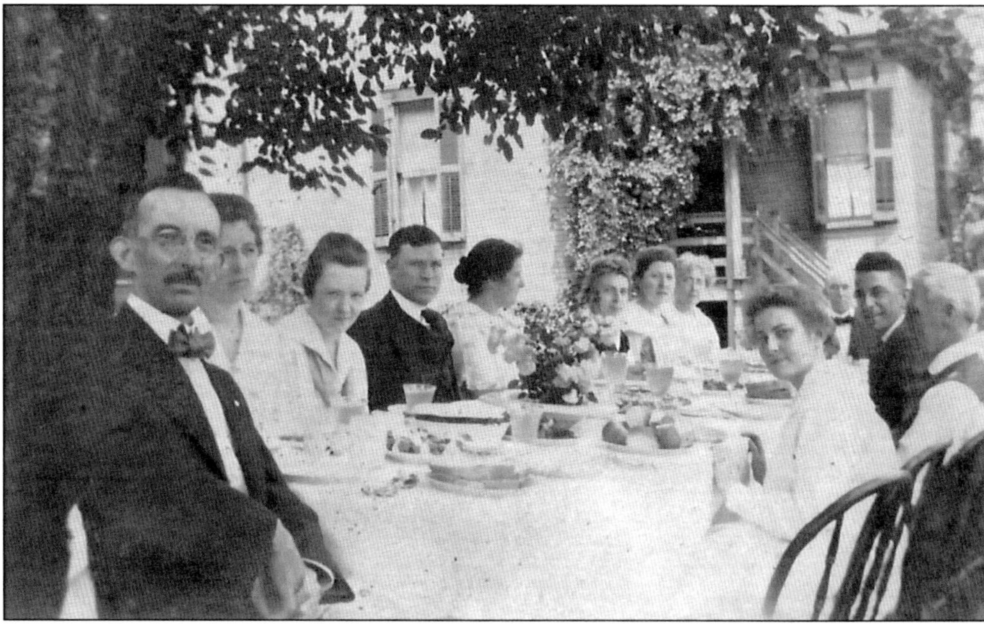

RINEY GARDEN PARTY. Pictured in the backyard of Dr. Fred Riney's home at 216 Steuben Street are guests and the good doctor (fourth from left) and his wife Elinor (Donohoo) Riney (third from left), who taught school in Mingo. (Courtesy Riney Robertson.)

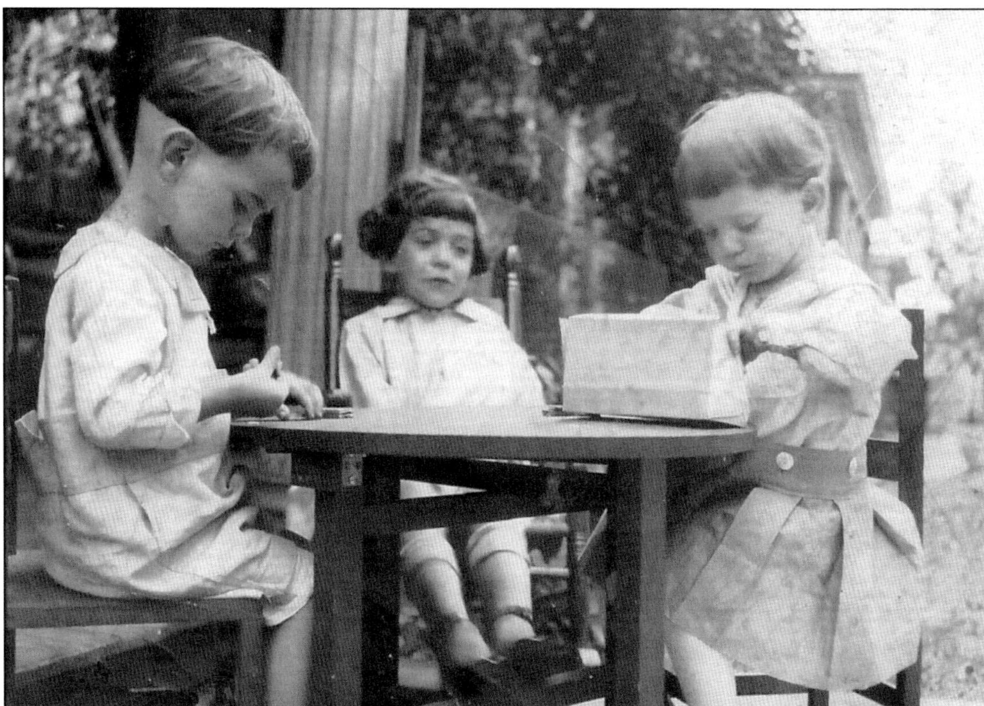

CHILDREN AT PLAY, 1923. Robert and Jane Quinn join Mary Alice Riney (right) at play in the backyard of Dr. Riney's home on Steuben Street, a beautiful two-tiered street lined with trees. (Courtesy Riney Robertson.)

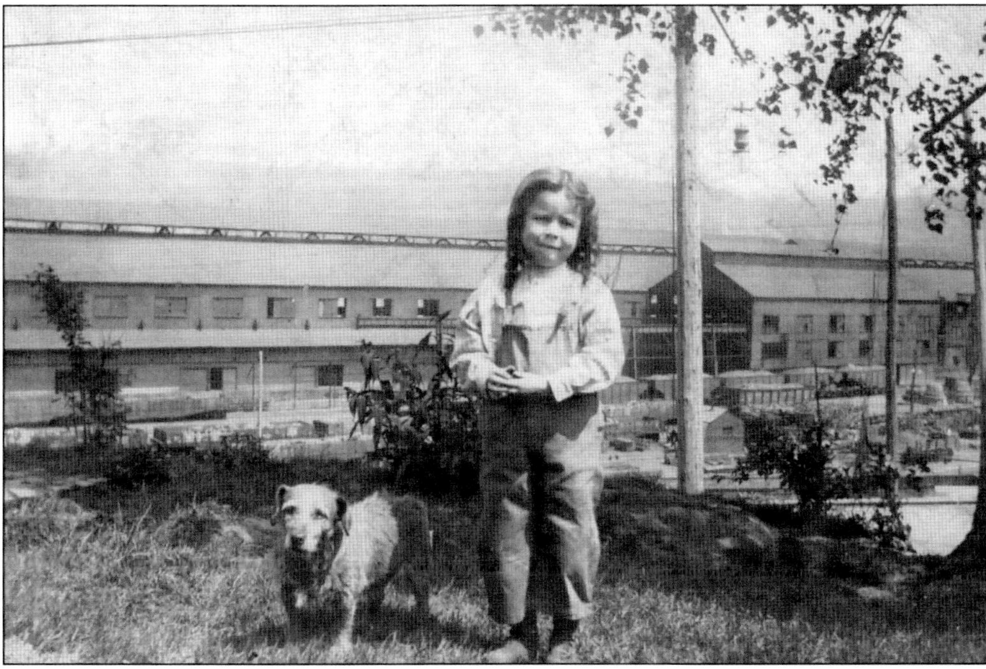

CHILDREN OF MINGO. In this working-class, immigrant town, children were prized and cared for. The young girl seen here with her dog stands on the treed rise before the ever-present steel mill. The houses built on the hills of Mingo faced into the mill, where noon whistles and sirens were a regular feature of the day. In the photograph below, five cousins in the first grade gather for this 1944 photograph before the old St. Agnes School building on St. Clair and Steuben Streets. Shown here from left to right are Judy Hagerty, Fredicka Hagerty, Mary Ann McCabe, Eileen Hagerty, and Elaine Pfister. (Both courtesy Eileen [Hagerty] Moody).

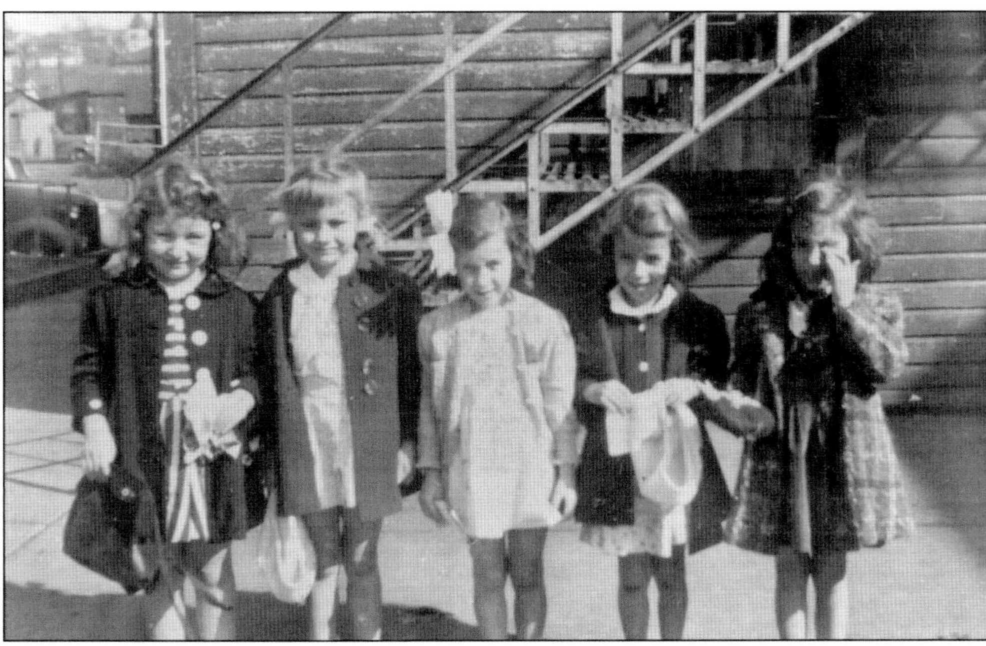

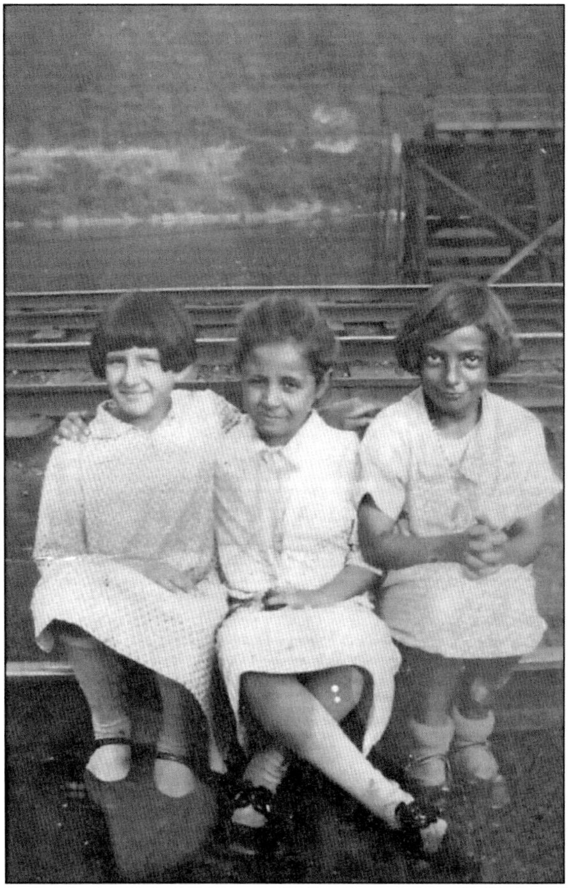

MINGO BOTTOMS, THE EAST SIDE. From Mingo's earliest times, the Bottoms area near Cross Creek has been a center of life, for the Mingo Indians, frontiersmen, settlers, and eventually for the waves of immigrant residents who sought affordable housing. One resident called the area "a regular League of Nations," recalling the ways the various nationalities supported each other. A bakery, restaurant, church, and school (Logan) existed here. By 1945, the area would disappear for the advancement of the Wheeling Steel industry. Here are some children around 1935, sitting along the railroad tracks. The girls are, from left to right, Bertha Dojonovic, Mildred Vokovich, and Mildred Visnic. They are shown again below beside their school and the Holy Resurrection Serbian Church. In the photograph below, from left to right, Bertha Dojonovic, Sue Dojonovic, and Millie Busic are joined by Mildred Visnic, who died when she was 14. (Both courtesy Mary [Visnic] Drzayich.)

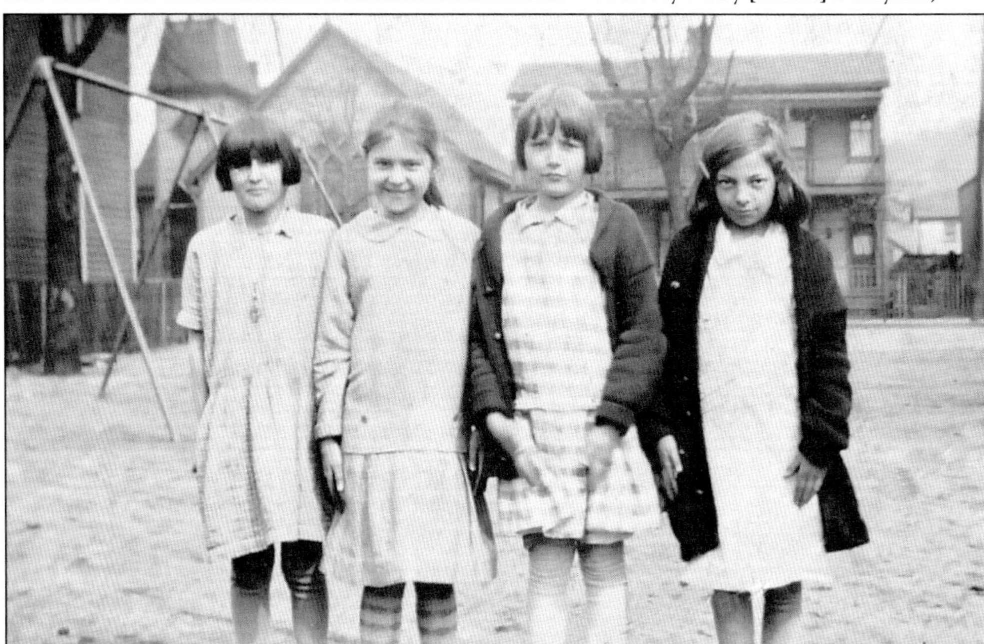

Working Man at Rest. Fred Visnic is shown resting at home in the Bottoms after a long day of work at Carnegie Steel as a railroad conductor, typically on the night shift. He died at 42 from lung problems, probably connected with his work in the mill. (Courtesy Mary [Visnic] Drzayich.)

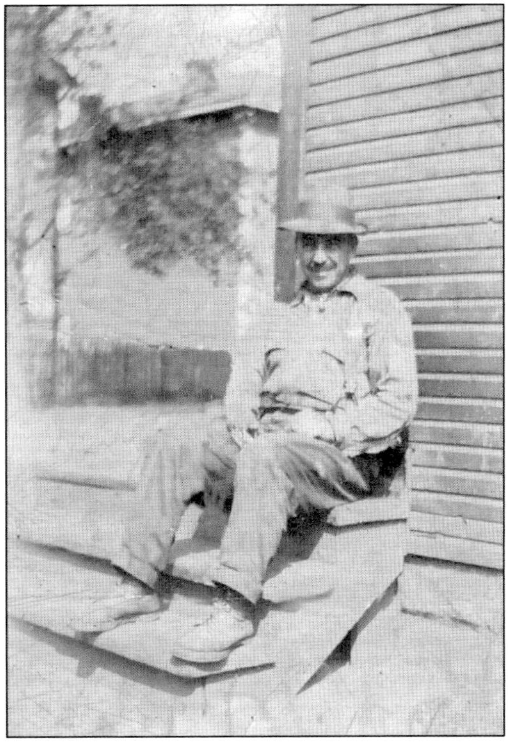

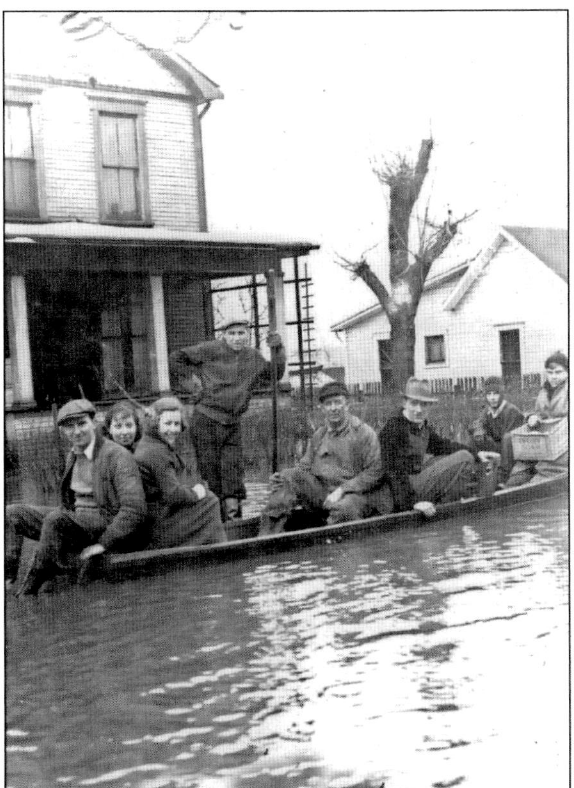

The Bottoms in Times of Flood. During the 1936–1937 flood on Wabash Avenue, rescue boats were a regular thing. Residents would move to upper floors and, on occasion, have to abandon their homes for a week during the worst floods. In the boat are, from left to right, Pete Kain, Kay Kain, Mary Visyak, Timothy Albaugh, Pete Hatfield, George Kain, Whitey McCain, and Bucky McCain. (Courtesy Mac Timcho.)

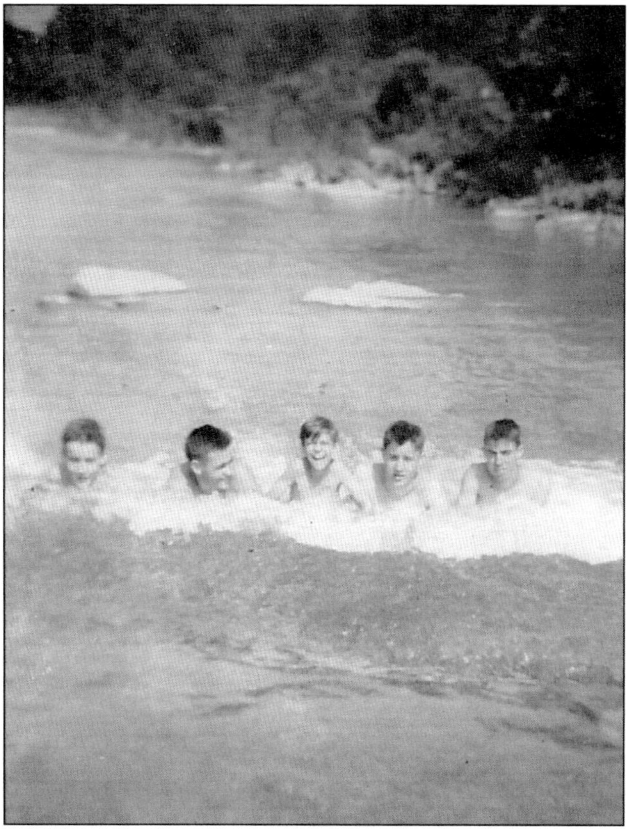

1920s Recreation. Cross Creek provided an area of free and natural recreation for the town youth. A mile from town out Gould's Road (nicknamed The New Road), one would find The Falls, an area of rapids where people could wade or swim, and at the Pennsylvania Railroad Stone Bridge one could jump from the bridge or swim in "Bare-Ass Beach." Here at The Falls are Charles Ferroni (second from left) and friends. (Courtesy Charles Ferroni.)

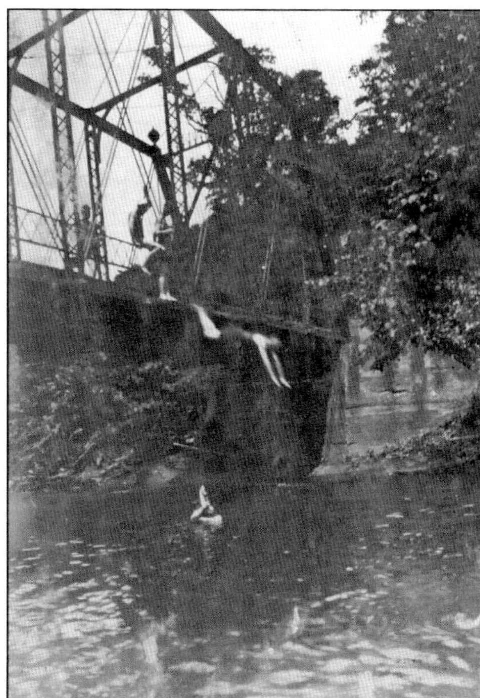

1920s Recreation. Daredevil boys dive off the Second Bridge into Cross Creek with its rocky bottom in the 1920s. (Courtesy Eileen [Hagerty] Moody.)

SWIMMING SITES. Other swimming and fishing sites existed along Cross Creek at what were termed First, Second, and Third Bridges. Pictured here in 1948 are a group of senior girls from Mingo High School who would walk or catch a ride out to Second Bridge to tan and cool off. Pictured here from left to right are Grace Gulino, Joanne Peeler, Nina Gulino, and Jane Mitchell. (Courtesy Joanne [Peeler] Sogan.)

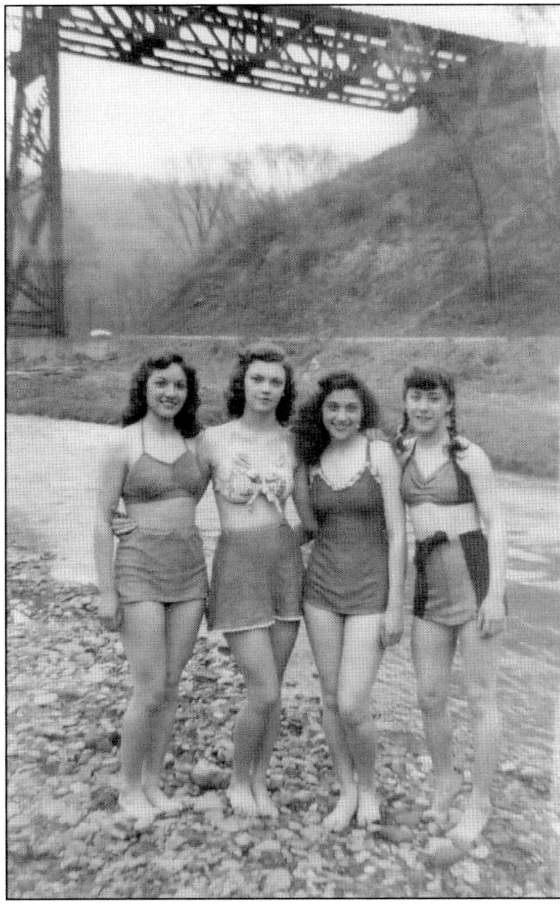

1920S RECREATION. A group of eighth graders from St. Agnes School take a picnic to the High banks area near Cross Creek. (Courtesy Eileen [Hagerty] Moody.)

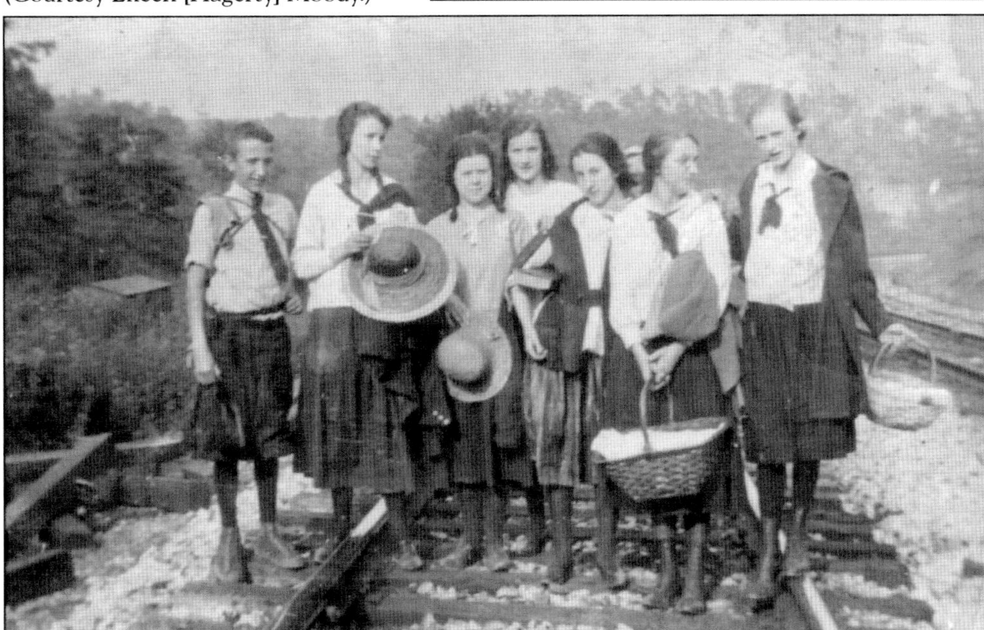

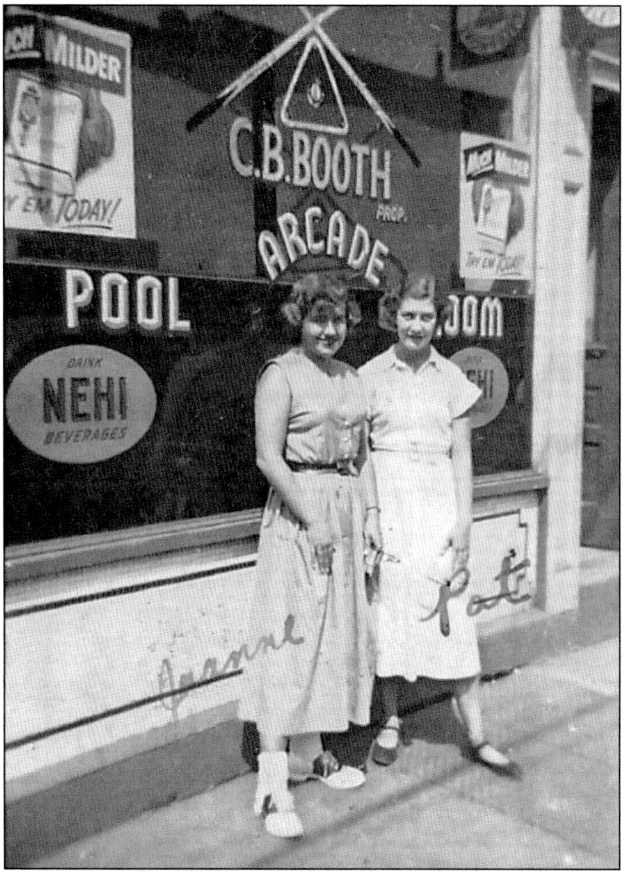

Recreation in the 1940s. Mingo's downtown area has had its share of pool halls, as here at C. B. "Chauncy" Booth's place on Commercial Street. Shown here in 1949 are Joanne Biggio (who lived in the apartment upstairs) and Patty Snyder. Joanne later became a physician. (Courtesy Bea [Petroskey] Daily.)

Shopping Downtown. Before shopping plazas and malls took over, one of the main activities of a small town life in places like Mingo was shopping. And during the thriving 1950s, Mingo had a Kroger, A&P, Isaly's, DiCarlo's, and Pesta's for groceries, as well as bakeries, butcher shops, a tailor-and-laundry shop, a shoe store and repair shop, flower shops, Weisberger's clothing store, Ann Scott's home store, Goodfriend's and Ardito's appliance and hardware stores, and the Gilchrist Lumberyard. (Courtesy Rochelle [Redin] Bouchet.)

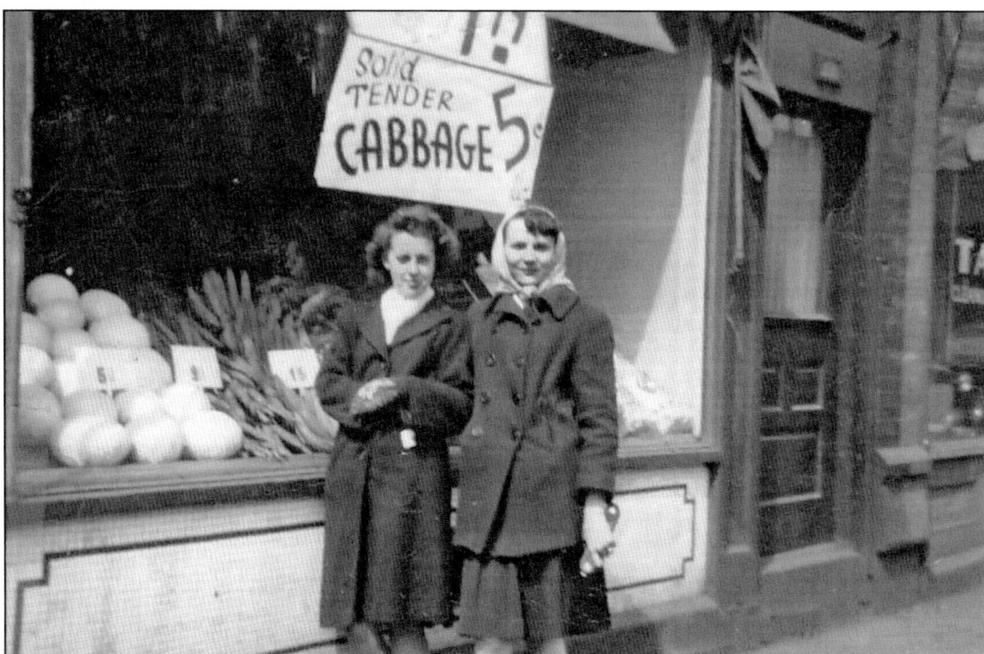

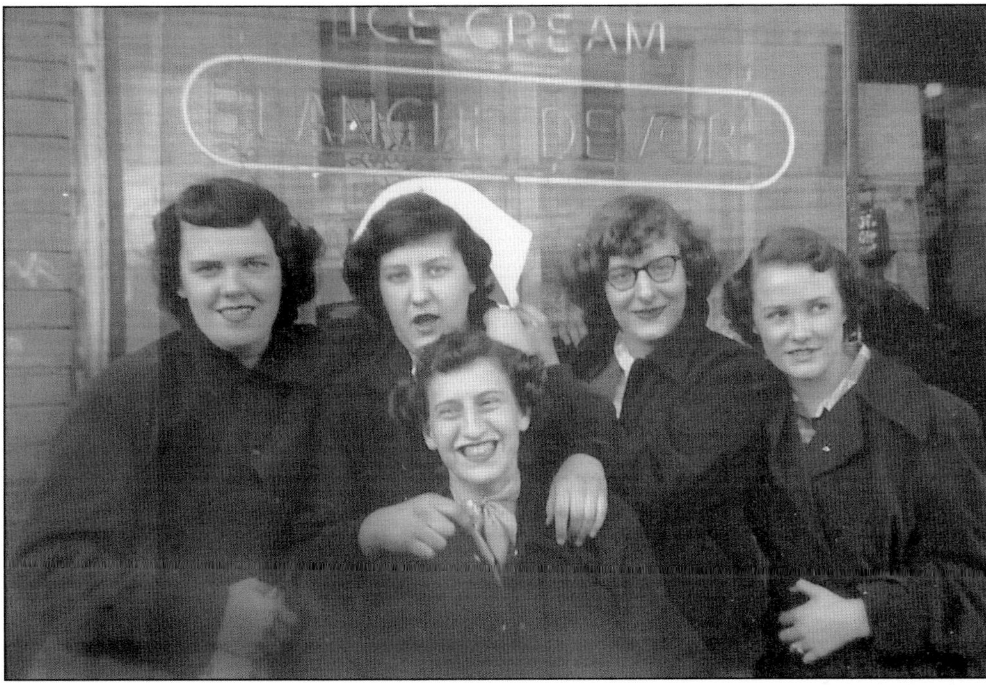

1940s Recreation. The downtown soda shop was also an after school attraction for high school youth as it is shown here at Blanch Devore's place on Commercial Street in 1949. In the photograph are, from left to right, Jane Ann Brettell, Darlene Caldrelli, Dottie Ashbaugh (in front), Lynn Rae Sanders, and Virginia Richardson. (Courtesy Bea [Petroskey] Daily.)

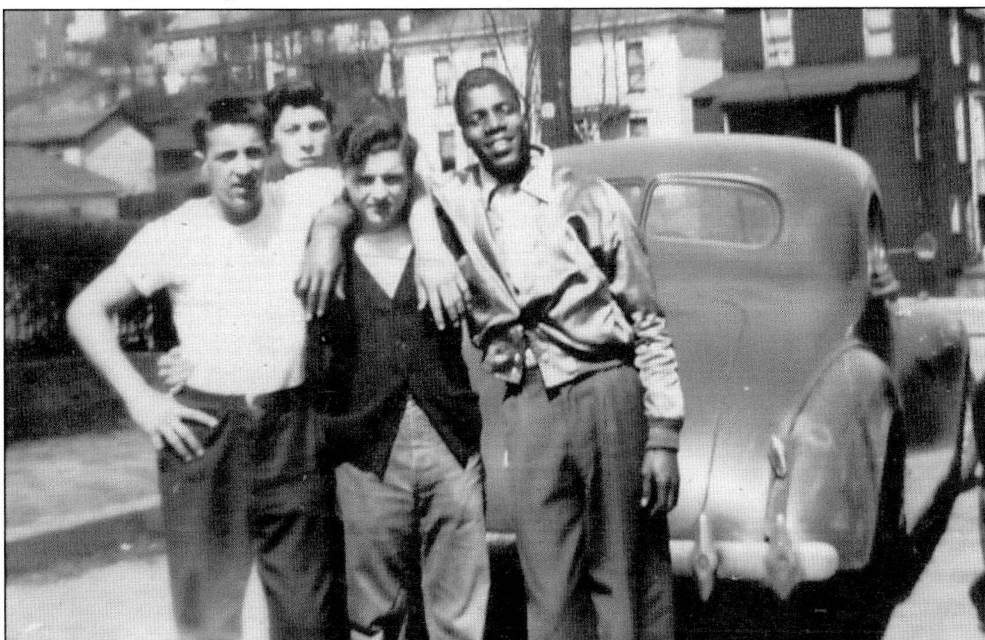

Fellow Classmates. Classmates hanging out on the neighborhood streets of town are, from left to right, Monk Potenzini, Richard Pizzeferraro, Busy Marcinko, and Moon William. (Courtesy Joanne [Peeler] Sogan.)

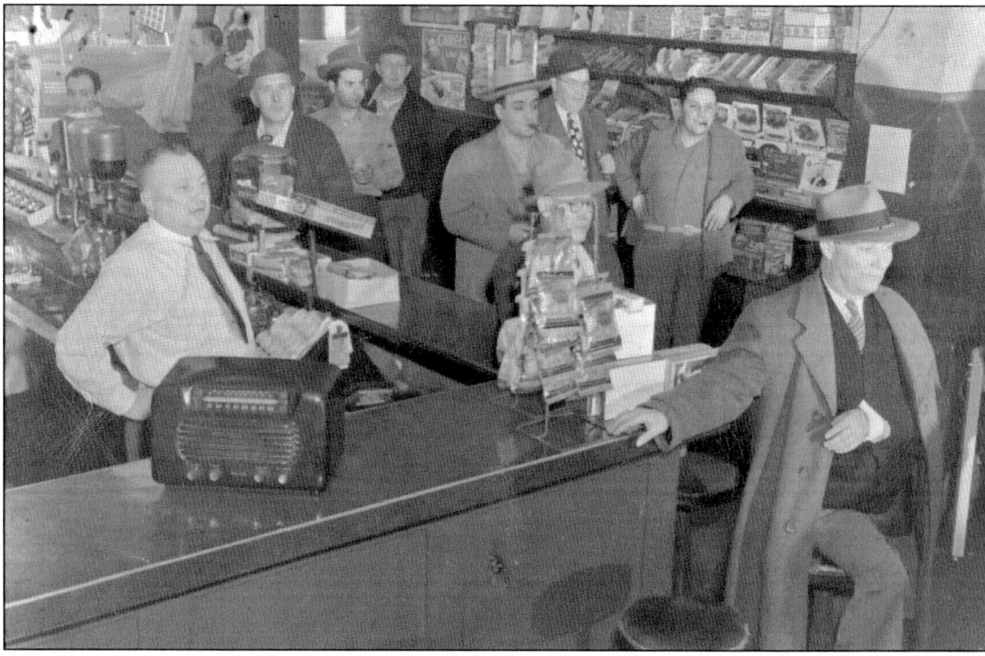

DUGAN'S CONFECTIONS AND POOL HALL, 1949. Dugan's was an institution in the town for over 60 years where people, young and old, would stand around the stoop or lean on the windowsill talking of the town. Behind the counter of Dugan's is George "Dugan" Kendrach; at the counter are Paul Sogan (far left), Lew Lane (with cigar and fedora), Fred Schaefer (polka dot tie), and Mario D'Alesio (leaning on cigar stand) with other regular customers watching the pool players. Below is the nightly mix of sports playing eight or nine ball while the crowd watches. There was some small time gambling in Mingo, and for many citizens stopping in to the sports and cigar store to play a number was a daily activity. (Both courtesy Paula [Kendrach] Kopcha.)

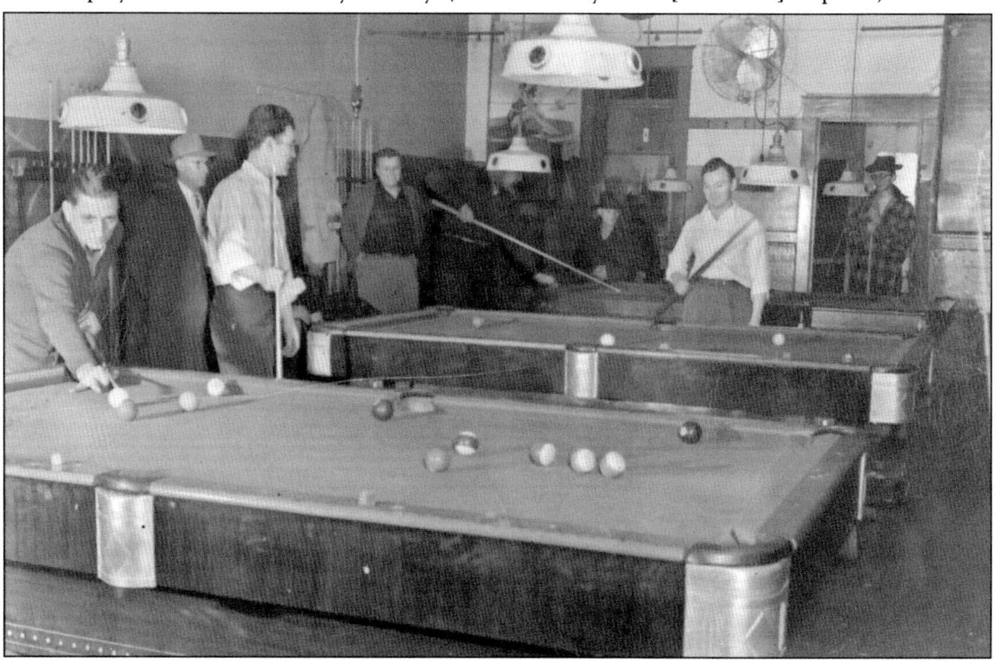

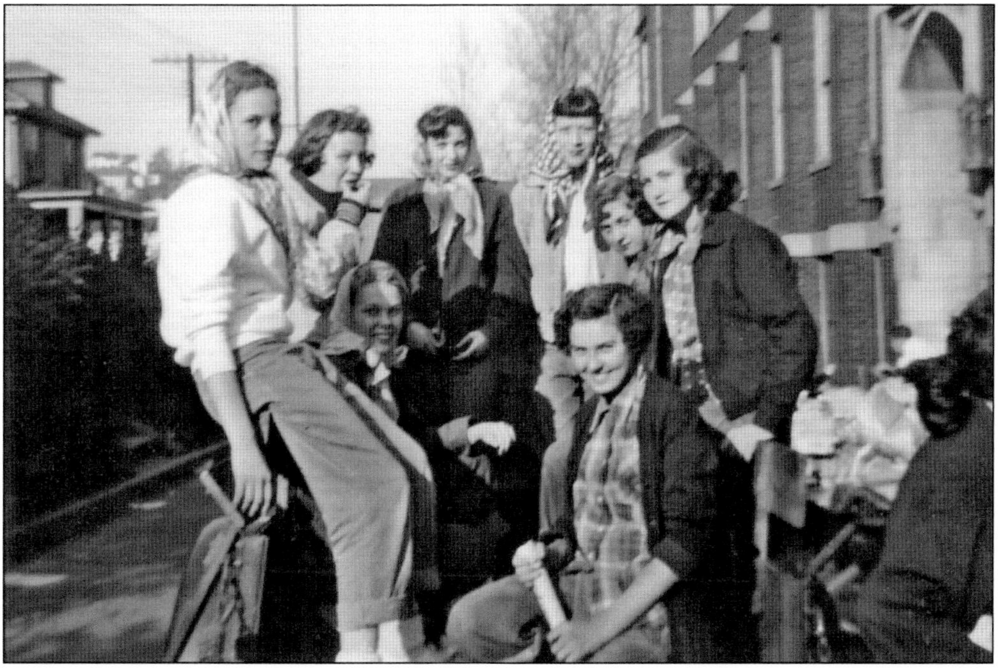

Community Support. Girls are rounding up old newspapers for the Mingo High School paper drive in 1954. They are, from left to right, Sonnie White, Sharon White, Barbara Blankenship, Mary Caranda, Evelyn DiCarlo, Judy Torrari, Angelina Pergi, and Betty Mitchell. (Courtesy Beatrice [Petroskey] Daily.)

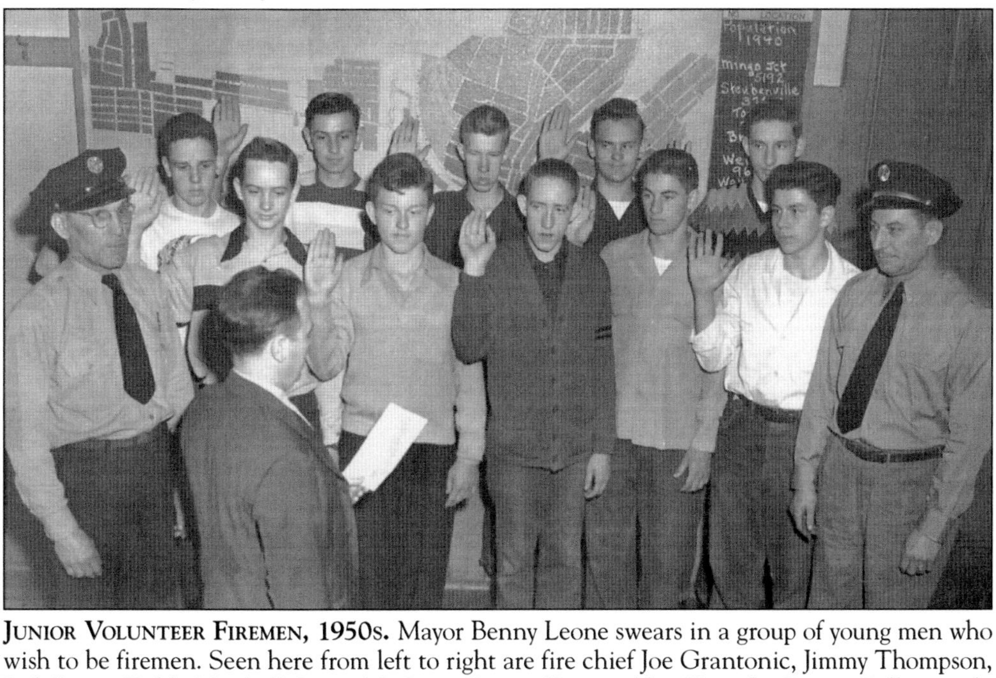

Junior Volunteer Firemen, 1950s. Mayor Benny Leone swears in a group of young men who wish to be firemen. Seen here from left to right are fire chief Joe Grantonic, Jimmy Thompson, Jack Jones, Teddy Mitchell, Larry McGuire, Lance Hauge, Alex Kovach, George Bellopatrick, Thomas "Wimpy" Mitchell, Jerry Stillwell, John Wade, and fire chief Orin Diamedi. (Courtesy Beatrice [Petroskey] Daily.)

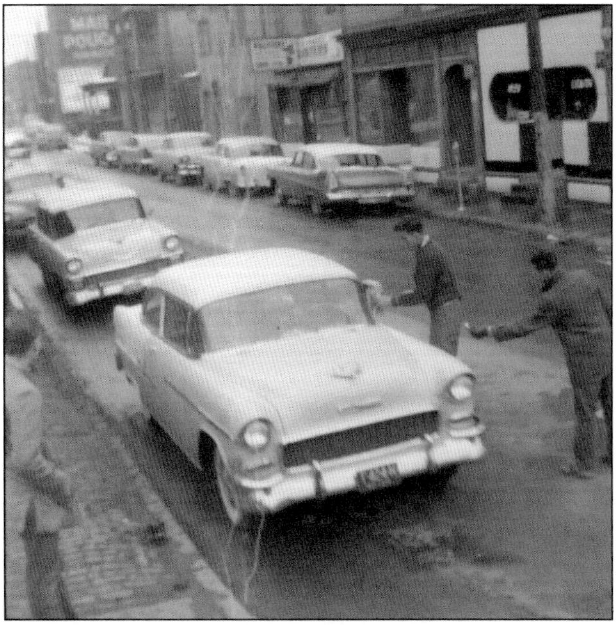

COLLECTING FUNDS. One of the most active service groups in the town was the Mingo High School Key Club, sponsored by the Kiwanis Club. The group, directed by business teacher Paul Sogan, went to state and national conventions and often brought home awards and national recognition to the town. It also broadened the experience of Mingo's high school youth. Seen here on Commercial Street in 1956, club members are collecting charity funds. (Courtesy David Kramarich.)

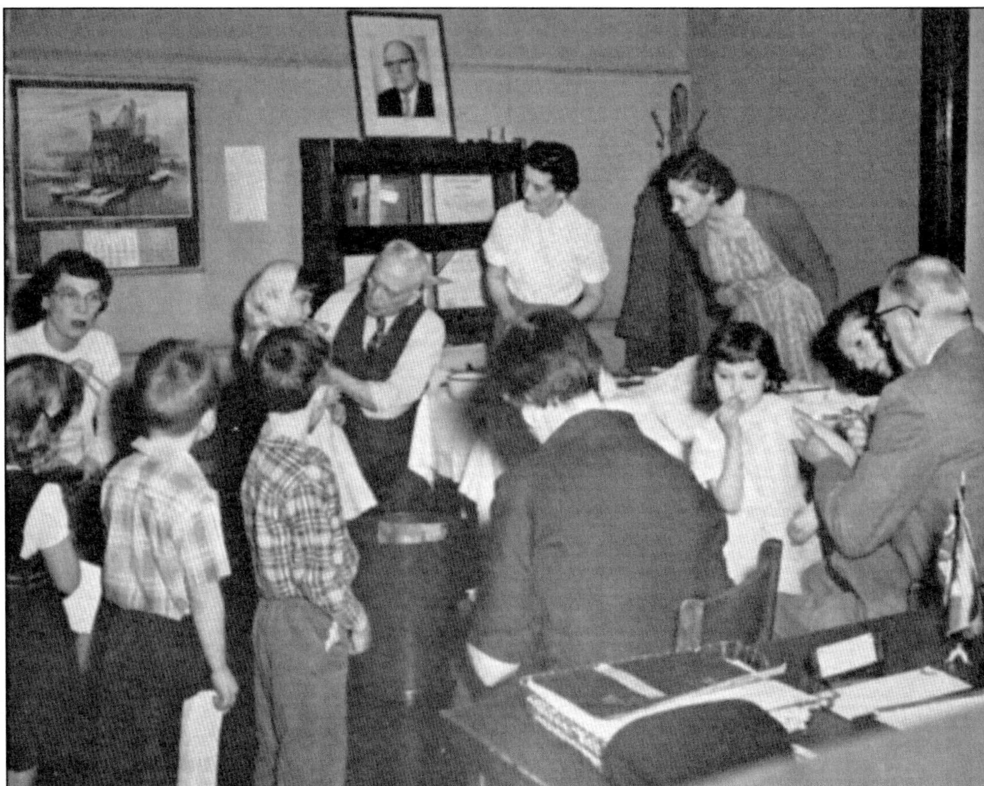

POLIO SHOTS, 1957. Dr. Fred Riney (left), Dr. Jason Albaugh, and nursing assistants Eleanor Smith (left), Aubrey Bainbridge (center), and Bertha Kendrach give much-needed Salk polio vaccine shots to schoolchildren in February 1957 in School Superintendent Dennis's office. (Courtesy Darlene Hoff, originally published in *Bicentennial History of Mingo Junction, Ohio.*)

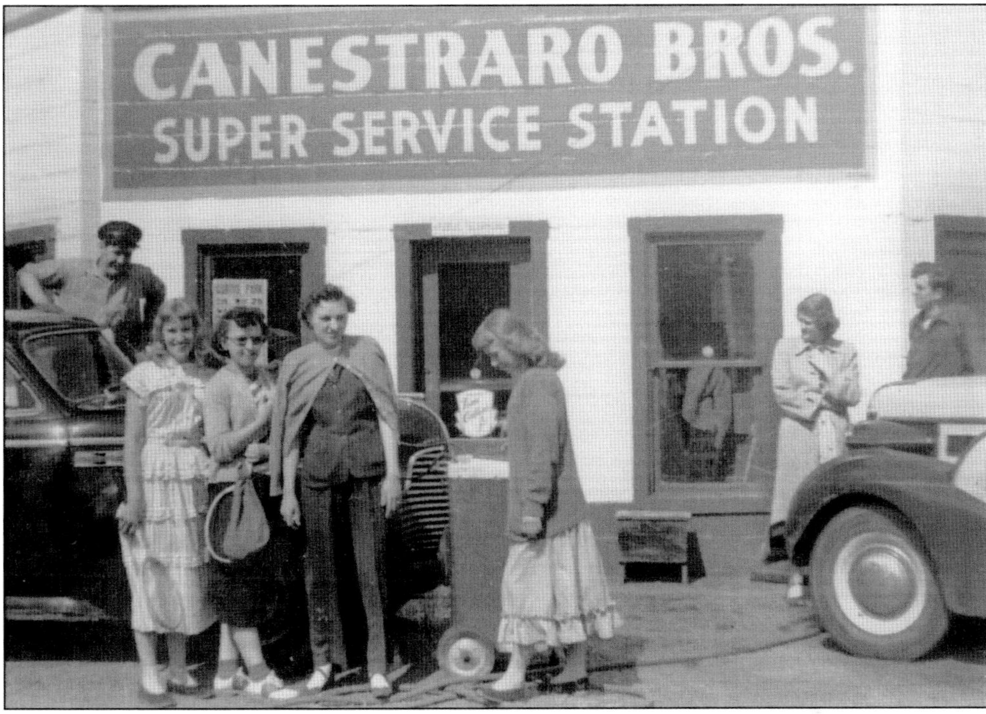

SERVICE STATION. Canestraro Brothers Service Station on North Commercial Street shows customers gathering in the late 1940s. In foreground, from left to right, are Karen Vasich, Helen Vag, Mary Vag, and Martha Vasich. (Courtesy Martha [Vasich] Trombetta.)

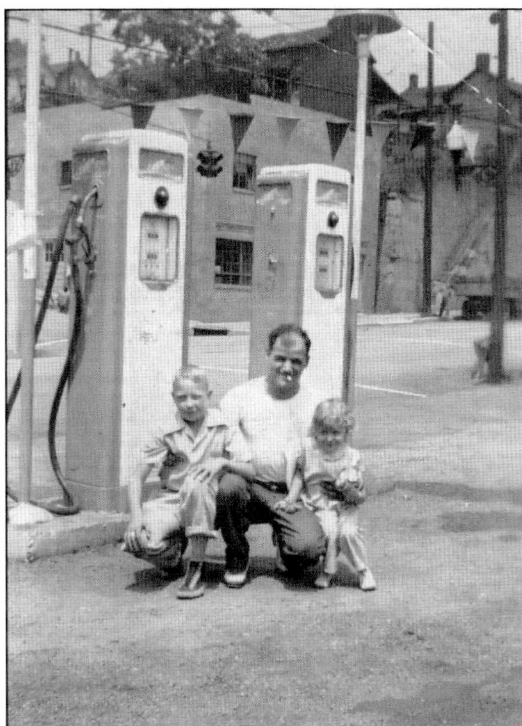

CHANGING HANDS. Like most of the businesses in Mingo, various owners have tried their hand at running them. The Canestraro station was later owned and operated by Daniel "Brownie" Falcone, shown here with Ted Smith and daughter Joyce in 1949. (Courtesy Joann [Seville] Tackach.)

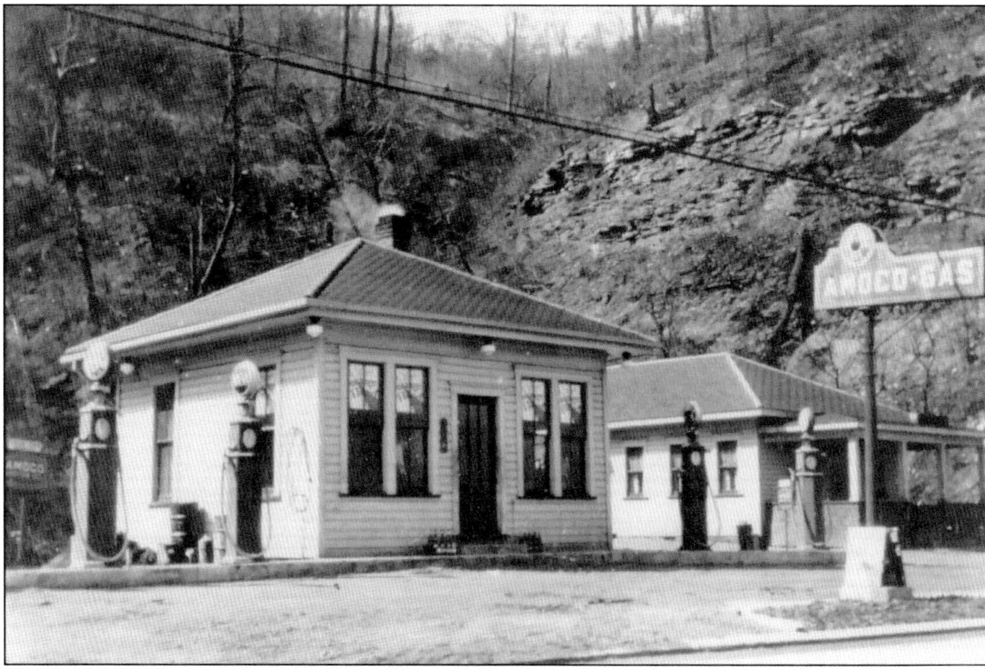

HAGGERTY'S AMOCO STATION. James Haggerty opened this station on old Route 7 on the way to Steubenville. Planted in the crevices of the rocky hills, it opened in the 1920s and ran until the 1950s. At this point in 1930, a dance hall was open beside it; later a trailer court would take its place. (Courtesy Eileen [Hagerty] Moody.)

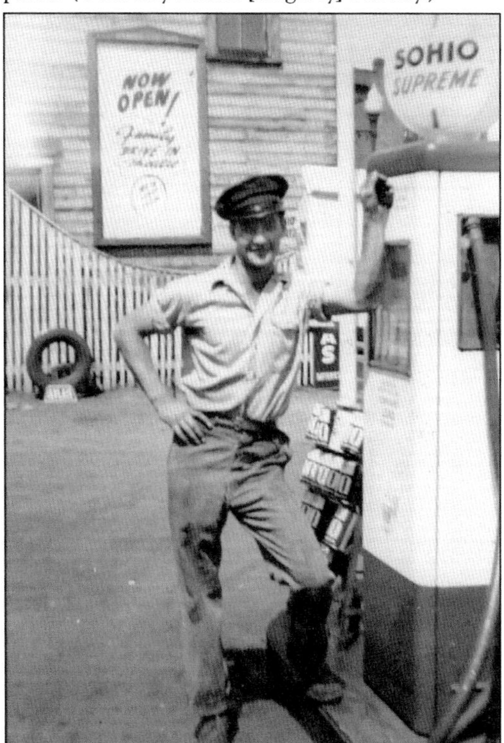

NEW BUSINESS OWNER. Al Ferroni, who at 16 falsified his age to enlist and serve in the military during World War II, returned home to finish high school, then launch his own service station on North Commercial Street in 1949. That service station changed hands many times during the years, and Al went on to work in the mill while owning one of the town bars, The Argo, with wife Maryann. The station was also owned by the Marcinko family and others. (Courtesy Joanne [Peeler] Sogan.)

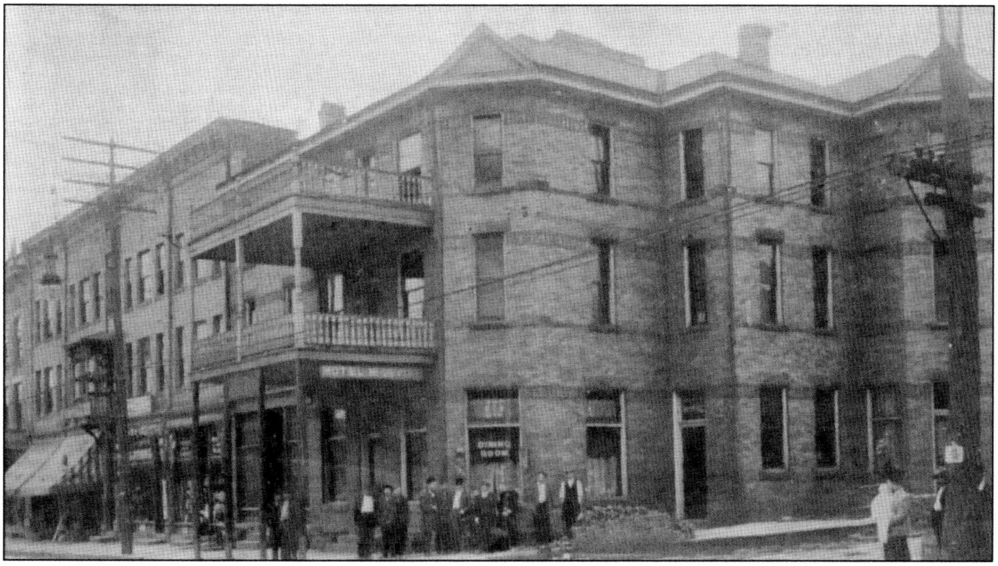

OLD HOTELS. At the turn of the century, Mingo was the home of two hotels, both at the north end of Commercial Street. Hotel McDevitt at the corner of McLister Avenue with its double balcony, though no longer a hotel, is still a key landmark of the town. Below is the Ash Hotel, which once stood on the corner of Potter and Commercial Streets near the city building. These hotels once were the quarters for salespeople and travelers and the temporary quarters of workers who soon moved into boardinghouses in town. (Above, courtesy Madeline [Brinskey] Campbell; below, courtesy Sondra [White] Hyde.)

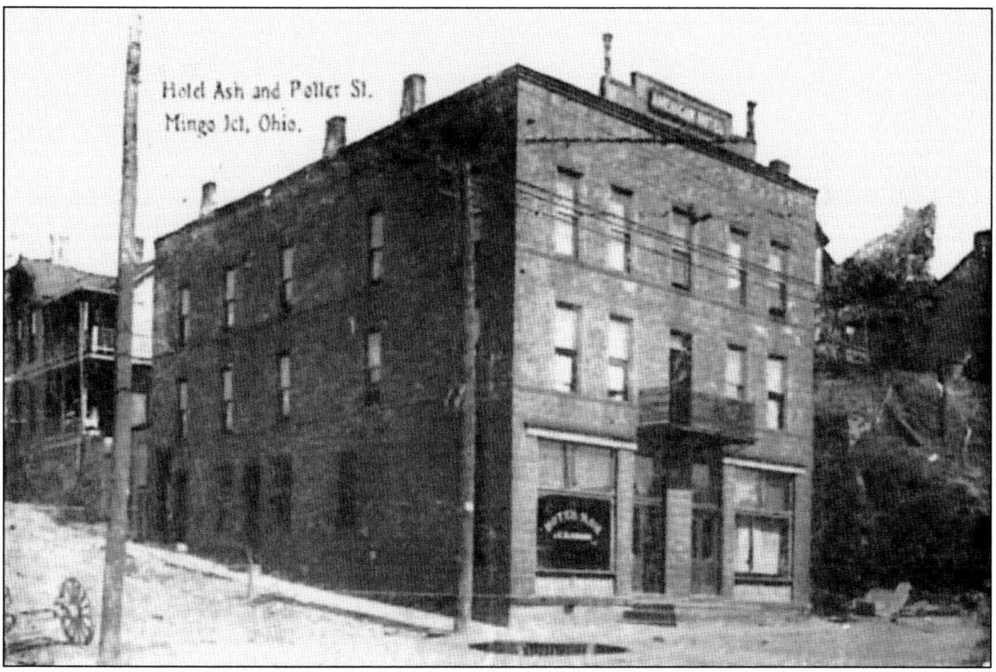

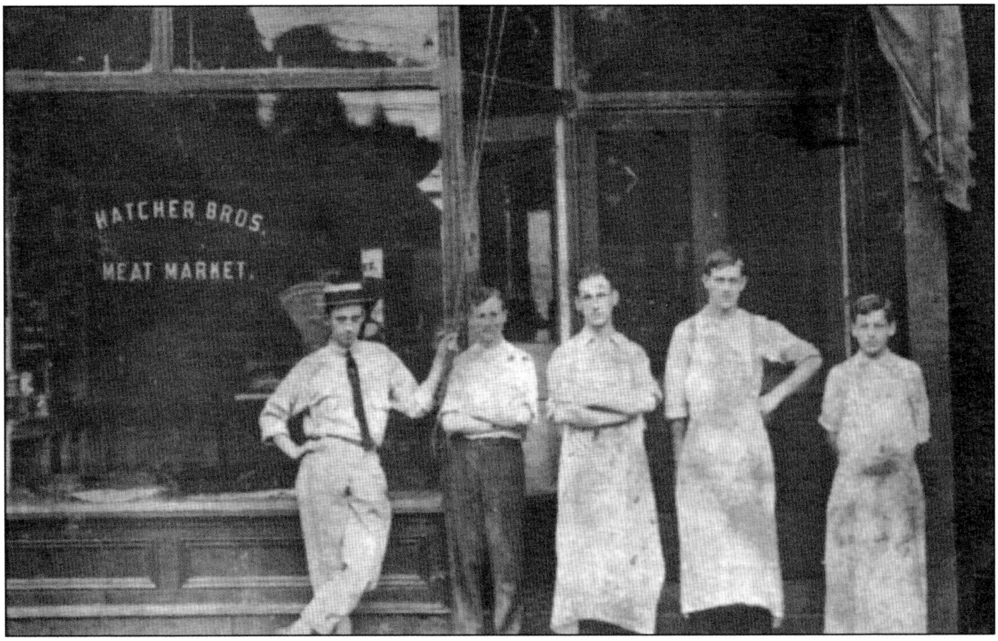

MEAT MARKET. Hatcher Brothers Meat Market operated on Commercial Street and delivered groceries by horse and buggy. Pictured is Earl Hatcher, second from right, who would later operate the Hatcher Construction Company in Mingo. This was one of many early meat markets in the town, which included Schwartz, Kundrats, Banaski, McNeal, Basil, and others. (Courtesy Darlene Hoff, originally published in *Bicentennial History of Mingo Junction, Ohio.*)

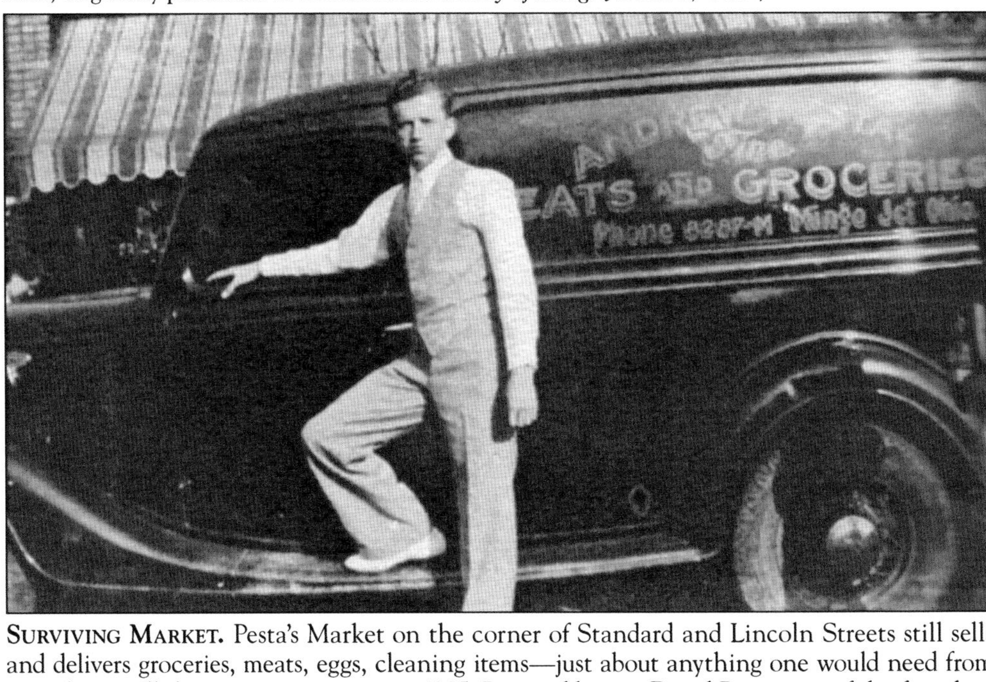

SURVIVING MARKET. Pesta's Market on the corner of Standard and Lincoln Streets still sells and delivers groceries, meats, eggs, cleaning items—just about anything one would need from its rather small shop, in operation since 1925. Pictured here is David Pesta, one of the founders, who ran the market most of his life. (Courtesy Darlene Hoff, originally published in *Bicentennial History of Mingo Junction, Ohio.*)

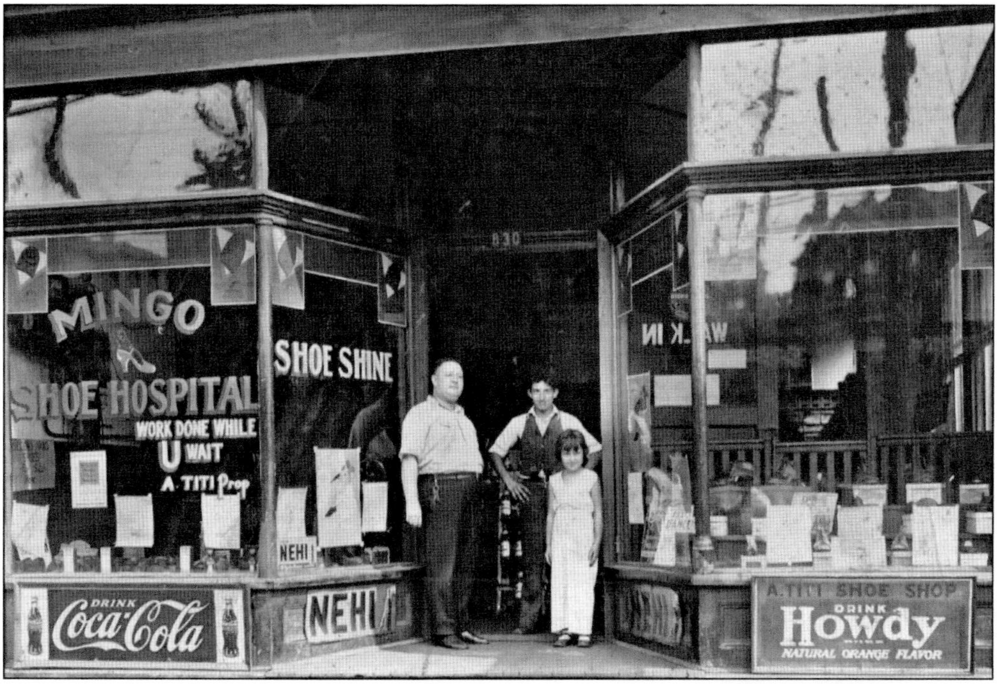

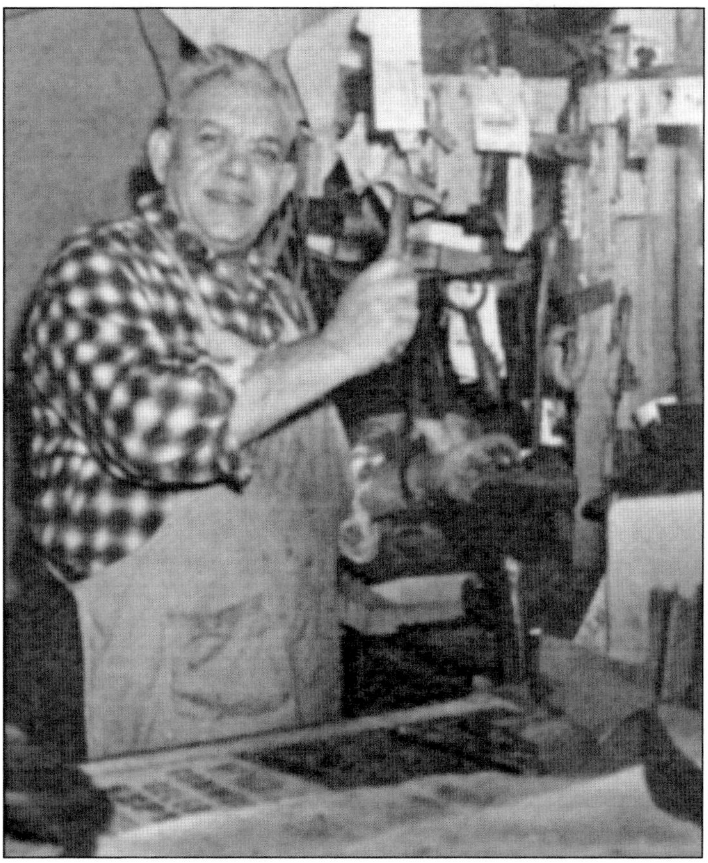

Shoe Shops. Mingo Shoe Hospital, opened around 1923, was located at 830 South Commercial Street. Pictured above are owner Amatore Titi, Kaiser Ciafradone, and Adrianna (Titi) Marangonibus. Among other shoe repair shops have been the Ardito and Mannarino shop on the corner of Ravine and Commercial Streets. The photograph at right shows the shoe repair store opened by Robert Ardito in 1947. Frank Mannarino, pictured here, ran it into the 1970s. (Above, courtesy Amatore "Sonny" Titi; below, courtesy Mannarino family.)

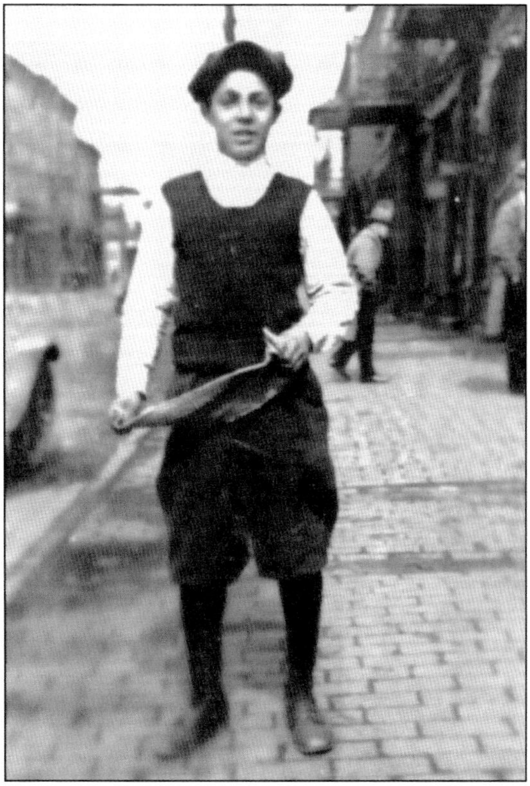

Shoeshine Boy. Liber D'Alesio shows his initiative even as a young boy in this 1922 photograph of him practicing his trade on Commercial Street. Note the brick sidewalks and his knickers from that era. (Courtesy Jim D'Alesio.)

Old Ferry Business. As to oldest businesses in town, the Maxwells may have it with their river ferry, which they rowed across the Ohio. Here are the William Maxwells, Junior and Senior, resting on their boat on the Ohio River banks. (Courtesy Darlene Hoff, originally published in *Bicentennial History of Mingo Junction, Ohio.*)

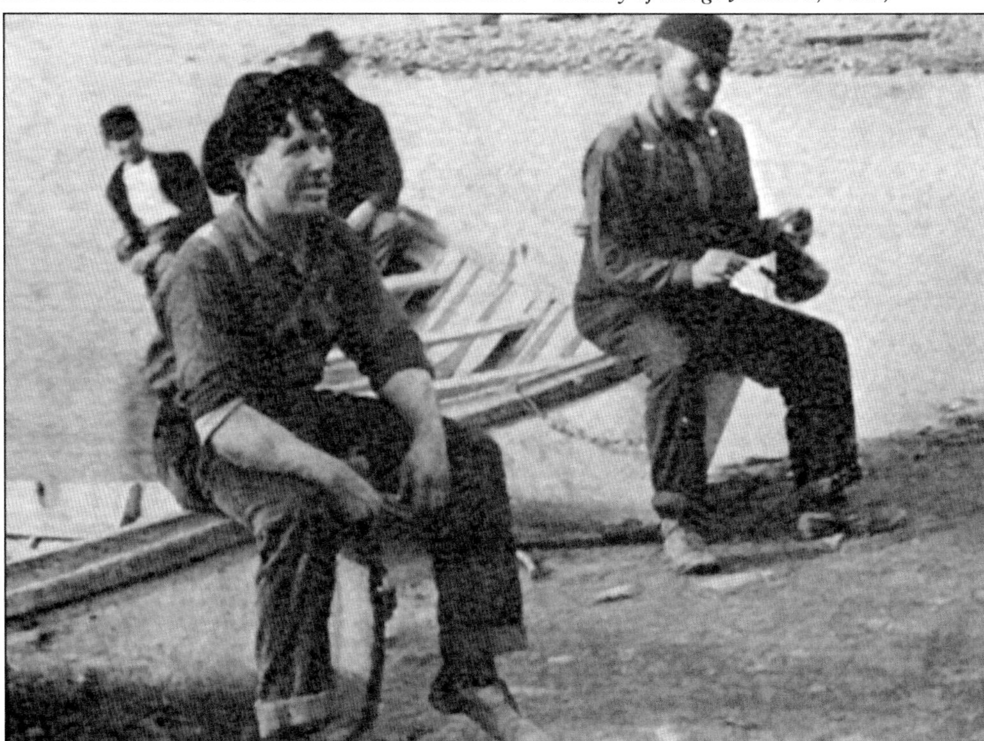

Town Drug Stores. One of the oldest drugstores in the town was that owned by William and Thomas Pelly, begun in 1897. Here is Pelley opening the shop on the east side of Commercial Street. It carried a variety of items and had the town's first soda fountain, which sold sodas for 10¢. The store was eventually sold to another pharmacist, Horace Weals. Other drugstores in the town would include Sharon and Mingo Pharmacies. (Courtesy Eileen [Hagerty] Moody.)

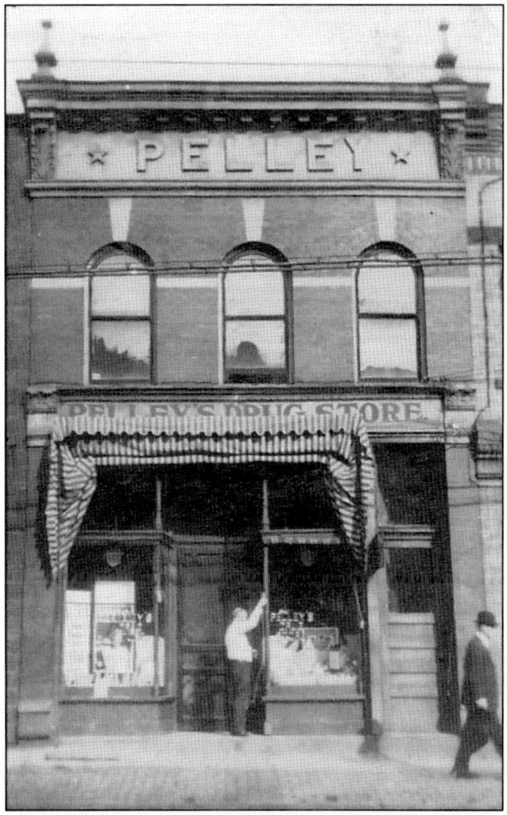

Beauty and Barber Shops. While the women often met at beauty salons such as Catherine's, Irene's, Flora's, and Maxwell's, for over a hundred years the men have gathered at the barbershops for a good hair cut, perhaps a shave, and talk of the town. The two oldest barbers were Nick Fortunato and Paul Rechichi, who both began in 1915. Later came Jimmy Paris, Santi Leonard, and Mike Timcho with shops along Commercial Street. Pictured here is Nick's at 708 Commercial Street. (Courtesy Darlene Hoff, originally published in *Bicentennial History of Mingo Junction, Ohio.*)

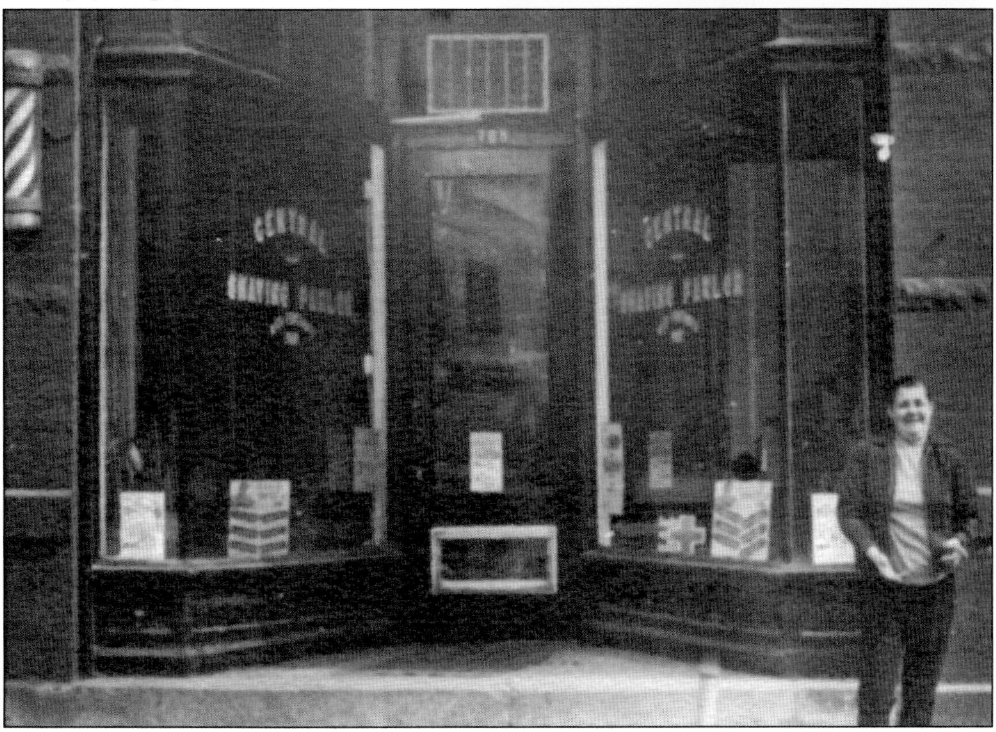

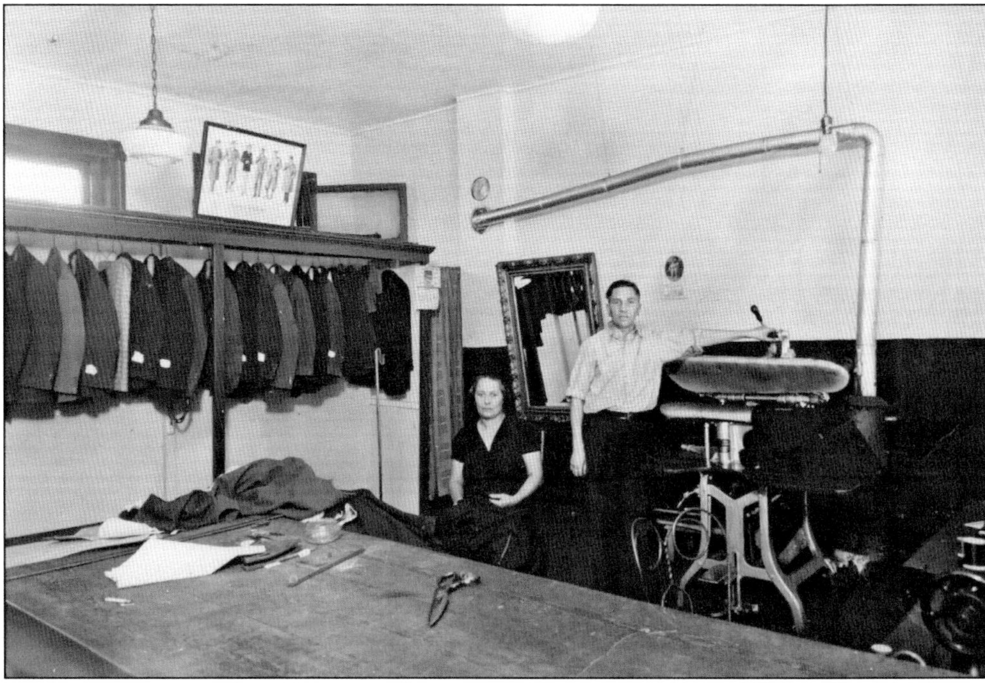

TONY ANTONELLI. Known as "Tony the Tailor," Antonelli and wife Cleonelda operated their tailor and dry cleaning shop at 622, then 635 Commercial Street for over 50 years, living upstairs in an apartment. They began in 1929; this photograph is from the interior in 1938. (Courtesy Elsie Cenci.)

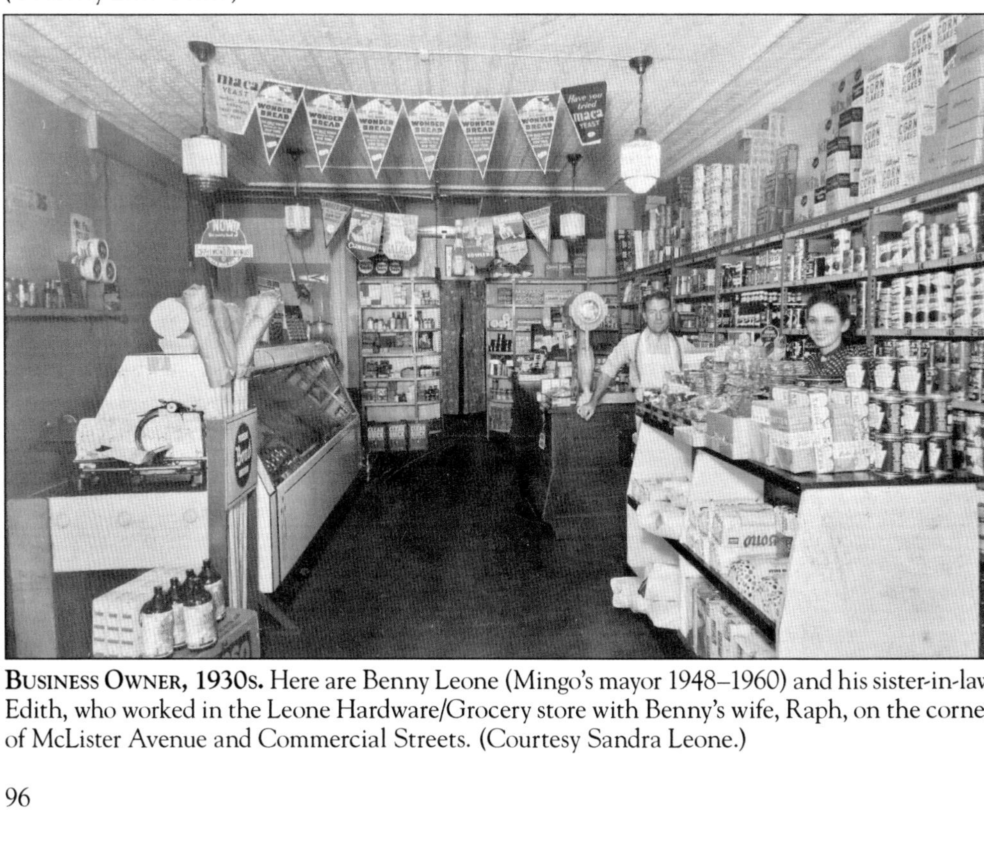

BUSINESS OWNER, 1930S. Here are Benny Leone (Mingo's mayor 1948–1960) and his sister-in-law Edith, who worked in the Leone Hardware/Grocery store with Benny's wife, Raph, on the corner of McLister Avenue and Commercial Streets. (Courtesy Sandra Leone.)

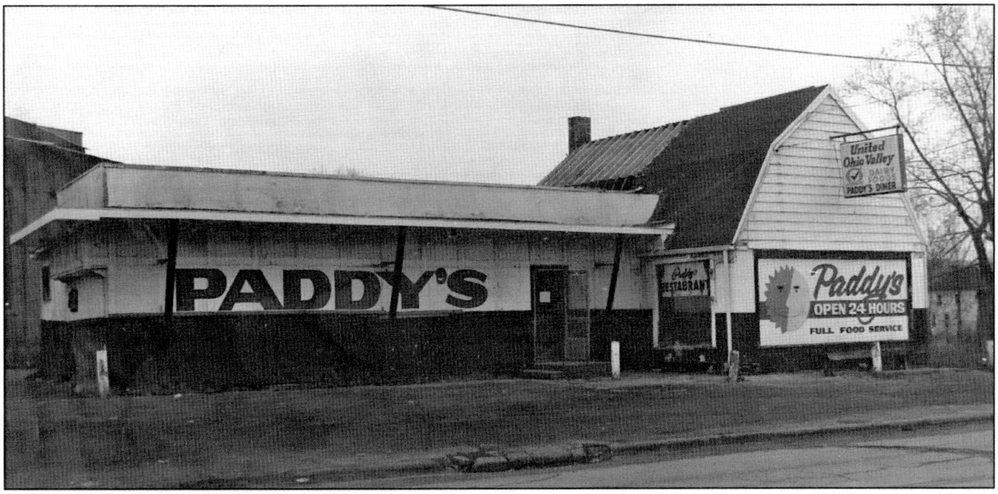

Town Meeting Places. Paddy's Diner, located in the Deandale area at the south end of town near the railroad roundhouse, became a meeting place where people would gather from breakfast until late at night. It served the town as an all-night roadhouse and meeting place and was owned by various people. (Courtesy Rocky Petrozzi.)

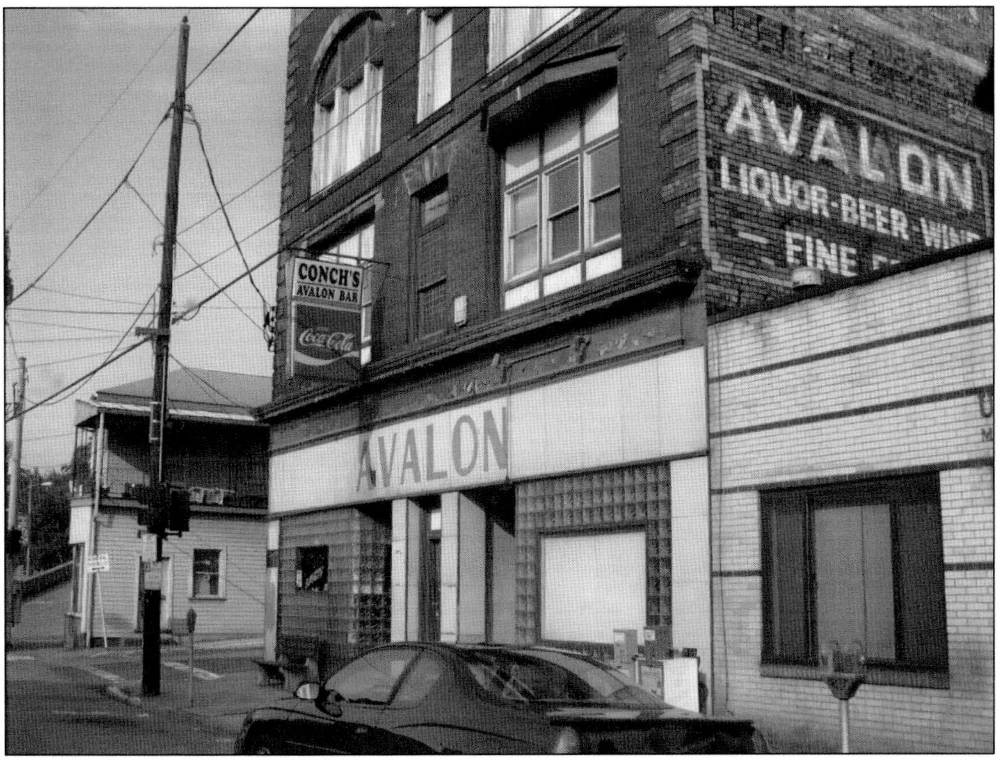

Town Taverns. The Avalon stood on the corner of Ravine and Commercial Streets where the first Mingo Post Office was. The R and A Hall on the top floor served the town for gatherings for half a century. Multiple social clubs exist on Commercial Street, and other taverns would include the Town House; Oasis; Lalich's, which became Welch's; Flora's; Scaffidi's; the Argo; Coochies; Franky and Johnnie's; Hillsboro Tavern; Parkview; the Schutzen Club; and the Slovak American Club. (Photograph by Joshua T. Buck, reprinted with permission.)

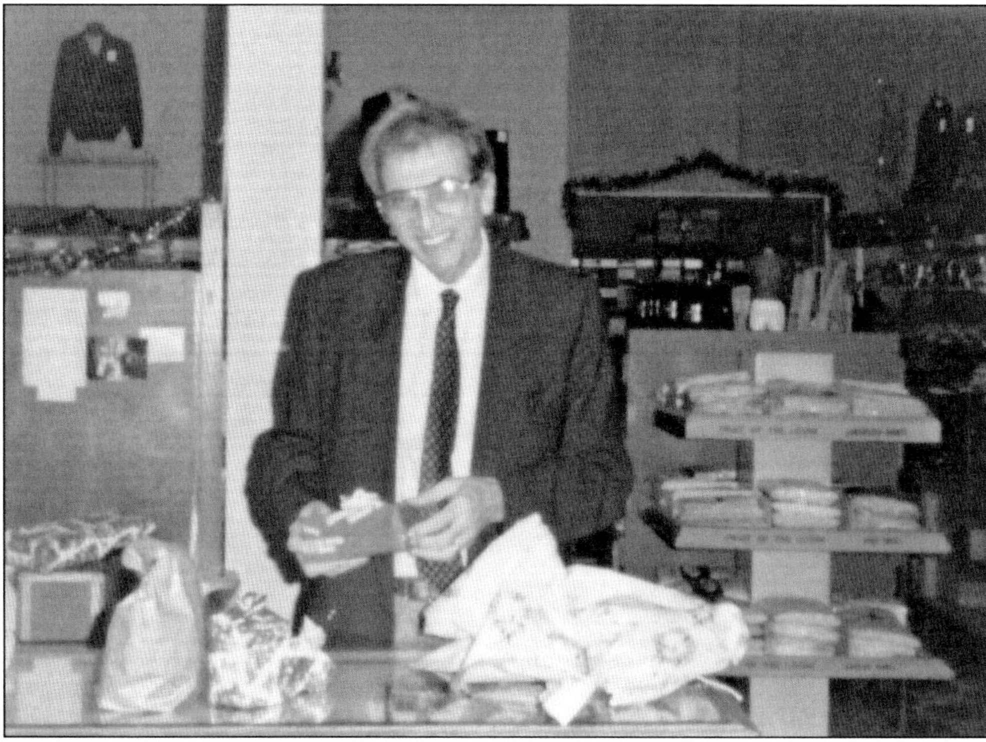

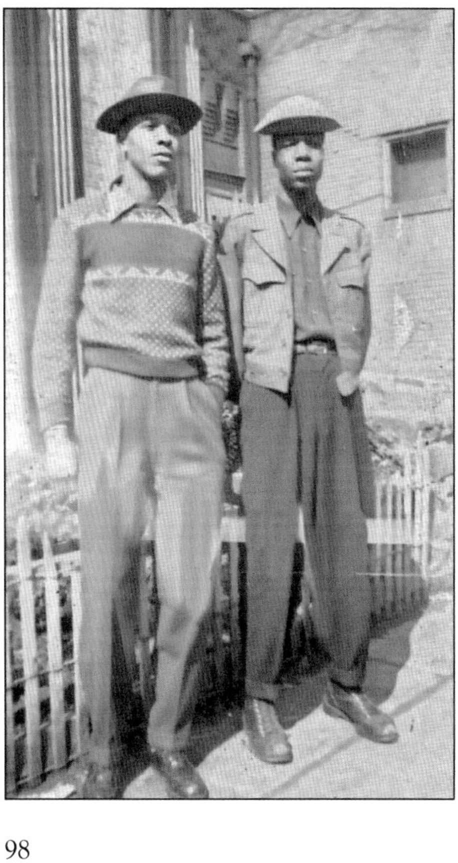

SHARP DRESSER. Not only did a smiling Freddie Weisberger dress well, as seen in his family's clothing store, but his family's store has helped the town dress well since 1893. During the Depression years and when new immigrants would come to town, the store would "carry them on the books" until they found work and could pay. (Photograph by Clara Sue [Stuber] Milewski.)

TWO WELL-DRESSED YOUTHS. Henry "Moon" Williams and Carl "C. A." Crossland show off their fine clothes in 1946 on the streets of Mingo. They pose here for classmate Joann Peeler, who used her first checking account to ride the bus to Steubenville and buy her first camera in 1944. (Courtesy Joanne [Peeler] Sogan.)

Six

Town Industry

As the lives of Mingo people are tied to their work, so their story is bound to the industry of that place. River, rail, and roads came together where natural resources were plentiful. Mingo became a junction not only for railroads, but also for industries of coal and oil, iron and steel, and their byproducts. As farming life gave way to industry in the late 1870, Mingo developed from a village into a town. Early days of grinding mills, blacksmith shops, and pottery-making gave way to iron and steel production.

In 1870, Lyman Potter's property in the lower "locust grove" was sold to capitalists, and by 1872, the first ironworks came to what is now downtown Mingo. It is hard to imagine today, but the area on West Commercial Street had a coal shaft, a coke oven on the hillside, and a trestle running above to a blast furnace on the east side of the railroad tracks where the present steel mill lies. By 1890, the Mingo Ironworks merged into the Junction Iron and Steel Company, running a steel-producing blooming mill and a nail factory. Renamed the Laughlin Steel Company, it was again sold in 1897 to the Aetna Standard Iron and Steel Company, which added a Bessemer furnace operation in 1899. The National Steel Company bought it in 1900 and sold it the following year to Carnegie-Illinois Corporation, a subsidiary of U.S. Steel, which began producing 8-inch and 10-inch sheet bars, slabs, and ingots. Carnegie ran the plant through World War II, during which it produced deck plates for submarines and warships. In 1945, the Wheeling Steel Company purchased it and expanded, buying up surrounding homes in the Mingo Bottoms area. In 1965, Wheeling Steel constructed a BOF (Basic Oxygen Furnace) continuous operation that made pig iron, ingots, slabs, hot bands, and sheets.

The town seems to rise and fall on this industry's health, riding high during years of productivity and enduring periods of long strikes and shutdowns, as in the Chapter 11 bankruptcy-filing of 1985 and again in 2000, the 300-day-plus strike of 1996–1997, and the 2009–2010 shut down by new owners Severstal Corporation. Other industrial employers have included the long-running Brettell Coal Company, the railroads, the defunct Ohio Nut and Washer Plant, Fotte Mineral Company (Vanadium Corporation), and the smaller Standard Slag, Belot Block, Tri-State Asphalt, Harmony Tool and Die, and Weldon Trucking.

Through good times and bad, Mingo Junction survives as a hardworking town.

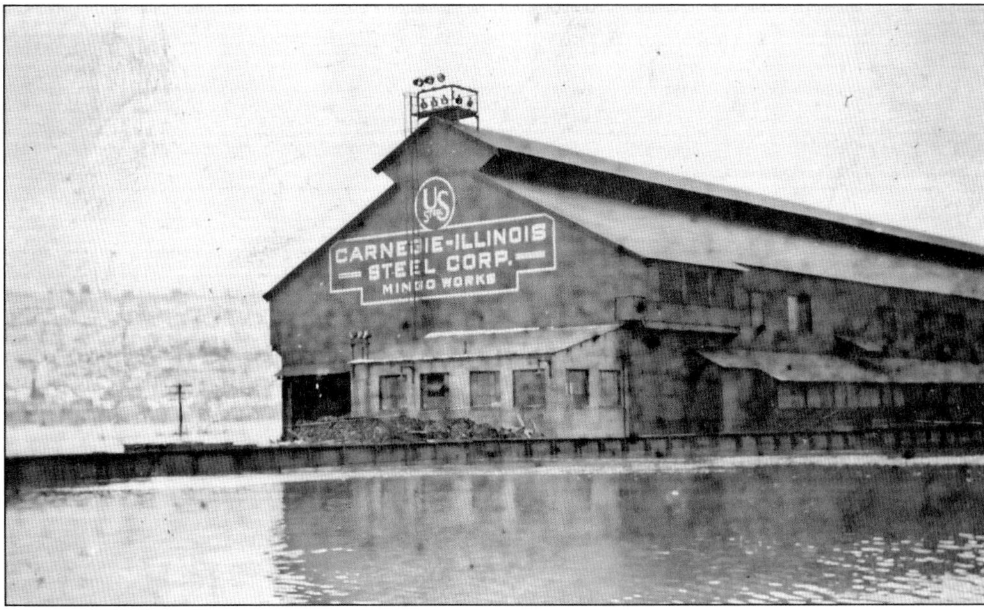

Carnegie-Illinois Steel. Carnegie Steel of U.S. Steel owned and operated these mills from 1901 until 1945, when it sold to the Wheeling Steel Corporation and workers were given the option of moving south or losing their pensions and being rehired at Wheeling Steel; most stayed. The 80-inch mill here is shown during the flood of 1936. (Courtesy Raymond Fox.)

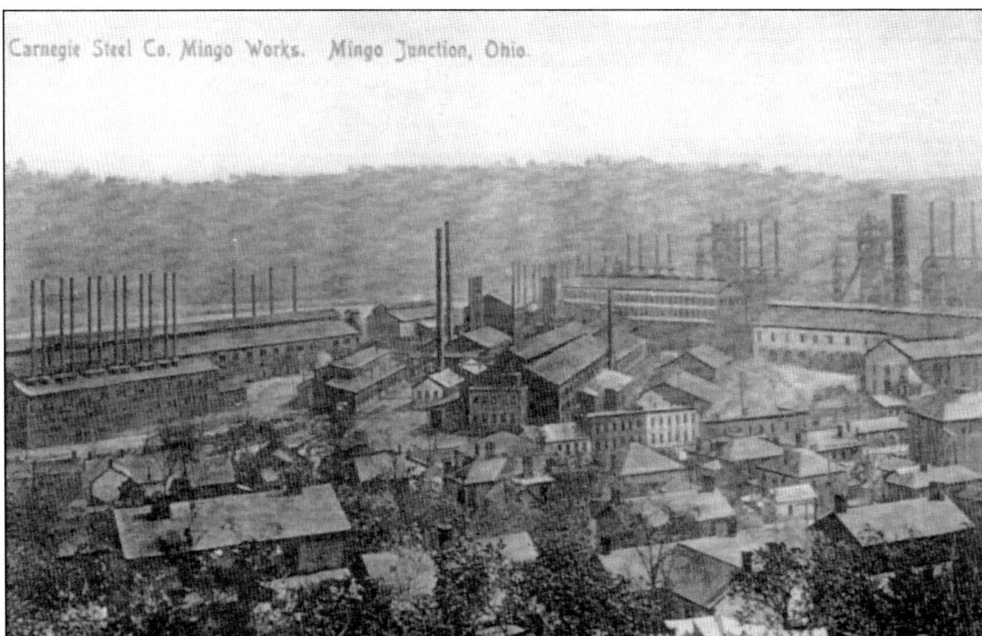

Carnegie Steel Mill and Town. This postcard image shows the extent of the steel mill in the town as it would be seen from North Hill. (Courtesy Madeline [Brinskey] Campbell.)

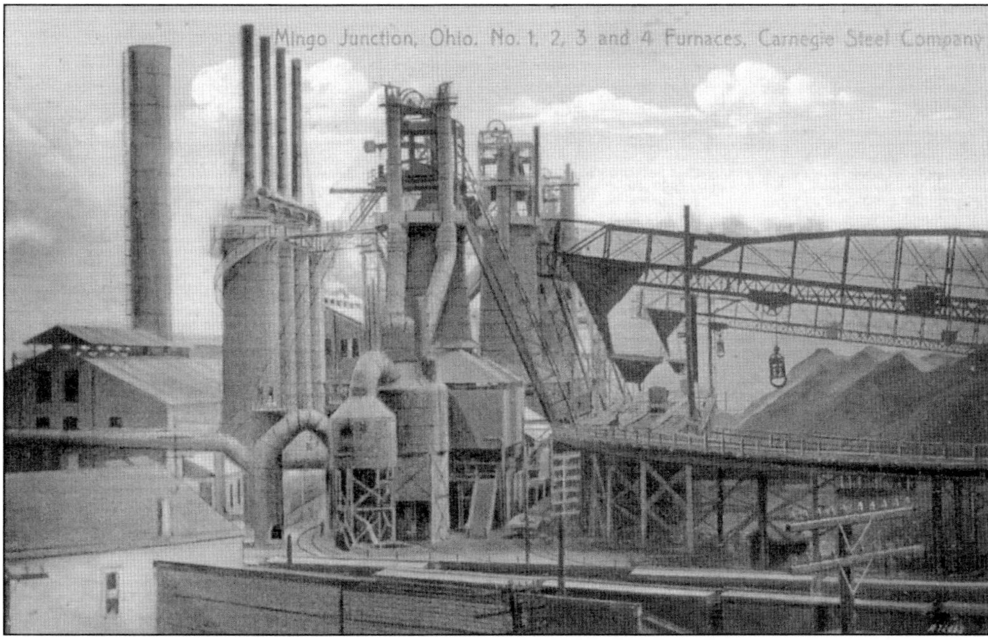

Blast Furnaces. Carnegie Steel is in full operation with four blast furnaces and the car dumper and crane operation in clear view. This view faced the Central School windows where the children could look out at the place where their families worked. (Courtesy Madeline [Brinskey] Campbell.)

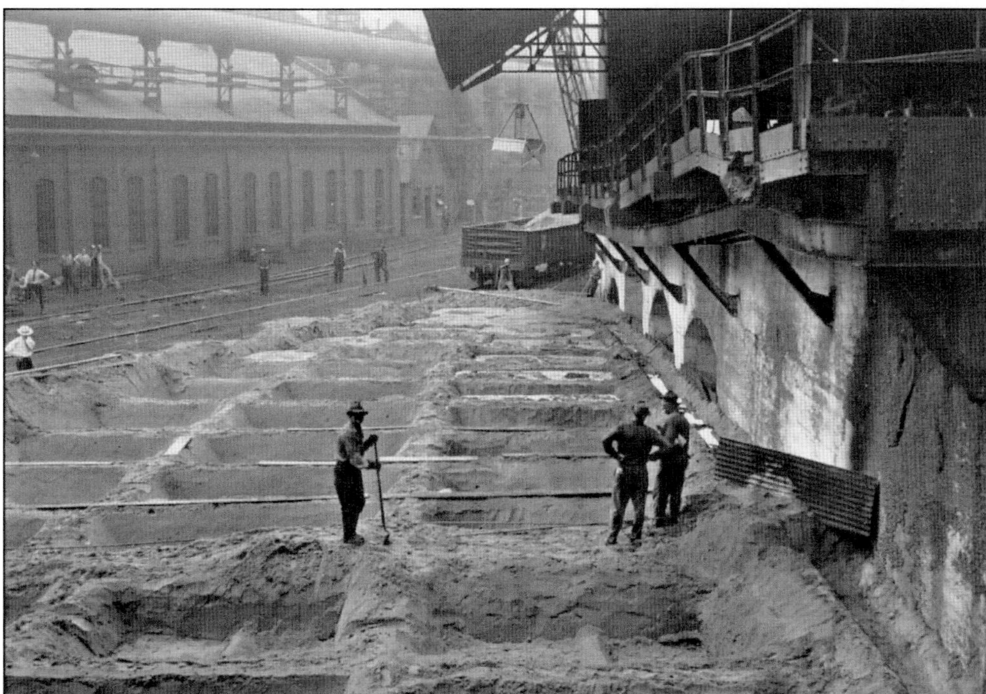

Salamanders at Mingo Works. These casting molds, nicknamed "salamanders," were used to receive the hot steel as it poured off of the blast furnace floor. (Photograph by Bessie [Priest] Quinn, courtesy her grandson David Quinn.)

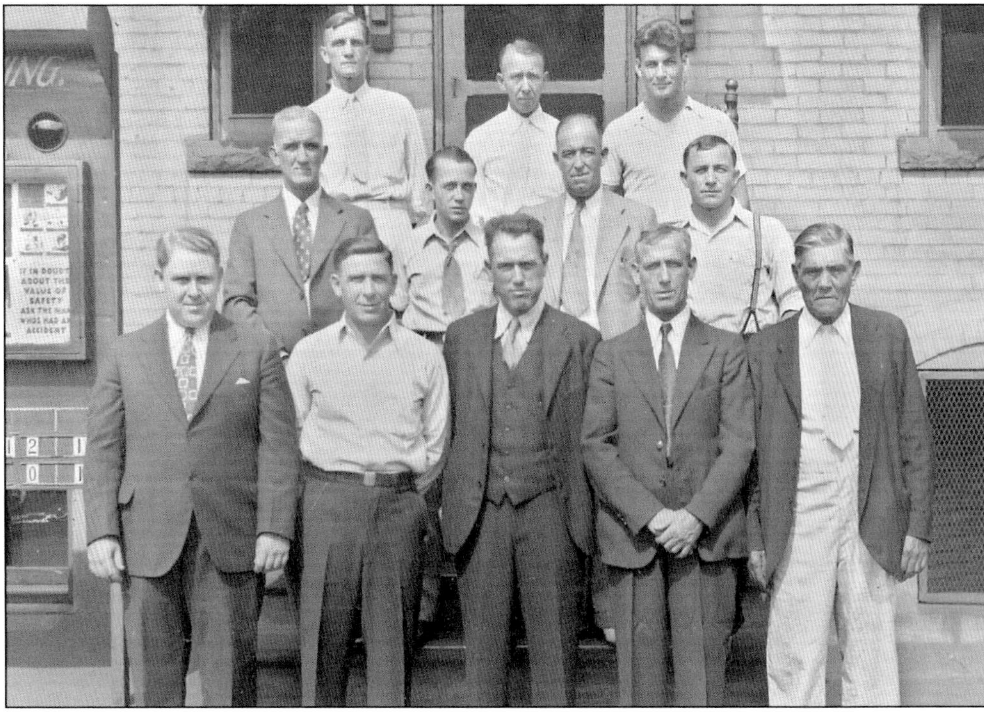

CARNEGIE STEEL SAFETY COMMITTEE, 1930. In this mixed group of workers and supervisors, the second person from left in the first row is Patrick O'Malley Sr.; in the second row at the far right is James Moody Sr. (Courtesy Ron and Eileen [Hagerty] Moody.)

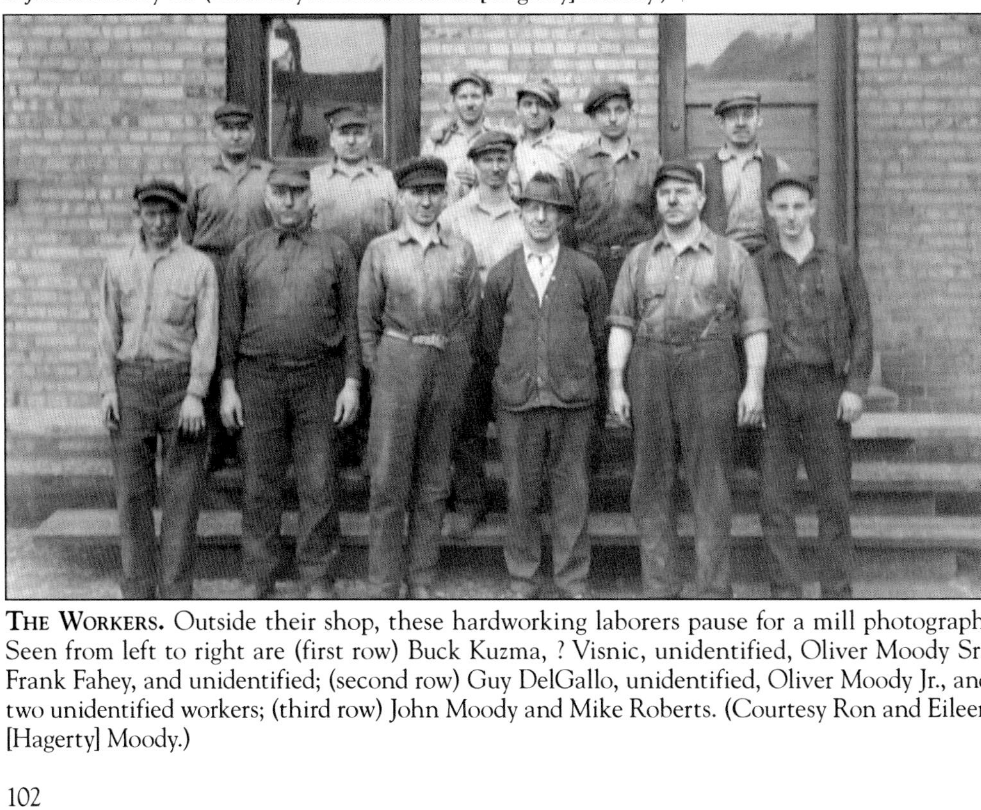

THE WORKERS. Outside their shop, these hardworking laborers pause for a mill photograph. Seen from left to right are (first row) Buck Kuzma, ? Visnic, unidentified, Oliver Moody Sr., Frank Fahey, and unidentified; (second row) Guy DelGallo, unidentified, Oliver Moody Jr., and two unidentified workers; (third row) John Moody and Mike Roberts. (Courtesy Ron and Eileen [Hagerty] Moody.)

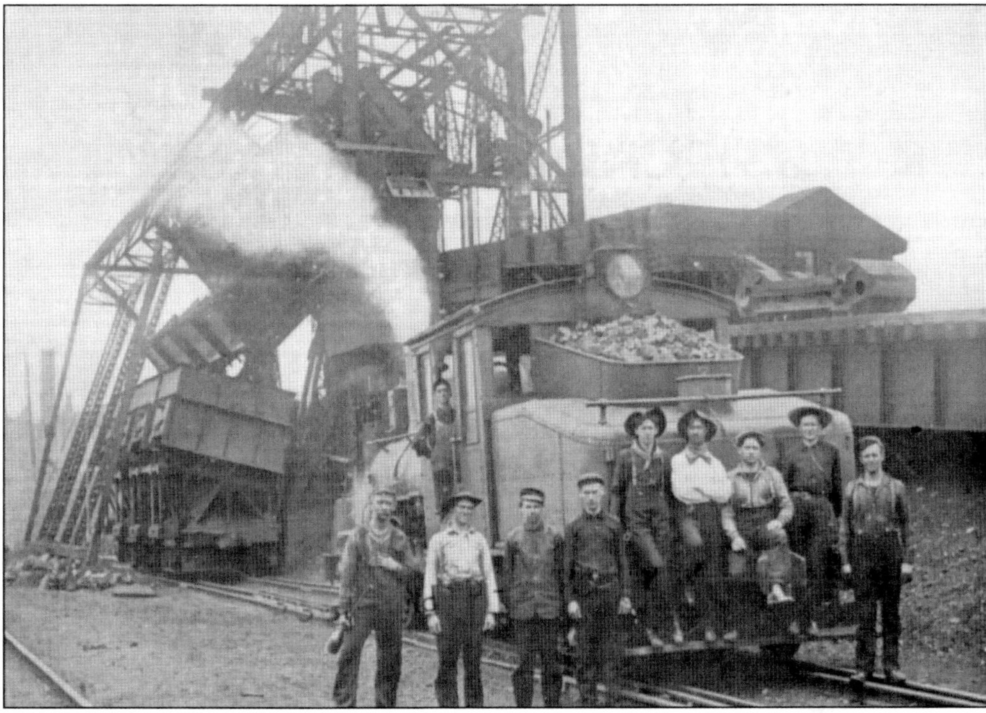

Carnegie Car Dumper Crew. The car dumper crew would throw the switches and guide in the ore railcars, which the huge car dumper would lift, dumping their contents onto the ore pile. (Courtesy Madeline [Brinskey] Campbell.)

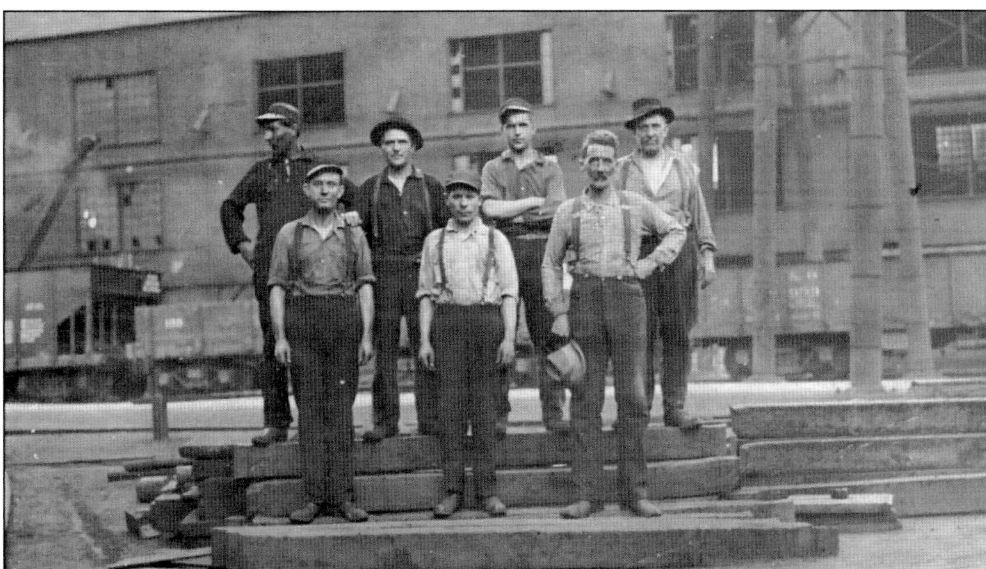

Carnegie Blacksmiths, 1930. Assembled here for this photograph are the rugged blacksmiths of Carnegie Steel. As time and technology advanced, the crew would shrink, then disappear. (Courtesy Ron and Eileen [Hagerty] Moody.)

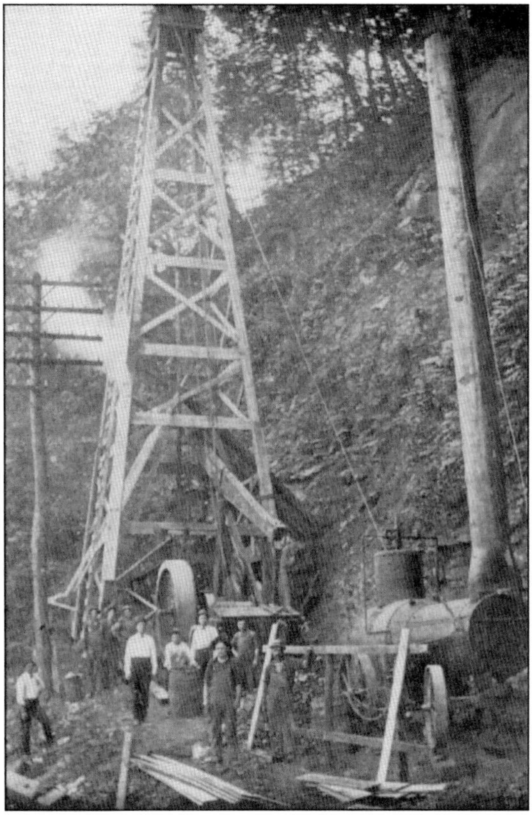

Oil Craze Comes to Mingo. In 1905, the first oil drilling took place in Mingo along McLister Avenue, which was then just a muddy trail into deeper woods and coal mines. Soon an oil fever took over the town and oil derricks like the one shown at left appeared up and down McLister Avenue on North Hill and Altamont. Joseph Conroy writes in *A Mill Town Pastor,* "The oil boom struck Mingo, shortly after Father Coffey was appointed as pastor. The whole district still bears the marks of the disease. Hundreds of skeleton derricks, like hideous gibbets, stud the land at intervals all about the scene (in many cases still active) of feverish diggings and drillings." In the photograph below, the scene on McLister Avenue looks like a scene from the Wild West. (Left, courtesy Madeline [Brinskey] Campbell; below, courtesy Darlene Hoff, originally published in *Bicentennial History of Mingo Junction, Ohio.*)

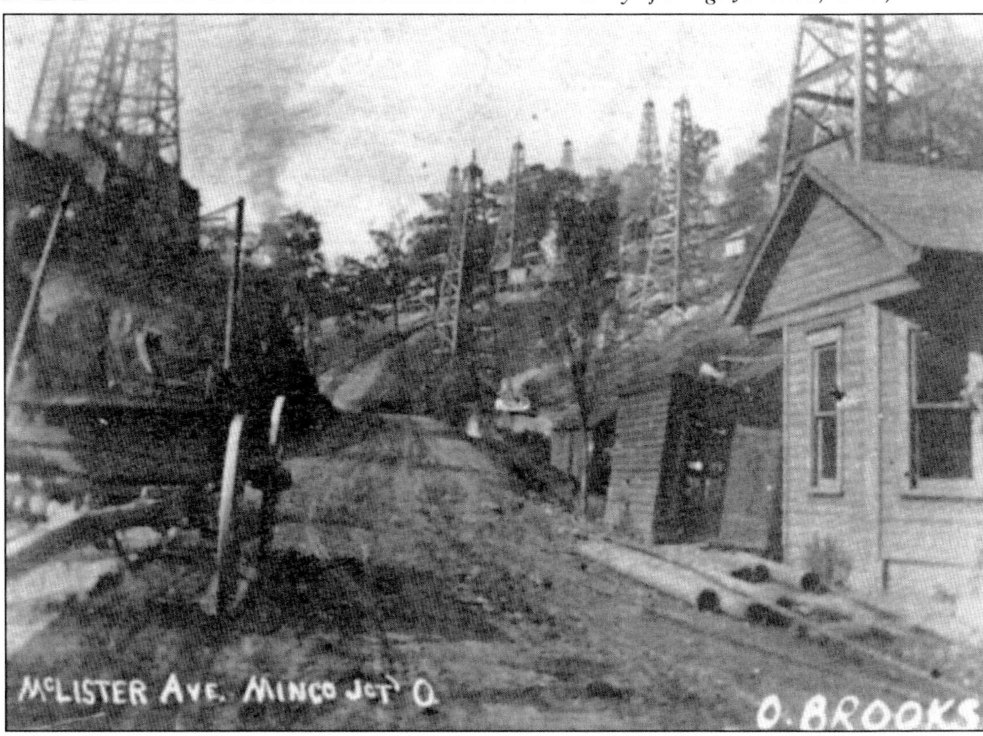

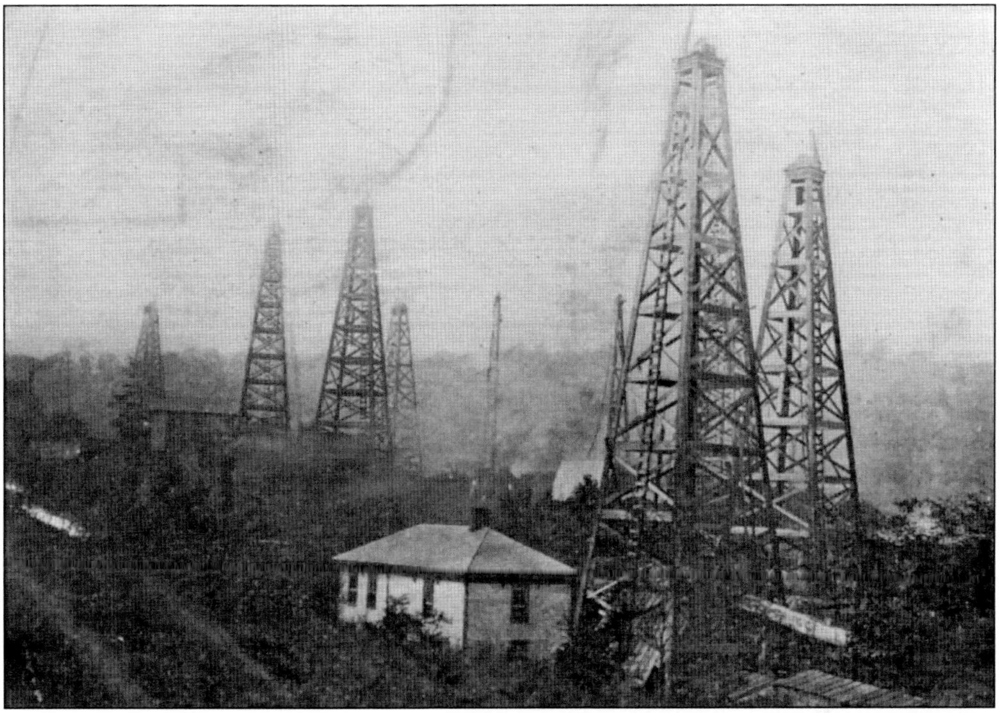

Buying into Oil. As Joseph P. Conroy explains in *A Mill Town Pastor*, partnerships in the oil wells were sold on the basis of shares of 19; however, misunderstanding or greed often found the shares sold again and again to 100, so that for some caught in this ignorance or scheming, the best bet was for the well not to come in, lest they face legal proceedings. And in fact, that proved the case for almost all of the oil wells. For a time, even his beloved Father Coffey (who often was given a share to bring luck) got caught up in the hope of returns for his church through oil. The photograph at right provides evidence that drilling even went into the farm fields. (Both courtesy Madeline [Brinskey] Campbell.)

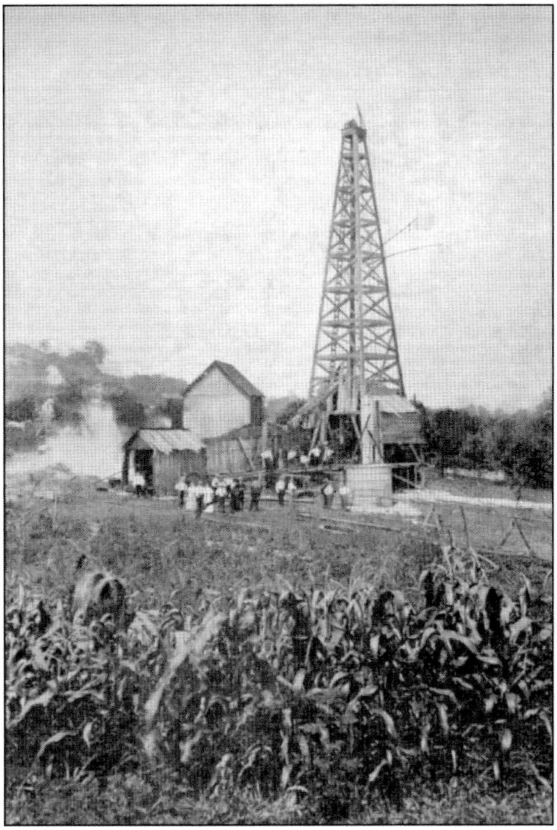

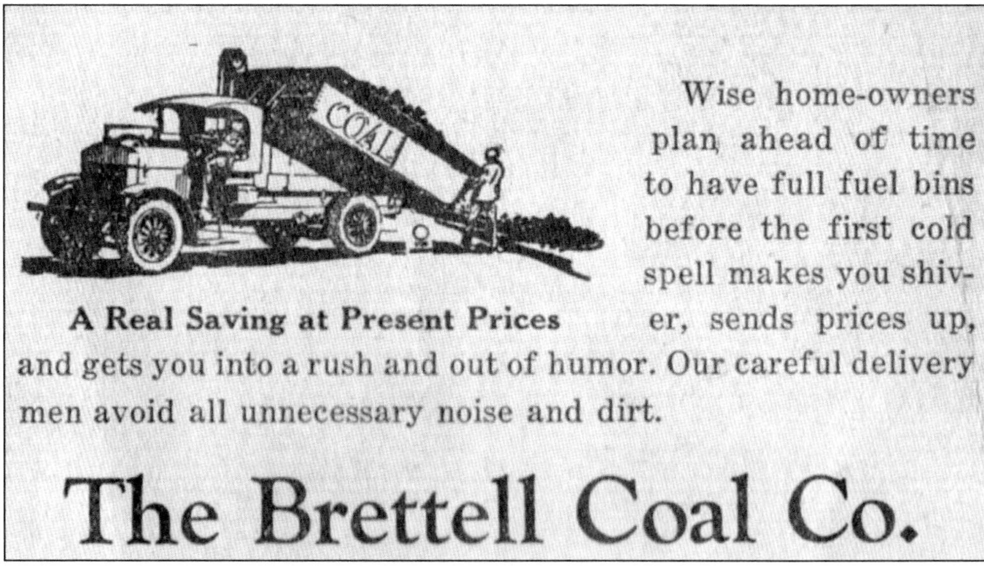

Brettell Coal Company. Perhaps the second largest industry in the town, and one that has gone on for over a century, Brettell Coal and Ice Company was formed by Thomas and Edward Brettell, who ran its delivery services off of Commercial Street. In 1900, they began mining their own coal a mile north of town along Route 7 from a drift mine where a tipple was erected. In 1915, they became suppliers for the Carnegie-Illinois mill. In 1921, the coal tipple was toppled by a cloudbursts and landslide, and so new land along McLister Avenue was bought and new mines were dug. By 1923, Brettell Coal Company employed 150 people. Below is the coal tipple north of town along Route 7, down the hill from Hagerty's Amoco station where company trucks or residents could pull up for a load of coal. (Above, courtesy Jack Brettell; below, courtesy Ron and Eileen [Hagerty] Moody.)

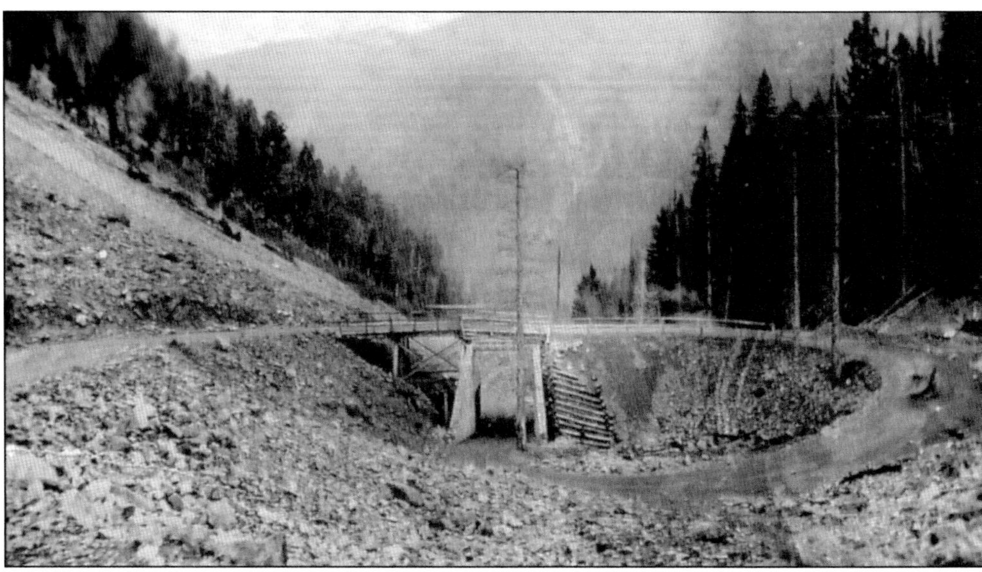

Trains and Trolleys. The first train lines were laid in 1853, the Steubenville and Indiana Railroad, for which three engines were brought in by barge from Pittsburgh. By the 1900s, industries of coal, iron, and steel brought the need for transportation, and the rails supplied the need. Train lines such as Nickel Plate, Wabash, Pennsylvania, Wheeling, and Lake Erie lines supplied the mills, which operated their own lines within. Here in the Mingo mill yard of 1927 are engineer Charles Roy Keys (left) and fireman W. D. Olney. In the photograph below, a steam engine pulls out of the Nickel Plate Railroad Roundhouse of 1925, a center for trains coming in and out of Mingo and the mills. (Right, courtesy Kay [Keenan] Kuebeler; below, courtesy Darlene Hoff, originally published in *Bicentennial History of Mingo Junction, Ohio.*)

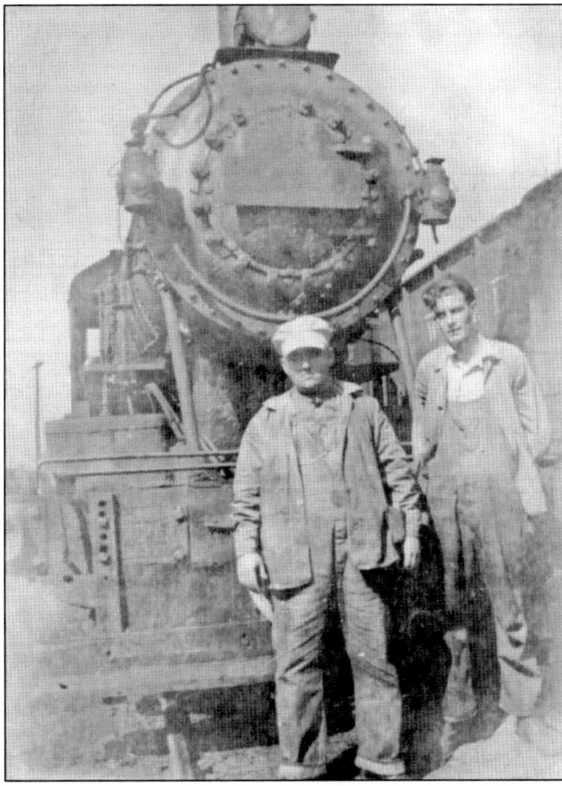

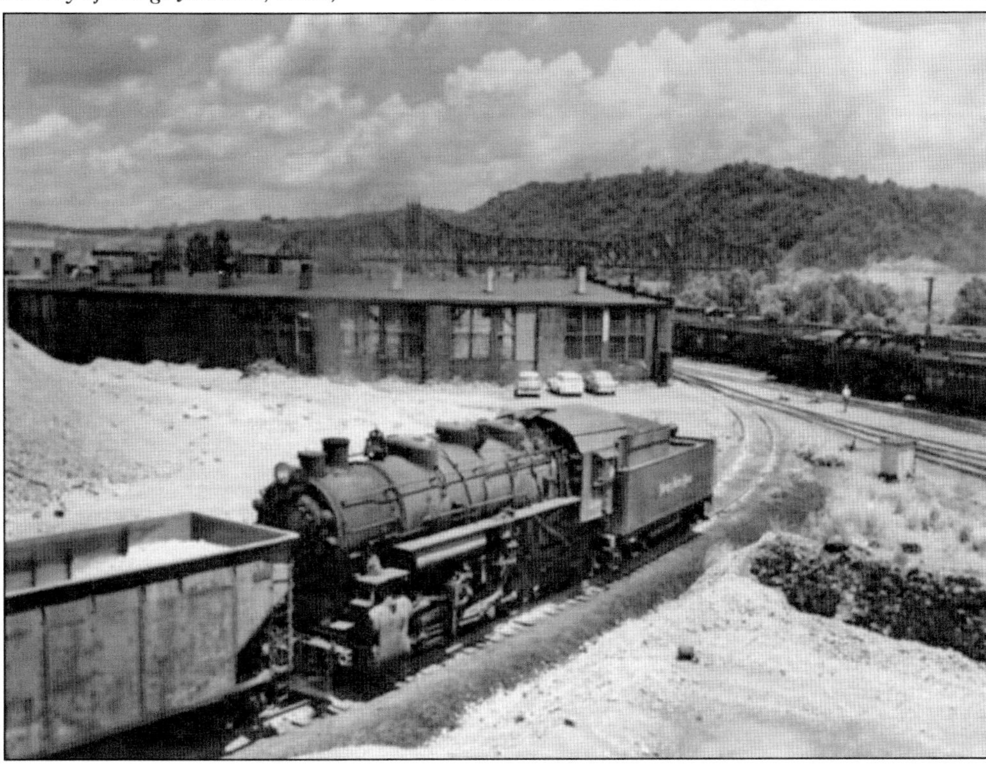

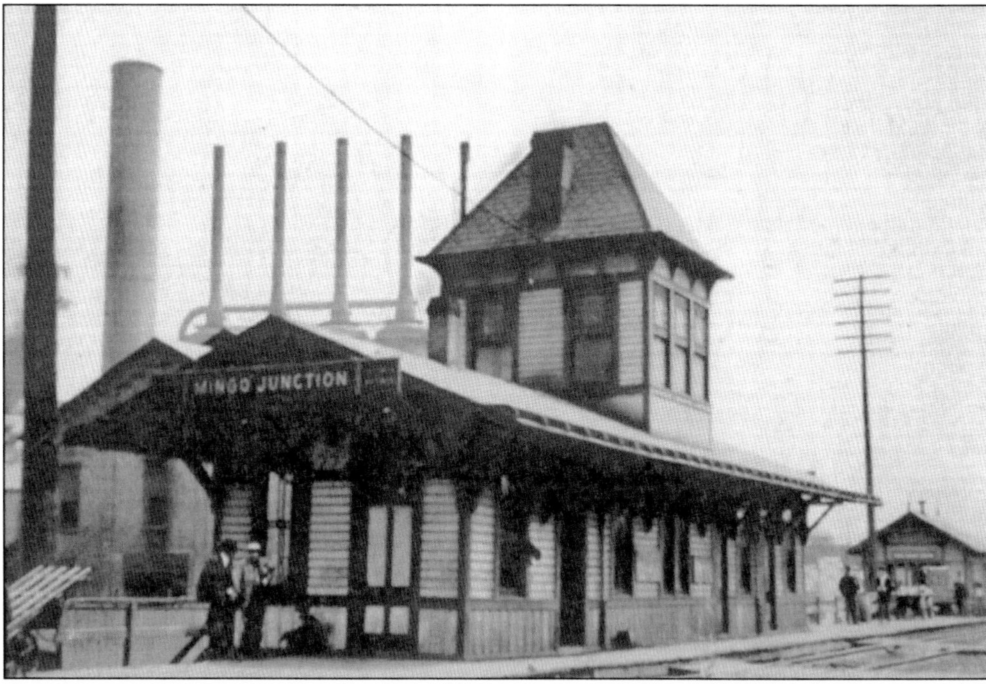

Pennsylvania Train Station. Train stations for passengers and for freight were located behind the mill gate where McLister Avenue meets Commercial Street. The War Memorial was located here as well. The station was often a busy scene for commuters and travelers before automobiles became the main means of transportation. The Mingo train station could be a busy place at times, as shown in the World War I–era photograph below, taken in 1918. (Above, courtesy Madeline [Brinskey] Campbell; below, courtesy Eileen [Hagerty] Moody.)

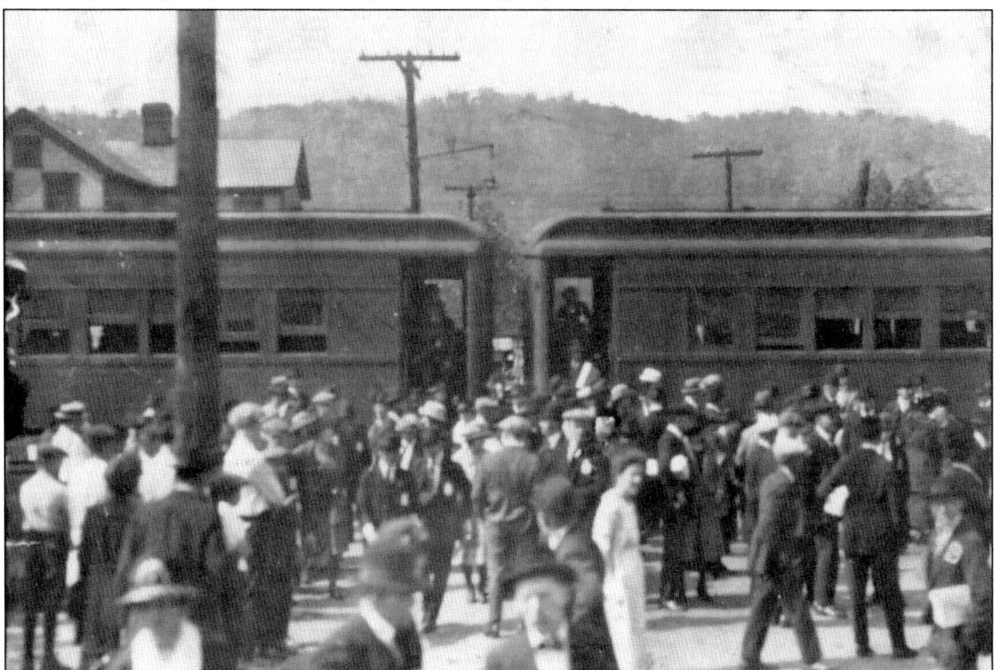

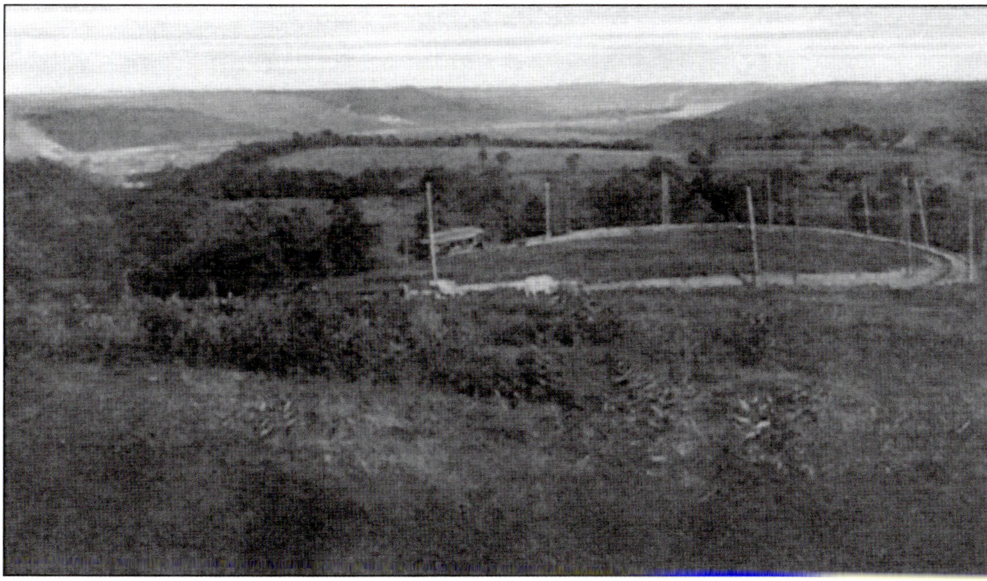

Traction Lines—The Trolley. In 1901, the Ohio Valley Traction Company ran the first trolley line through town and over the Altamont hills to Steubenville. Often viewed as the "scenic route," it certainly offered great vistas of the valley, yet was considered slow, even by 1900 standards. Pictured above is "The Loop" over the hill in the Altamont area. (Courtesy Madeline [Brinskey] Campbell.)

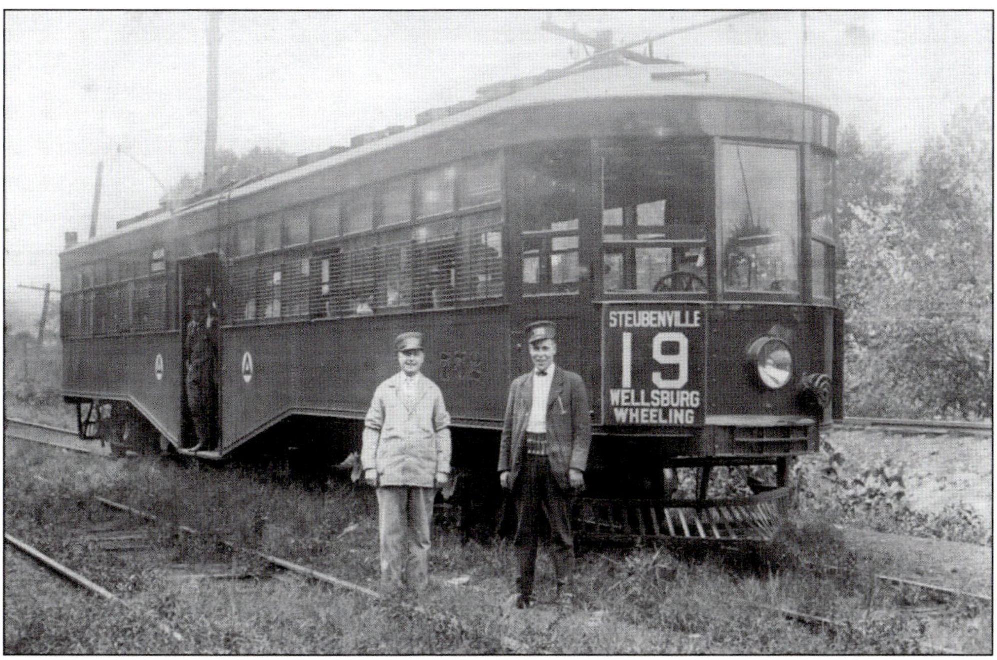

Ohio Valley Line. In 1905, this line was replaced by a competing Steubenville and Wheeling line that ran near the railroad tracks along the river. This c. 1925 photograph of the Steubenville and Wheeling trolley shows conductor Harry Merrill Barr on the left. (Courtesy Kay [Keenan] Kuebeler.)

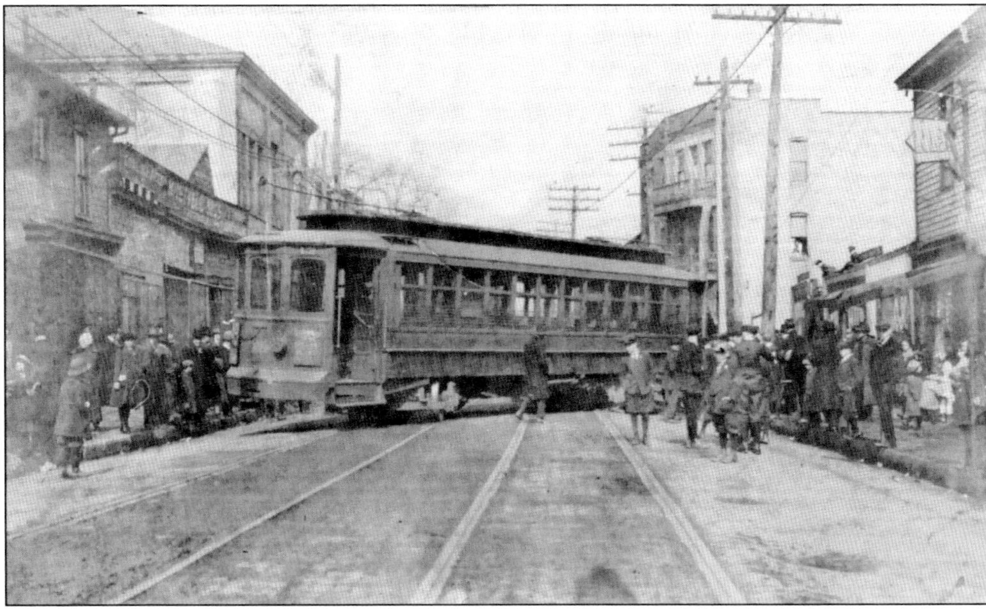

Trolley Accident. Things did not always run smoothly on the trolley, as shown in this *c.* 1918 accident scene on Commercial Street where the trolley has come off the tracks. The tracks of the Steubenville and Wheeling line ran right through downtown Mingo along Commercial Street. The photograph below shows another essential in the industrial traffic of the area: the near-continuous flow of river barges moving up and down the Ohio. (Above, courtesy Ron and Eileen [Hagerty] Moody; below, courtesy Charles Ferroni.)

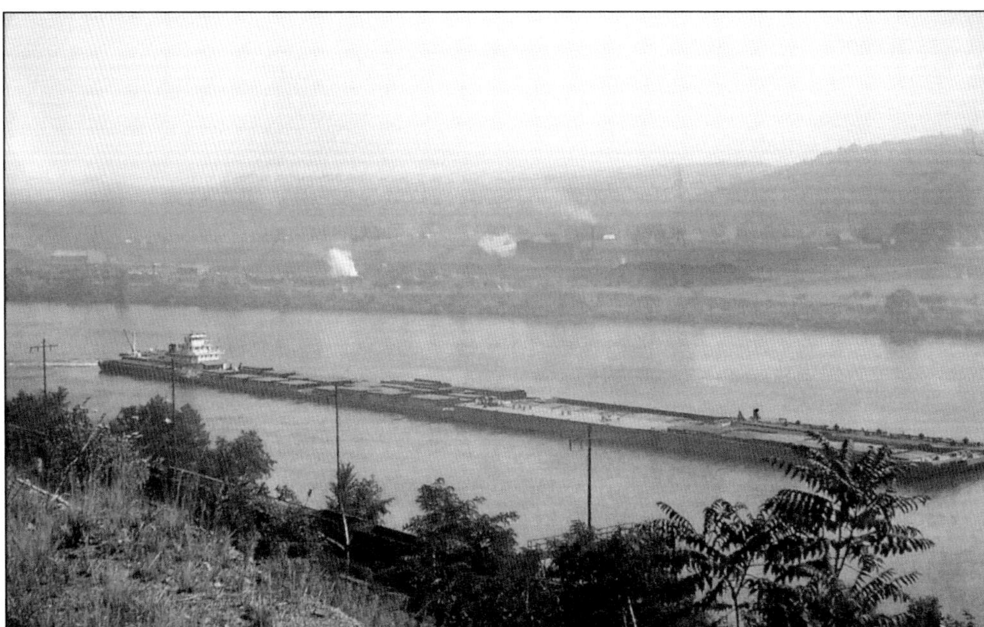

Seven

FAMOUS MINGO RESIDENTS

What do professional sport heroes, a legendary football coach, menthol cigarettes, a rock star, and Squirt soda pop all have in common? Mingo is represented in every one of the above-mentioned categories. Much like Ripley's Believe it or Not, the town has had more than its fair share of super achievers. All but one was born and raised in this small, no nonsense steel mill town and was forever bound to the Ohio Valley.

Most travelers on Route 7 pass Mingo Junction without a second thought other than a quick double take at the huge blast furnaces and dark structures of the steel mill. Yet what was it that enabled Mingo to have this inordinate number of famous people? Was it something only found in the Mingo waters, the powers of the ancient Indian burial grounds, the rich diversity of the tough, blue-collar, ethnic-melting-pot community, or a combination of all of the above?

The town's diverse cast of famous and colorful characters includes "Little" Billy Albaugh from the Mingo-Deandale area, who became the living icon for one of the major soda pop companies in America. Two early-1930s Mingo High School athletes, Arthur "Jake" Strutt and George "Bunco" Kakasic, went on to play football for Duquesne University and later became teammates and starters for Art Rooney's 1936 Pittsburgh Pirates (today's Steelers). Ohio State's renowned Woody Hayes had his first coaching job fresh out of college in the Mingo schools (1935–1936) under head coach John Muth. A now-legendary young man, Lloyd "Spud" Hughes, invented and patented the process for producing menthol cigarettes. Following in the footsteps of earlier area rock vocalists and musicians, Wild Cherry's lead singer, Bobby Parissi (MHS 1968), wrote a song that became the number one hit in America. Joe Fortunato (MHS 1948) enjoyed a very successful 12-year career as an NFL linebacker with the Chicago Bears. Bea (Petroskey) Daily moved from the Mingo High School Camera Club to work at Nossett's Photograph Studio and then for the military as a professional photographer of celebrities.

One fact should be obvious: little Mingo Junction eclipses many a larger community when it comes to the success and fame of its offspring—the sons and daughters of the Red and Black.

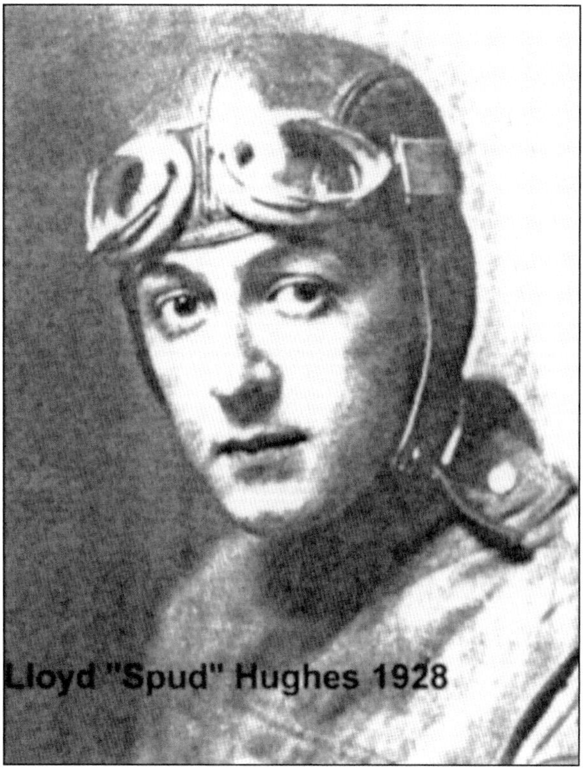

Lloyd "Spud" Hughes. Spud's father owned a restaurant in Mingo where he helped out occasionally, but fact has long since passed into legend for him. As a young man, he invented and patented the menthol cigarette process and sold it for $90,000 in 1926. Always an enigma, Spud used the money to buy and race cars and airplanes, and in two years, the $90,000 was gone. Asked in a November 1932 *Fortune* magazine article if he regretted blowing all the money on airplane and car racing, he replied that at least he had fun with his windfall rather than losing it all in the stock market crash. (Courtesy U.S. Tobacco Institute.)

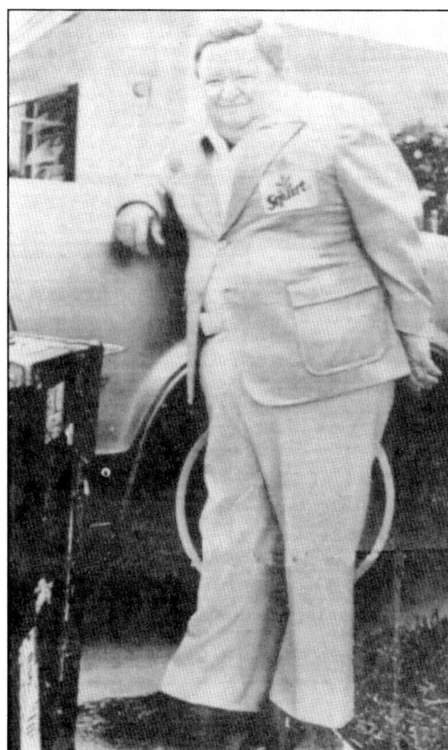

Call Him "Squirt." Jovial "Little" Billy Albaugh was 4 feet, 7 inches tall and graduated from Mingo High School in 1946. As the mascot for the Buffalo Bills football team, he was spotted interacting with both children and adults in the crowd, which impressed Milton Bonn, owner of the Squirt Beverage Company. Billy was hired to represent the "Little Squirt" trade symbol and went on to become the living trademark for Squirt and Company for the next 35 years. (Courtesy Paul Yates.)

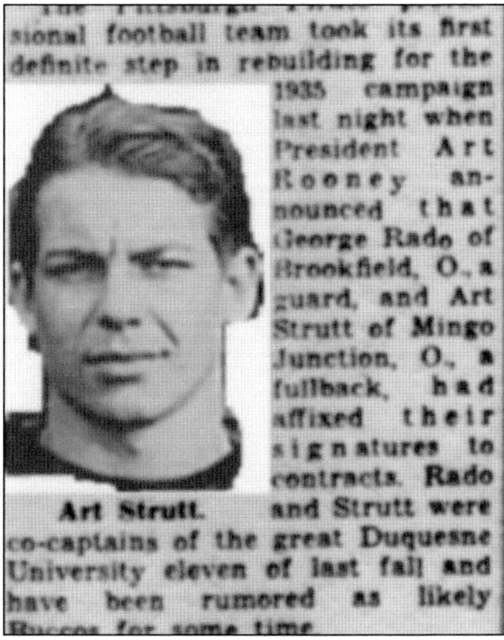

...sional football team took its first definite step in rebuilding for the 1935 campaign last night when President Art Rooney announced that George Rado of Brookfield, O., a guard, and Art Strutt of Mingo Junction, O., a fullback, had affixed their signatures to contracts. Rado and Strutt were co-captains of the great Duquesne University eleven of last fall and have been rumored as likely Buccos for some time

Art Strutt.

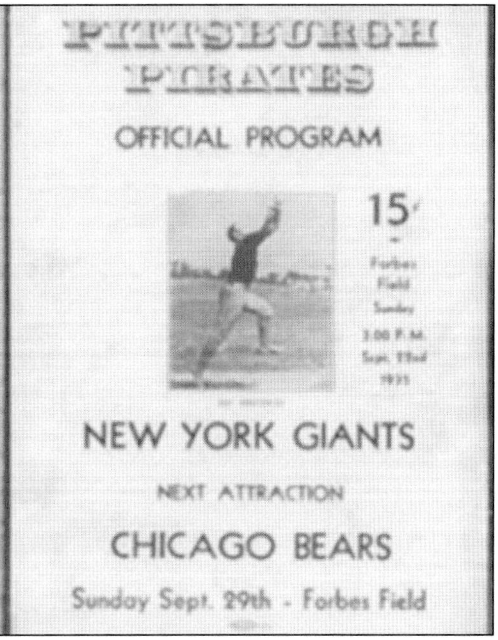

ARTHUR "JAKE" STRUTT. A 1931 Mingo High graduate, Strutt (sometimes spelled "Strott") excelled in all sports—particularly football and baseball. He went on to Duquesne University and, in his senior year, was the second leading college scorer in the nation. Strutt was signed by Art Rooney's Pittsburgh Pirates football team and started for the 1935 and 1936 football seasons, then was sidelined with a shoulder injury. He also played professional baseball and starred in the Pittsburgh Pirates minor league system. He was one of the first people to play two sports professionally and, even today, possibly remains Mingo's best all-around athlete, ever. (Courtesy *Pittsburgh Post Gazette* and Pittsburgh Steeler Archives.)

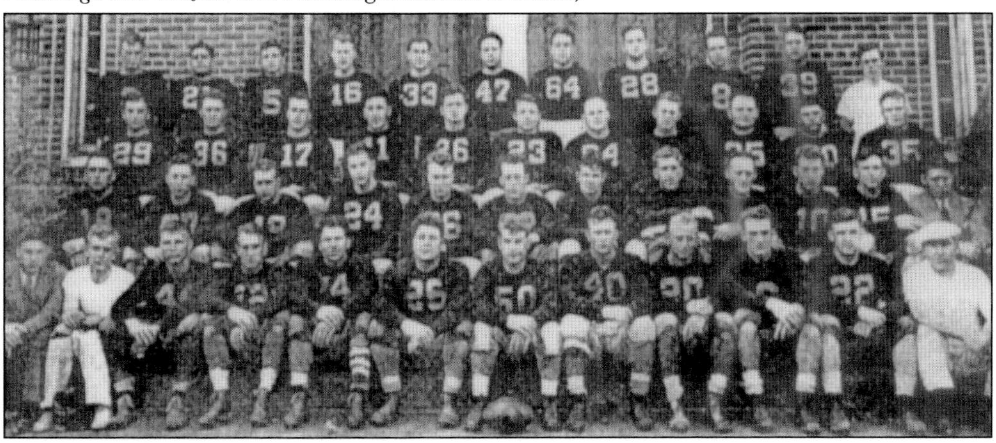

GEORGE "BUNCO" KAKASIC. George graduated from Mingo in 1930 and also attended Duquesne University, then signed and started at tackle for the Pittsburgh Pirates from 1936 through 1939. In this 1938 photograph, Kakasic is fifth from the left in the first row, wearing no. 74. He and Arthur Strutt were starting teammates on the 1936 Pittsburgh Pirates football team. In the second row of this team photograph are three legendary figures: Byron "Whizzer" White, no. 10, former Supreme Court Justice (third from right), and Hall of Famers John "Blood" Mcnally, no. 15 (second from right), and Pittsburgh team owner Art "The Chief" Rooney (far right). (Courtesy Pittsburgh Steeler Archives.)

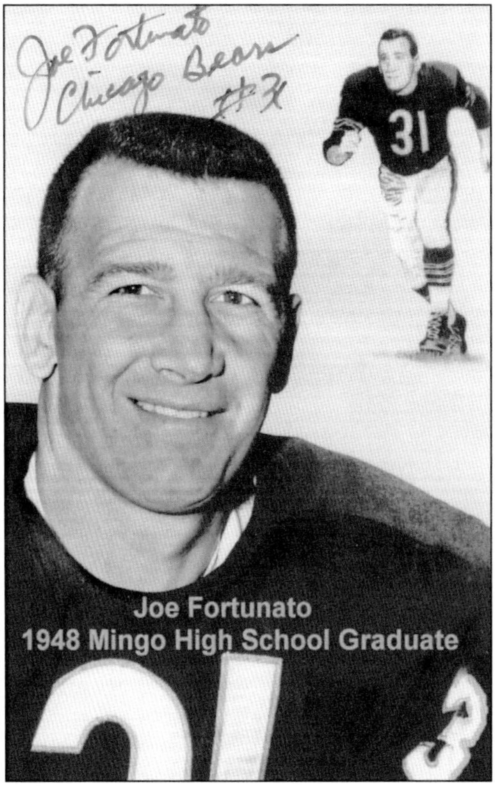

JOE FORTUNATO. Joe graduated from Mingo High in 1948, where he excelled in all sports, particularly football. Joe received a football scholarship to Mississippi State, where he was Senior Bowl defensive captain. Joe was drafted by the Chicago Bears in 1952. After serving two years in the military, he became starting linebacker for the Bears (1955–1966). He was selected All Pro five times and cocaptained the Bears' 1963 championship team. Below Joe is seen on November 4, 2007, Joe Fortunato Night, held at the packed Knights of Columbus Hall in Mingo. Joe thanked his hometown supporters and announced that he and the Mingo Business Association had set up a continuing high school scholarship. Joe and wife Catherine live in Natchez, Mississippi. (Left, courtesy Joe Fortunato family; below, courtesy Jim and Kathy Frieling.)

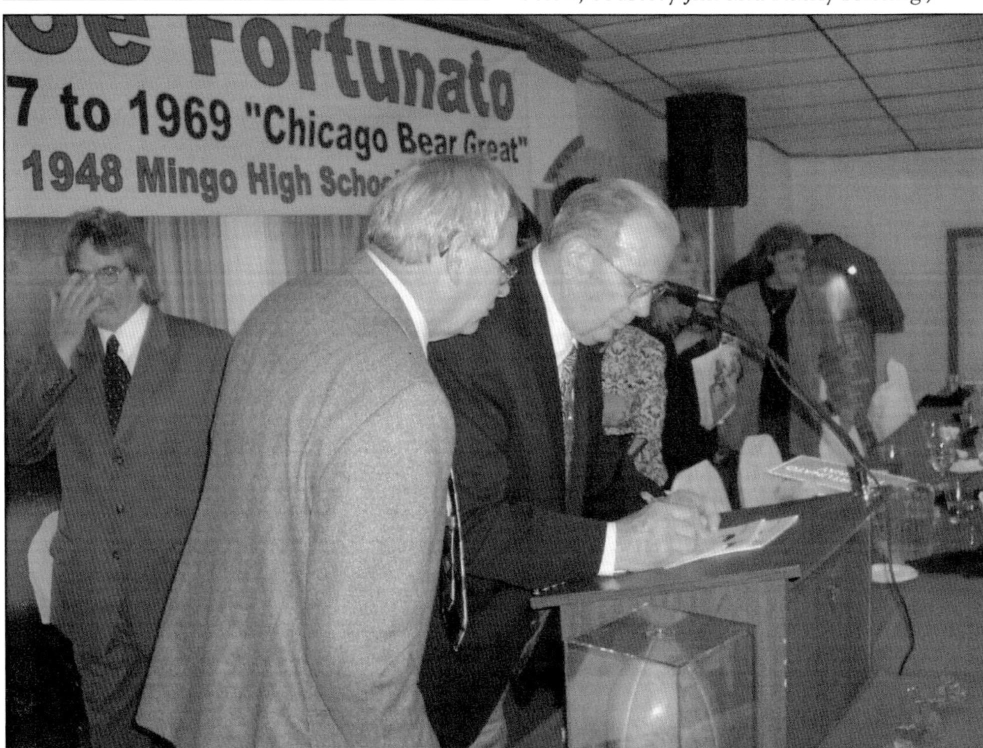

THEY CALL HIM WOODY. The year was 1934, and a young man named Wayne Woodrow Hayes had just graduated from Dennison University and was seeking employment. "Woody" was offered a teaching position in Mingo for the 1935–1936 school year. He taught and was assistant football coach under John Muth that year. Woody Hayes, left, and John Muth are pictured when Hayes returned one last time to honor his old head coach and longtime friend as Mingo Stadium was renamed John Muth Stadium. (Courtesy Lewis and Sandy Leone.)

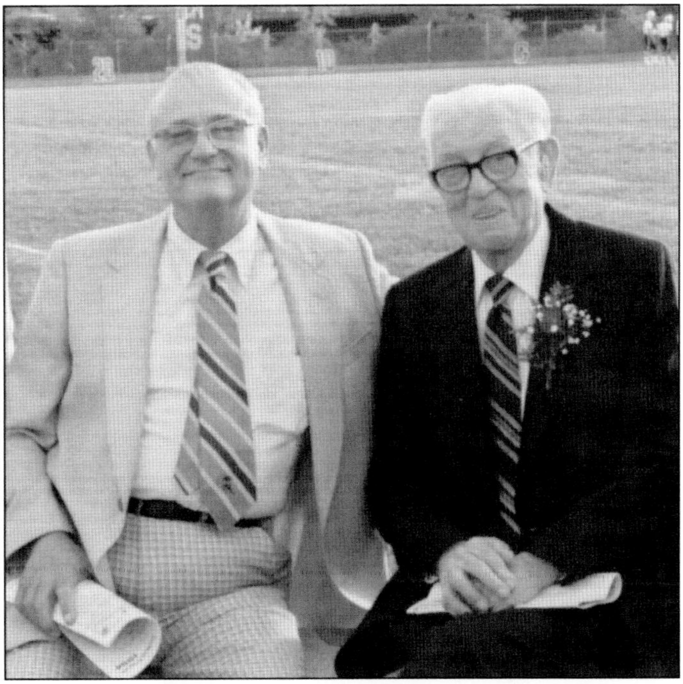

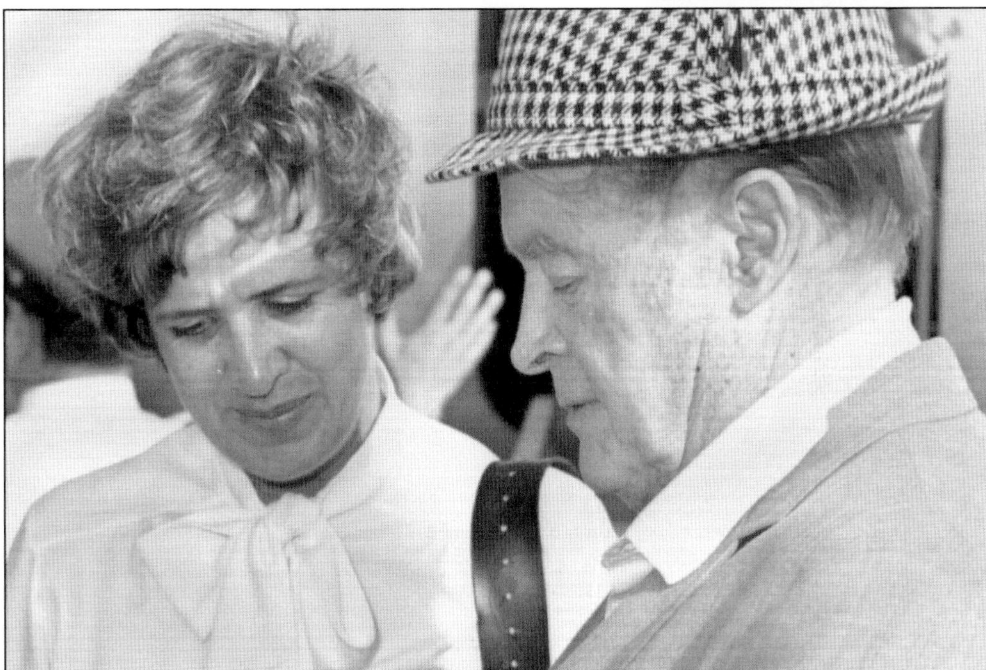

BEA (PETROSKEY) DAILY. Bea joined Mr. Hendon's Mingo High School Camera Club and went on to work at Nossett's Photograph Studio in Steubenville. She later joined the U.S. Air Force and trained as a professional photographer. She was hired by Bob Hope Village, the Air Force enlisted widow's home, as their official photographer. Bob Hope came yearly for a benefit show, and Bea (left) would meet him and other stars to work out their schedules. (Courtesy Bea [Petroskey] Daily.)

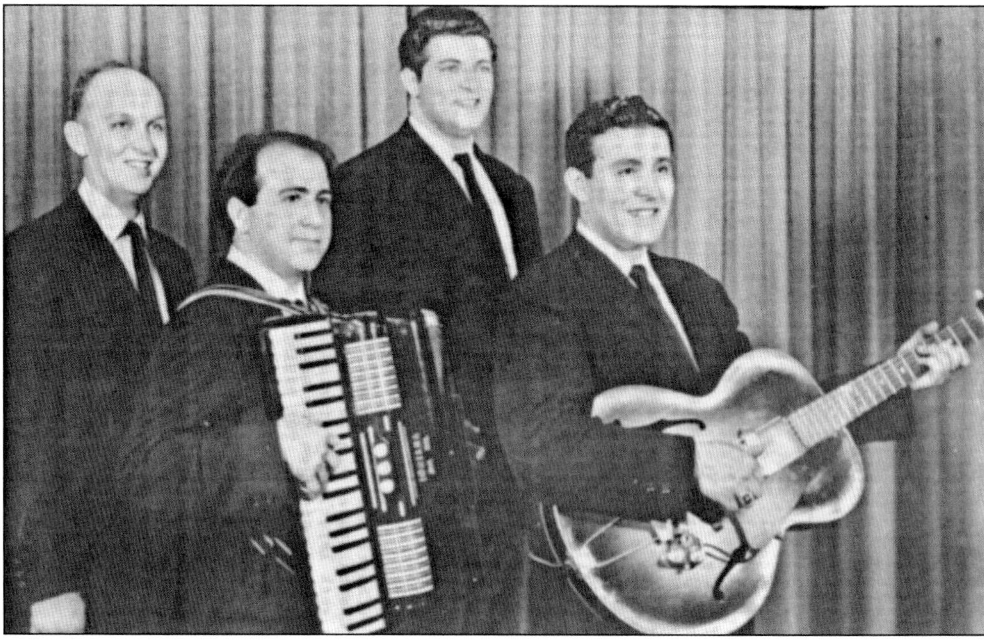

THE ORIGINAL ANTONES. Three Mingo graduates were members of what was possibly the first rock-and-roll group in the Ohio Valley. Paul Visyak (left), Joey Pizzoferrato (third from left) and Pete Graceffa (guitar) also worked on the Pennsylvania Railroad. Chatta Johnson (accordion) owned a barbershop in Steubenville where many times they practiced deep into the night. They released two records that had great success locally but ultimately had to disband in August 1957 because they—like many groups of that era—were not receiving any royalties. (Courtesy Paul Visyak.)

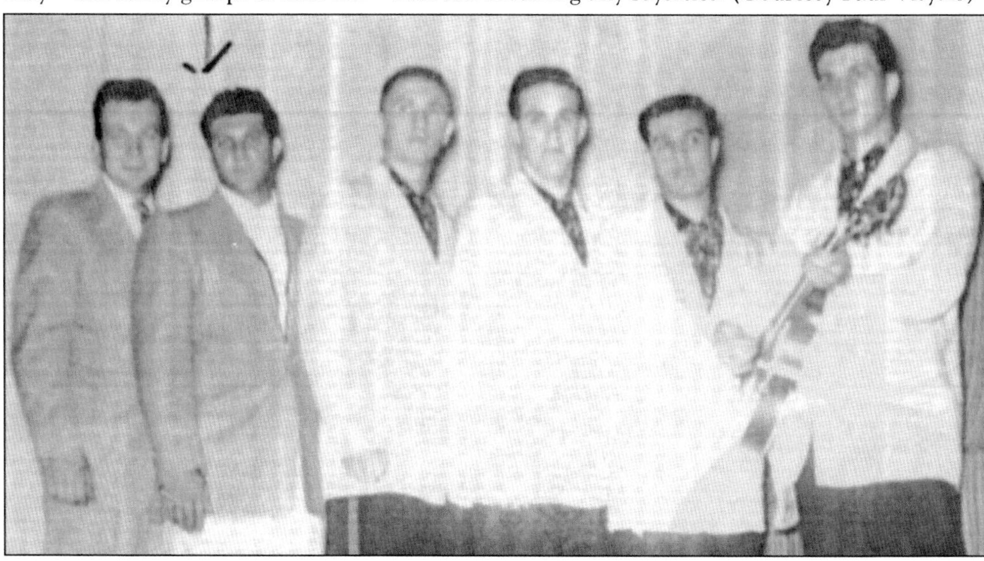

THE MINGO MEN. Joey "Farr" Pizzoferrato continued to manage and sing and joined forces with four guys from Mingo called the Savoys; they became Joey Farr and the Mingo Men. In the summer of 1958, they set out for a New York recording studio. Their session produced two tracks, "Devotion" backed with "Moving On Down." The renowned King Curtis did the saxophone work on the latter. From left to right are Bill Dem John (disc jockey), Joey "Farr" Pizzoferrato, Bill Mitchell, Ron Morris, Bob Cutri, and Dan Pizzoferrato. (Courtesy Paul Visyak.)

WOODIE YINGST, GUITAR PLAYER. Woodie graduated from Mingo in 1956 and, in 1957, joined up with a newly formed group, Buddy Sharpe and the Shakers. The left-handed Woodie played by simply flipping the guitar over—with no string changes. At a New York recording session, they cut one single, "Linda Lee," with "Bald Headed Baby" as the flip side. Their one record is still played regularly on oldies stations 50 years later. (Courtesy Buddy Sharpe.)

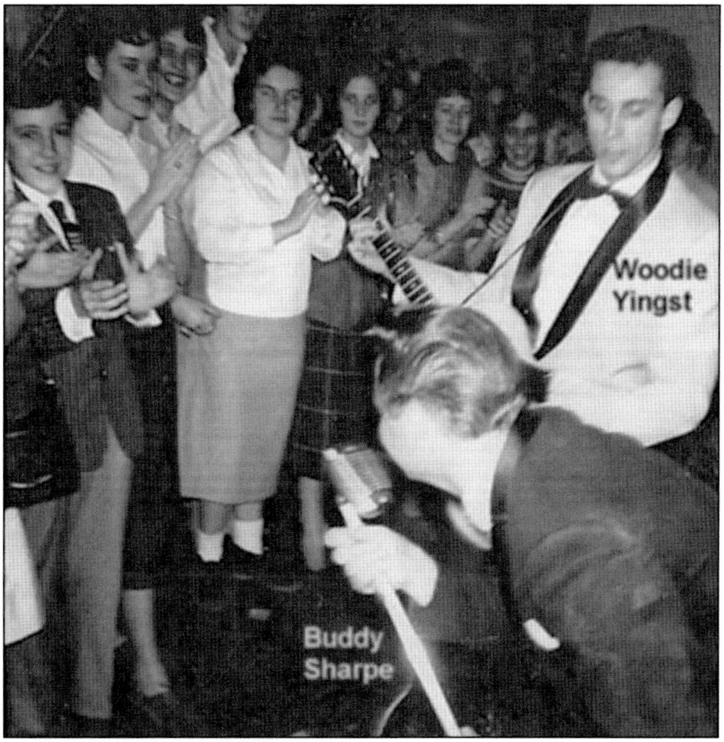

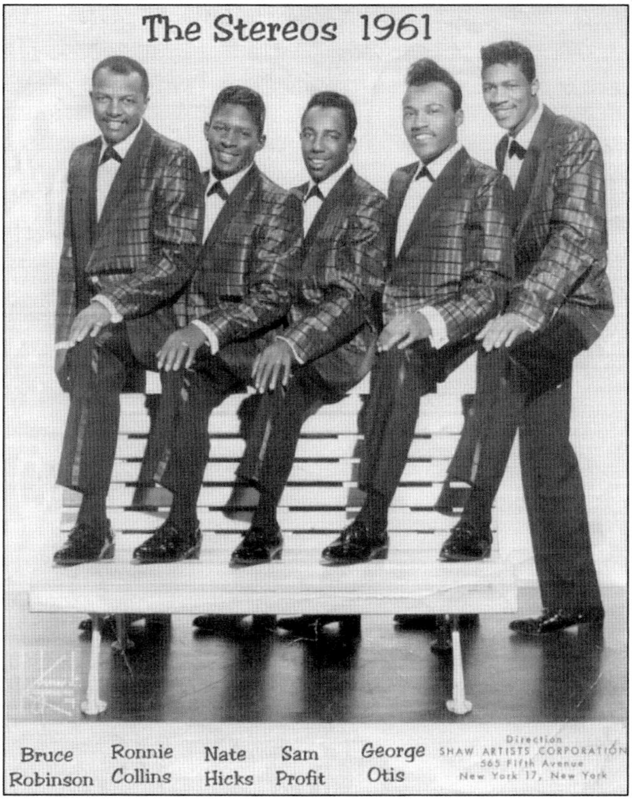

GEORGE OTIS, BARITONE. George Otis, a 1954 Mingo graduate, was asked to join in with four Steubenville guys to form the doo-wop group the Stereos. He sang with them from 1959 through 1966. They had 10 single releases over that time, and one song, "I Really Love You," gained national attention and made it to no. 19 on the R&B charts and no. 29 on the national pop charts. They also performed at Harlem's legendary Apollo Theater. (Courtesy Gail Otis.)

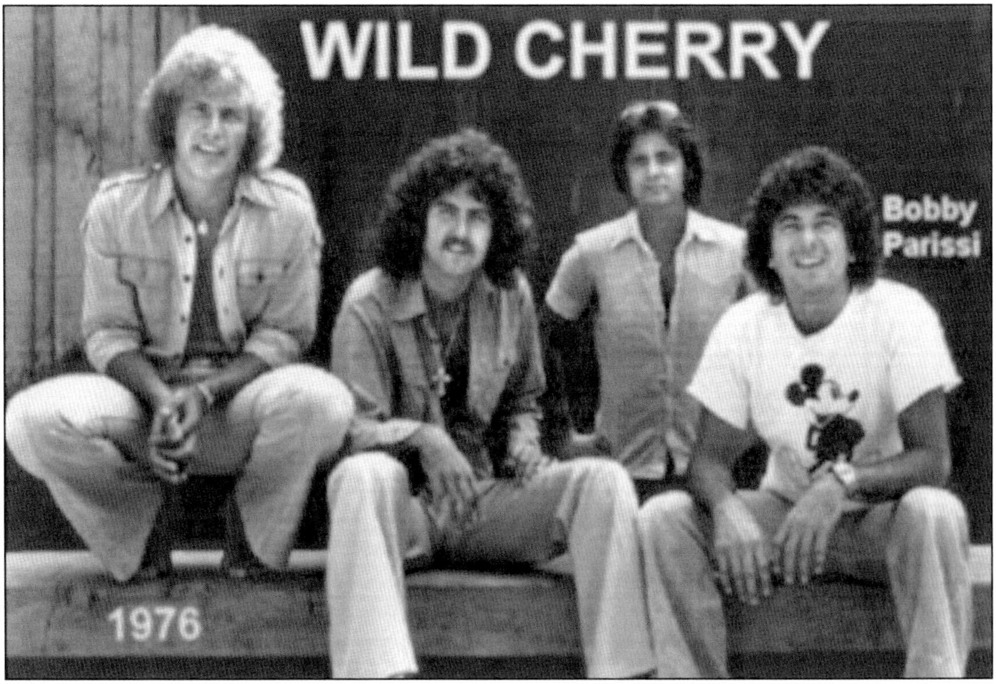

Wild Cherry Lead. Lead singer and songwriter with Wild Cherry, Bobby Parissi made it all the way to the top. He graduated from Mingo High School in 1968 and was somewhat influenced by every Mingo group or member previously mentioned. Bobby wrote and sang lead on the 1976 American no. 1 single "Play That Funky Music," helping the group to earn *Billboard*'s Best Pop Group of the Year honors. (Courtesy Rob Parissi.)

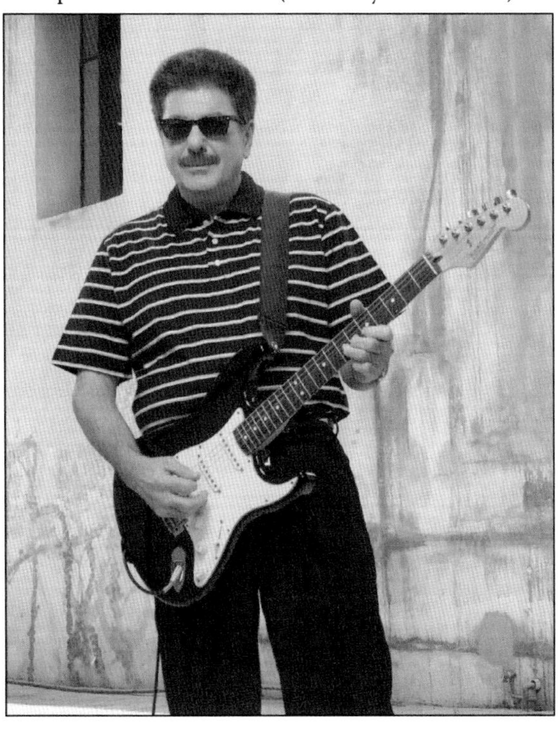

Bobby Parissi in Florida. As always with Bobby, it is about the music and that sound. He still manages to make it back home to Mingo to visit his family and some old, old friends. He continues to search for that new sound through a blending of Adult Contemporary and Smooth Jazz. He still makes occasional appearances and is listed in Cleveland's Rock and Roll Hall of Fame. (Courtesy Rob Parissi.)

Eight

Films Made in Mingo Junction

If visitors take the Mingo Junction Logan Avenue exit, make a left turn at the stop sign, drive down the steep hill toward the steel mill, and make a right turn at the bottom stop sign, they will find themselves in the central block of Mingo. In that one-block area between the two stoplights, three major movie production back drops would be recognizable. In fact, the Logan exit and drive under the Route 7 overpass and down the hill into Mingo is the same one taken by the roaring, smoking truck in the opening scene of 1978's *The Deer Hunter.* The movie won critical acclaim and five Academy Awards, including Best Picture. Many of the movie's steel mill scenes were filmed in Mingo.

The climactic closing scene of *Hearts Of Steel*, a 1983 made-for-television movie, and Michael's poignant homecoming scene from *The Deer Hunter* were filmed at the first of Mingo's two stoplights on Commercial Street, near the millworkers' main entrance bridge. Moving further down the street, a stop at the second light on Commercial Street and a look off to the right reveals several backdrops out of the 1984 movie *Reckless*. These include the Paul Sogan Gymnasium and Mingo Central School.

Larry Smith and Tom Koba also filmed their 1987 documentary, *James Wright's Ohio,* around Mingo and in the Wheeling-Pittsburgh Steel mill. Several other lesser-known movies were also filmed in the Mingo area, and the movie filming continues right up to the present day. Just recently, some scenes of *Unstoppable*, starring Denzel Washington and Chris Pine, were shot here on location.

Mingo seems to have the right stuff when it comes to interesting film location imagery. Its atmosphere resonates well with the blue-collar mystique, unions, family values, economic struggle, and traditional pride.

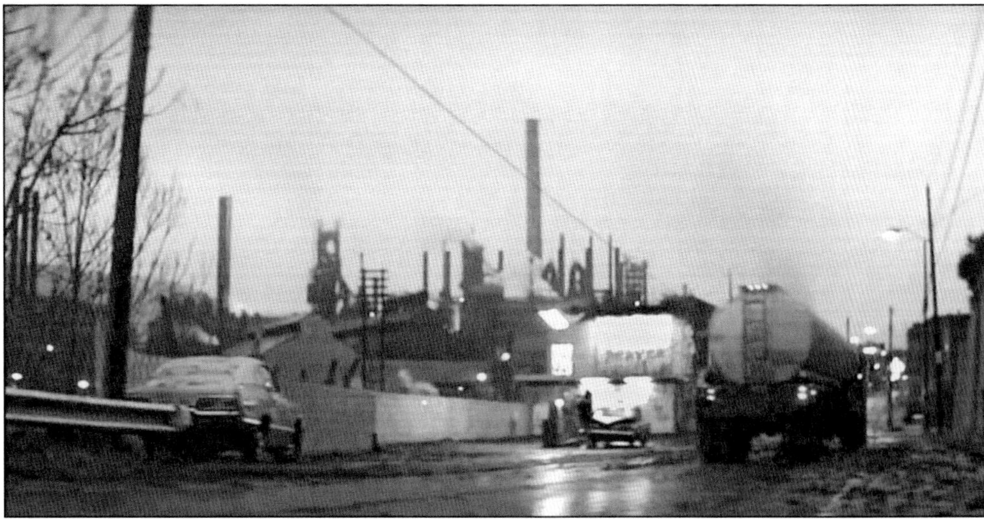

OPENING SCENE OF *THE DEER HUNTER*. The huge tanker truck spewing sparks and black smoke roars down steep Logan Avenue and makes the sharp right turn onto Commercial Street. The ever-present blast furnaces loom darkly in the background. Downtown Mingo is straight ahead, and it is about to enter movie lore and legend. Mingo was a major contributor of locations to the 1979 classic, which won five Oscars, including Best Picture. (Courtesy NBC Universal.)

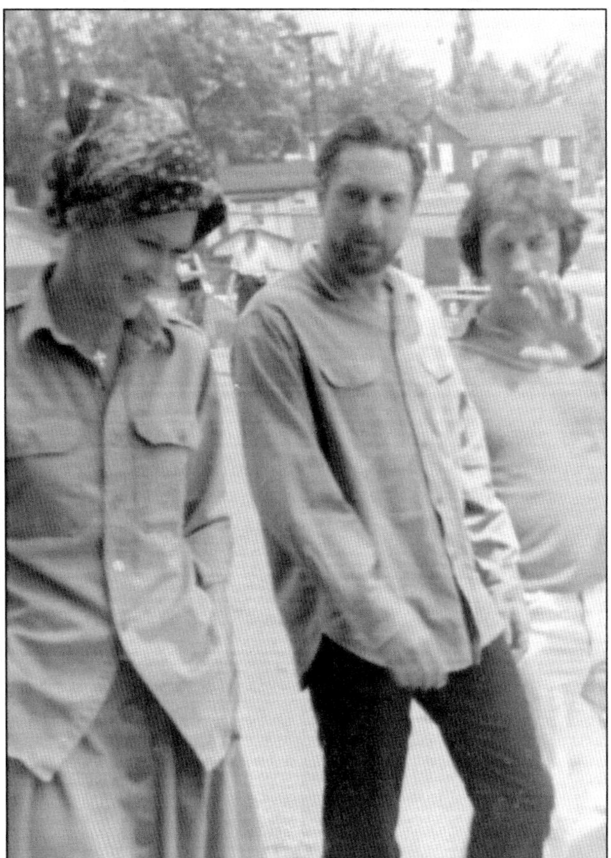

THE STARS HAVE ARRIVED. Meryl Streep, Robert De Niro, and director Michael Cimino stroll down McLister Avenue discussing the filming of the De Niro character's welcome home scene. Soon there will be lights, camera, and action as some scenes are filmed and reshot time after time. De Niro and others arrived weeks ahead of shooting to live in the town and get the feel of the place before the cameras began to roll. Meryl Streep and all the cast and crew seemed to enjoy the people and their time in Mingo. (Courtesy Lou DelGallo.)

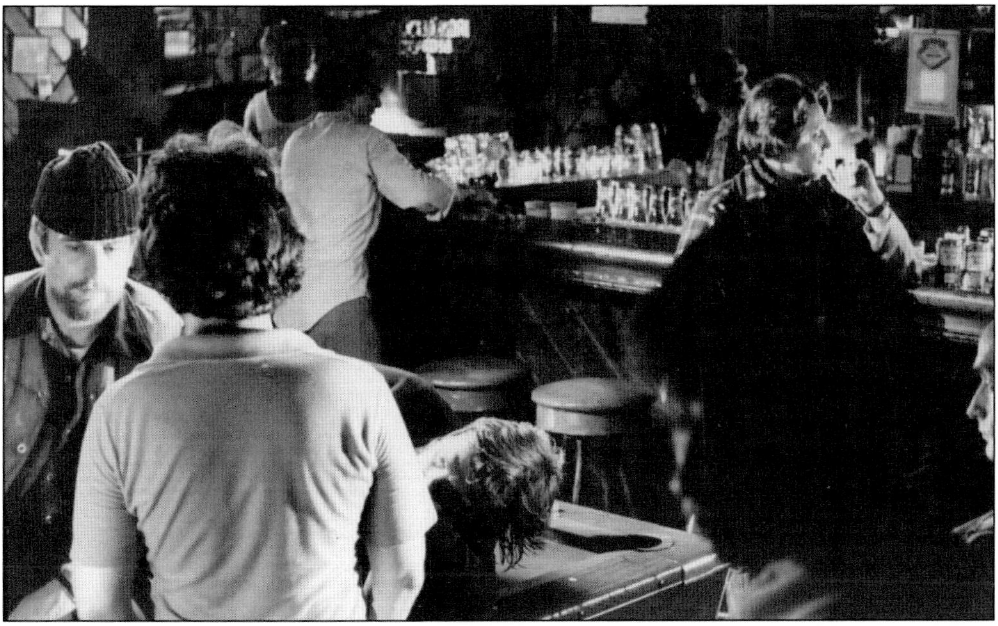

WELCH'S LOUNGE—END OF LONG DAY'S SHOOT. All the actors were exhausted as it neared 2:00 a.m. on South Commercial at Welch's Lounge in Mingo Junction. The filming had begun early in the morning. John Savage and John Cazale are in the right foreground; Christopher Walken is at the bar; George Dzunda is behind the bar; and Chuck Aspegren is listening, stretched out on the pool table. Director Michael Cimino has his back to the camera as Robert De Niro listens intently and Cimino lays out the next film sequence. (Courtesy Guy Mason.)

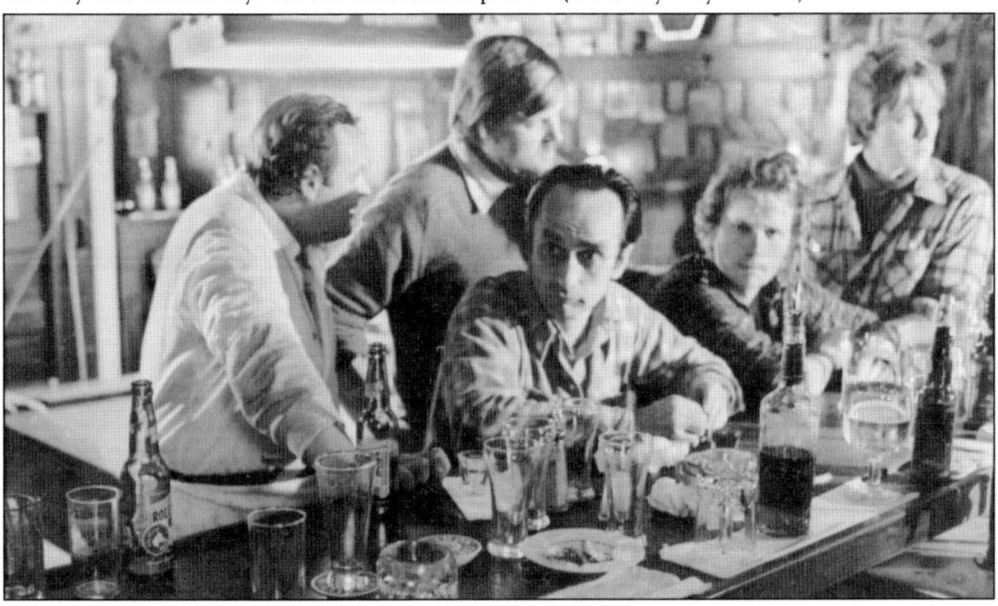

***THE DEER HUNTER* GANG AT BAR.** The actors from *The Deer Hunter* are keeping their positions, listening and watching on the set as Robert De Niro and director Michael Cimino (out of frame to the right) discuss more script changes. The two movie cameras and lights are also being repositioned behind the bar and off to left of the pool table. Soon there will be lights, camera, and action once again. (Courtesy Frank Devore family.)

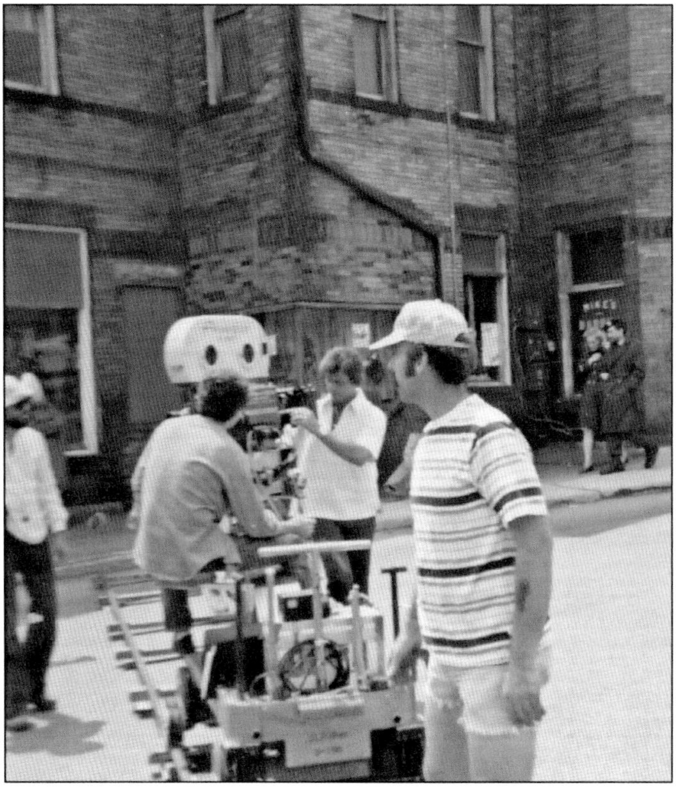

Michael Cimino Directs. Meryl Streep and Robert De Niro do a walk-through of Michael's reluctant homecoming scene from Vietnam. One can see Streep and De Niro walking down McLister Avenue. The cameras are in position but not yet ready to start filming due to last-minute angle adjustments. The building in the background is the old McDevitt Hotel. Director Cimino is off camera to the left, viewing the "walk-through" scene for effect. (Courtesy Lou DelGallo.)

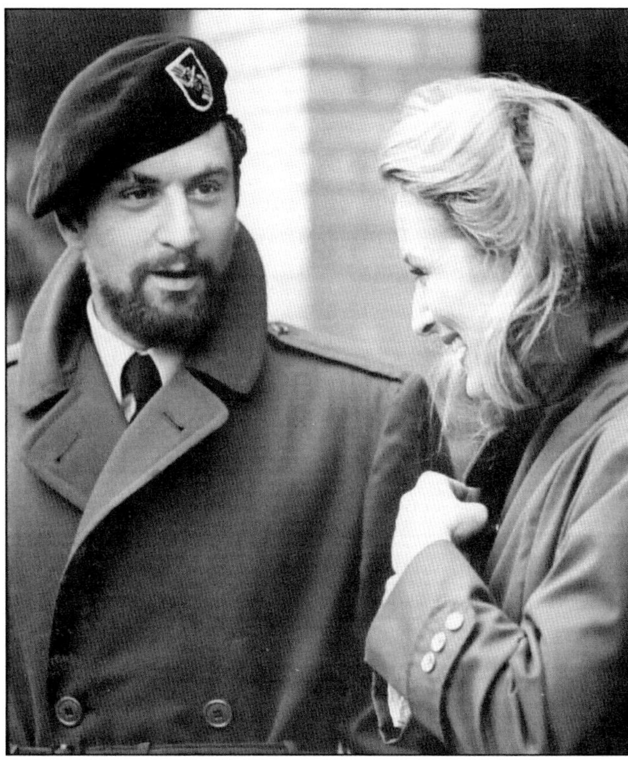

Welcome Home, Mike. This is the film image as seen on the big screen, filmed at the corner of McLister Avenue and Commercial Street just below Mike's Barber Shop. Linda (Meryl Streep) is happy and proud to have Mike (Robert De Niro) back home from Vietnam, and he accepts the "Welcome backs" from the town's residents. This sequence of the film's story was set in the winter, but the temperature reached the low 90s at times. After each take, Streep and De Niro immediately had to remove their heavy coats and be cooled off. (Courtesy NBC Universal.)

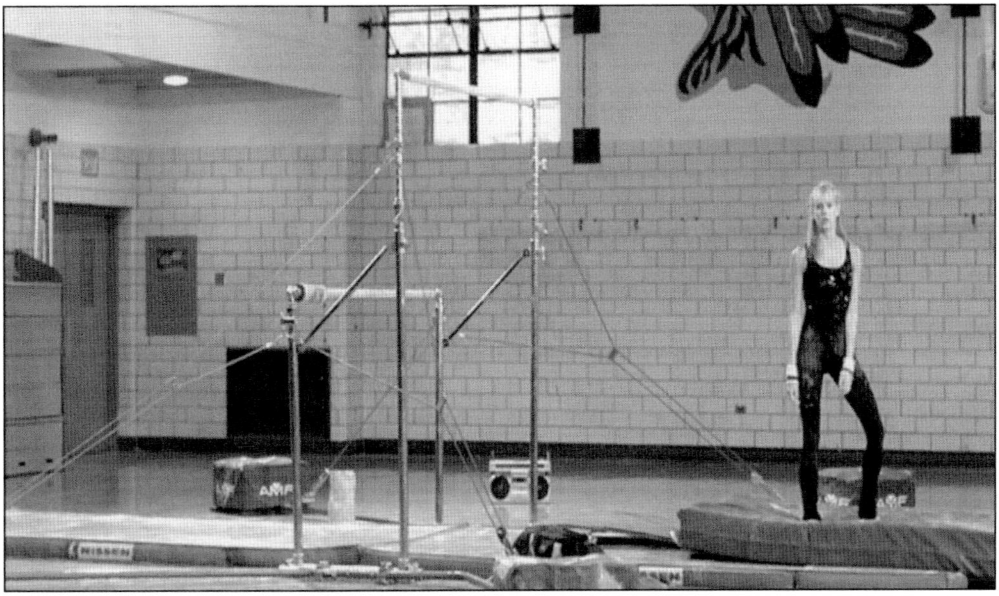

RECKLESS, 1984. Daryl Hannah stands poised in Mingo's Paul Sogan Gymnasium. The Mingo Indian logo was there long before Daryl Hannah arrived. The Mingo Indian head is still on the Sogan Gym wall. *Reckless* kept the Mingo Indian theme. One may recognize the familiar Mingo band and football uniforms in the film, and the movie football fight song is actually the Mingo "Sons of the Red and Black." (Courtesy Metro-Goldwyn-Mayer.)

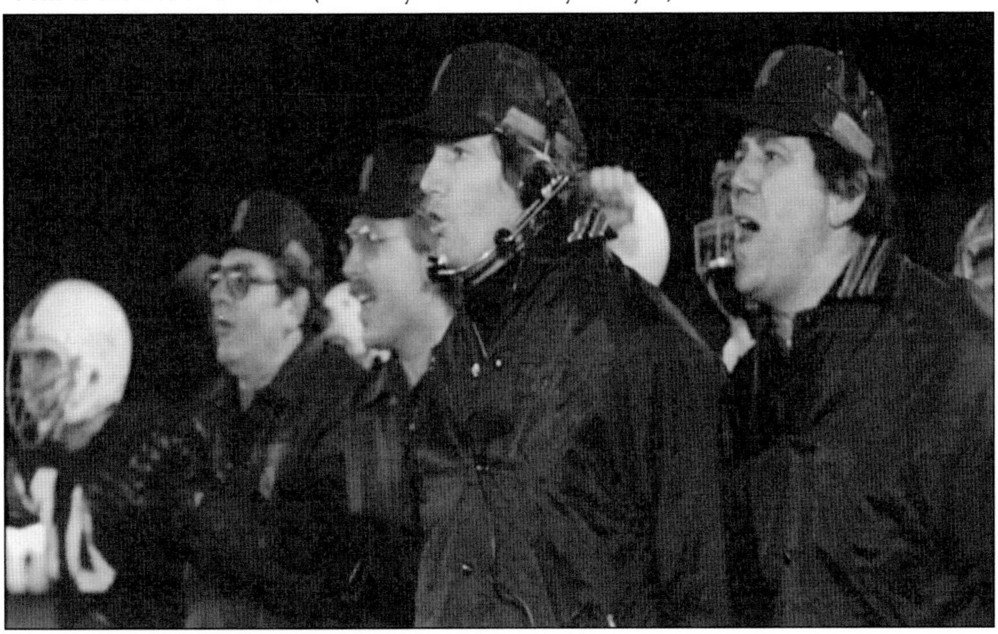

MINGO FOOTBALL COACHES IN FILM. Two Mingo coaches were selected for small parts and on the sideline with celluloid head football coach Cliff De Young (playing "Coach Barton"). To the right is former Mingo Indians head football coach Mike "Satch" Herrick. To the left is John "Bragan" Bracone, Mingo's assistant football coach. The romantic youth movie included a fire in the Central Building and scenes in the furnace room that earned it an R rating. (Courtesy Metro-Goldwyn-Mayer.)

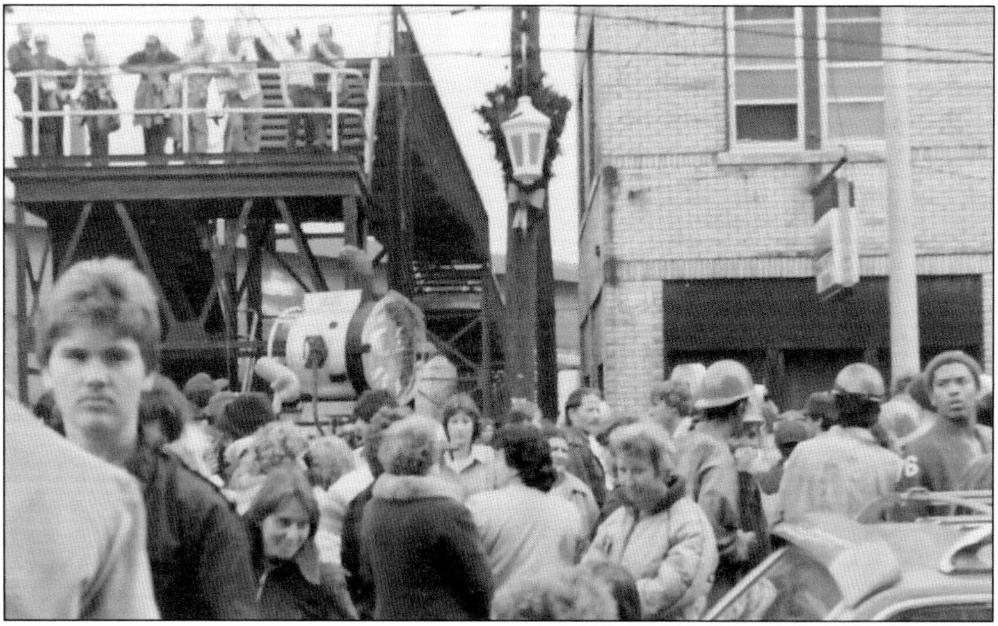

HEART OF STEEL, 1983. Peter Strauss played the starring role in this hard-hitting film about America's working class, made for HBO. Extras are seen here milling around the set on Commercial Street in downtown Mingo. Peter Strauss can be seen in the middle-back of the image under the Christmas decoration, discussing an upcoming scene with director Donald Wyre. Strauss's onscreen wife, actress Pamela Reed, can also be seen in front of the movie light looking towards the camera. (Courtesy Jim Huggins.)

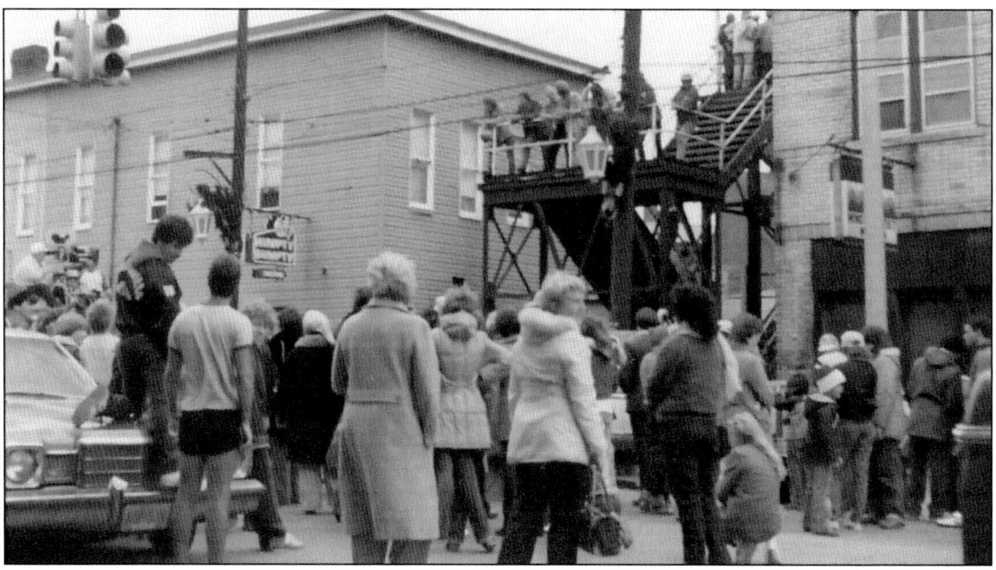

ANOTHER LONG DAY OF FILMING. The movie camera on the hydraulic lift to the left is in position. People on the mill crosswalk are watching the suicide scene as it is being filmed in the middle of the walkway. Later would come the triumphant ending scene after the workers had filled the room wall-to-wall with the steel pipes. Though judged unrealistic by locals, the film did reveal the all too real tensions of workers made useless by mill shutdowns. Peter Strauss was warm and always willing to pose for a picture or sign an autograph. (Courtesy Joann [Takach] Silvane.)

JAMES WRIGHT'S OHIO, DOCUDRAMA, 1987. Tom Koba and Larry Smith, codirectors, are checking the lighting and focus for the next film sequence of their *James Wright's Ohio*. It was filmed completely on location. Many of these same locations inspired James Wright's poetry. Larry Smith is also the author of *Milldust and Roses: Memoirs* and *The Long River Home*, a novel set primarily in Mingo Junction. (Photograph by Paul Ferguson, courtesy Bottom Dog Press.)

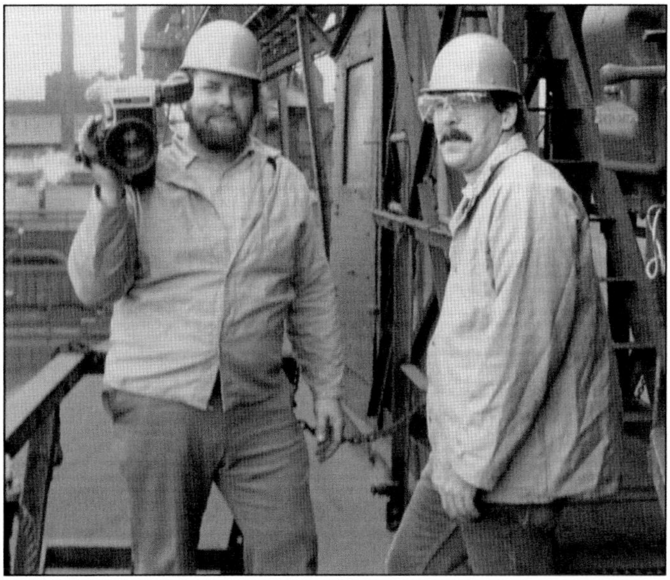

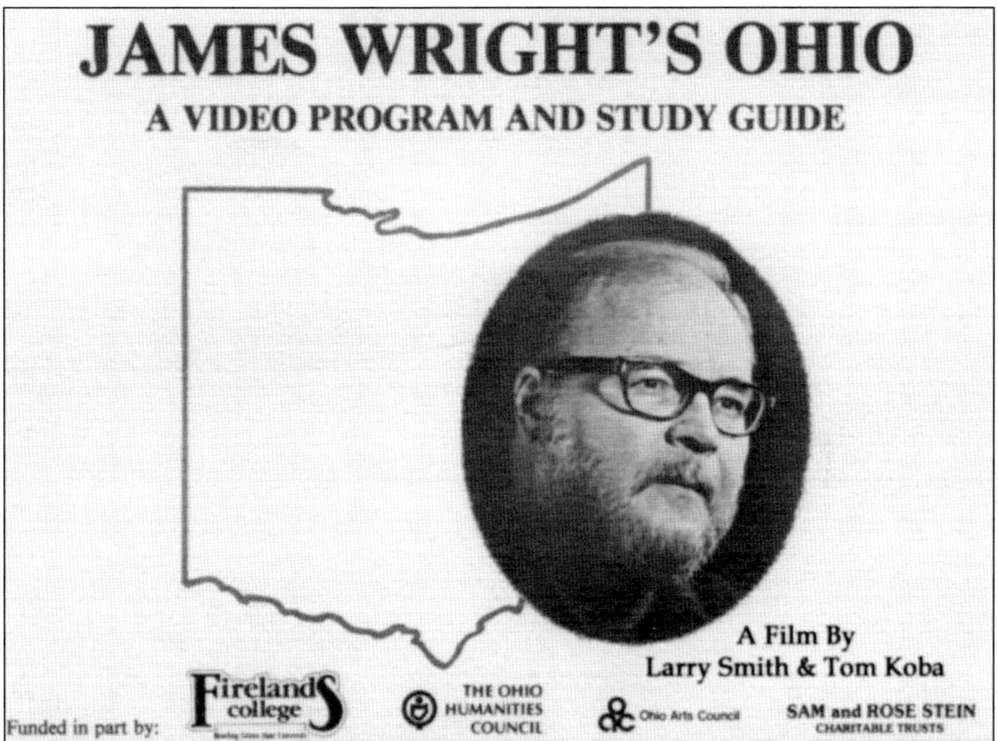

JAMES WIGHT'S OHIO. James Wright was a Martins Ferry native from a working-class family in the Ohio Valley, so it was a natural subject for Mingo native Larry Smith. Wright's 1971 Collected Poems won him the Pulitzer Prize. Smith and Koba's locally filmed docudrama skillfully captured the essence of Wright's sense of place in Ohio. It is a well-regarded and enlightened study of an exceptional poet. Smith and Koba also produced a docudrama on renowned Ohio poet Kenneth Patchen. Both films were funded in part by the Ohio Humanities Council and the Ohio Arts Council and aired on PBS stations. (Courtesy Bottom Dog Press.)

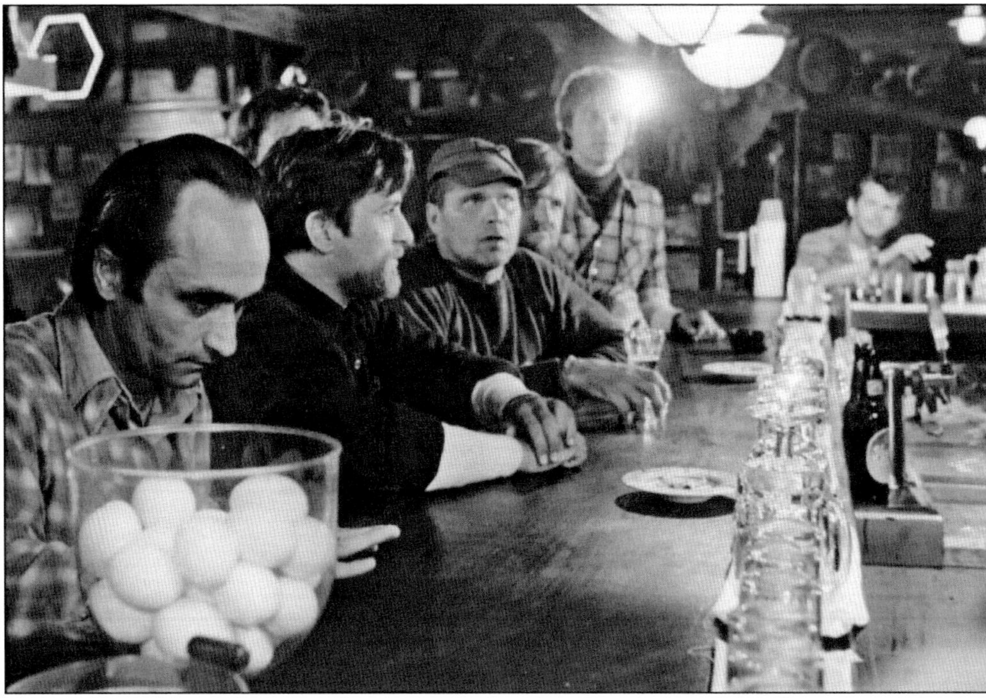

John "Boom Boom" Buchmelter, Local Actor. John is a lifetime Mingo resident and a retired Wheeling-Pittsburgh Steel employee. He received a role in the Academy Award–winning 1978 film *The Deer Hunter* and is seen in several different scenes throughout the movie. Here Boom Boom (in hat) is at the bar with his buddies John Cazale, Robert De Niro, John Savage, Chuck Aspergren, and Christopher Walken. Some of Buchmelter's suggestions for dialogue and voice inflections were used in the movie. (Courtesy Frank Devore family.)

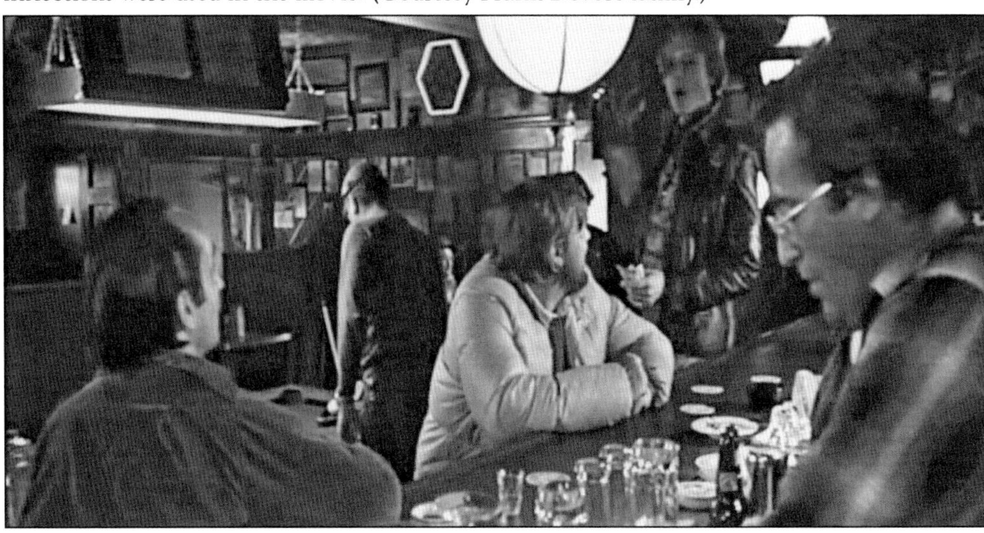

Frank Devore Plays a Role in Films. Frank graduated from Mingo High School in 1956. He was a bartender in real life and felt right at home behind the bar in the film, trading stories and pouring drinks. Here Frank (in glasses) is serving John Cazale and Chuck Aspergren. Devore loved working in *The Deer Hunter* and told many interesting stories about what was going on behind the scenes. (Courtesy Frank Devore family.)

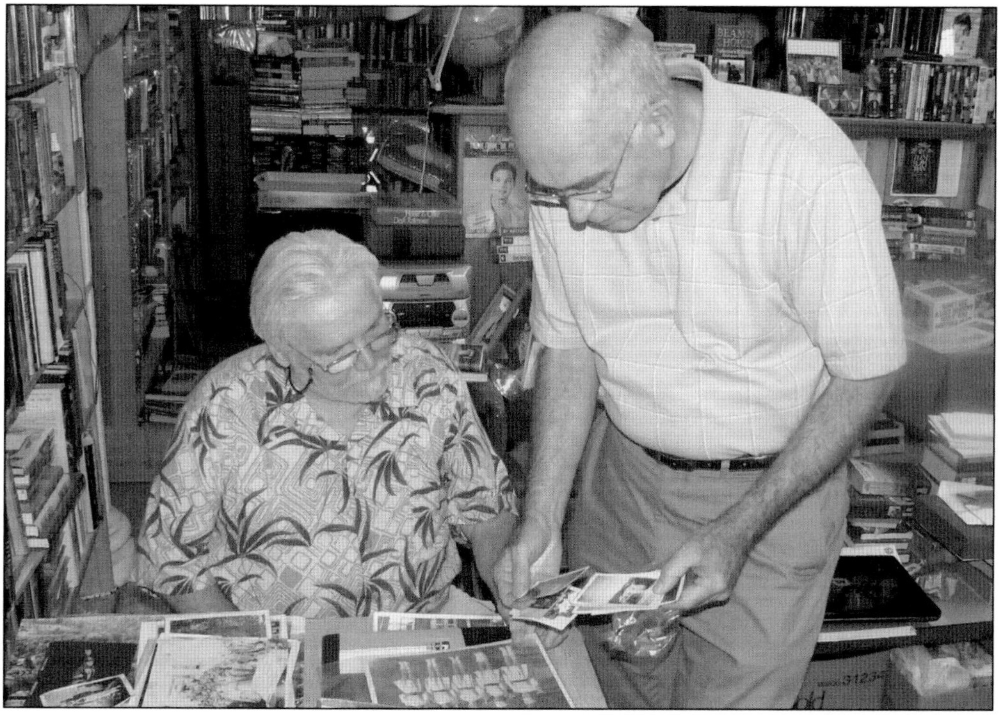

MASON AND SMITH AT WORK. These two Mingo natives and retired doctors, Guy Mason (a dentist) and Larry Smith (a professor of humanities), work to select, scan, and arrange the many images that the citizens of Mingo Junction shared with them. Though they are not shown here, Eileen (Hagerty) Moody, Joanne (Peeler) Sogan, Madeline (Brinskey) Campbell, and Sondra (Hyde) White provided the authors with key assistance. This photograph appeared in the July 4, 2010, issue of The *Steubenville Herald Star* along with an article by Julie Ghrist. (Courtesy Julie Ghrist and the *Steubenville Herald Star.*)

BIBLIOGRAPHY

Brettell, Anna. *History of Mingo Junction*. 1937.

Caldwell, J. A. *History of Belmont and Jefferson Counties, Ohio and Incidental Historical Collections*. Wheeling, WV: West Virginia Historical Publishing Company, 1880.

Conroy, Joseph. *A Mill Town Pastor: The Story of a Witty and Valiant Priest*. Cincinnati, OH: Benziger, 1921.

The Diaries of George Washington. Donald Jackson, ed. Vol. 2. Charlottesville, VA: The University Press of Virginia. 1976.

Hoff, Darlene and Margaret Novotny. *Bicentennial History of Mingo Junction, Ohio*. Sugarcreek, Ohio, 1970.

Jones, Mary Harris. *The Autobiography of Mother Jones*. Chicago, IL: Charles H. Kerr Publishing 1990.

lucky-13.com

smithdocs.net/mingojunctionhistory.html

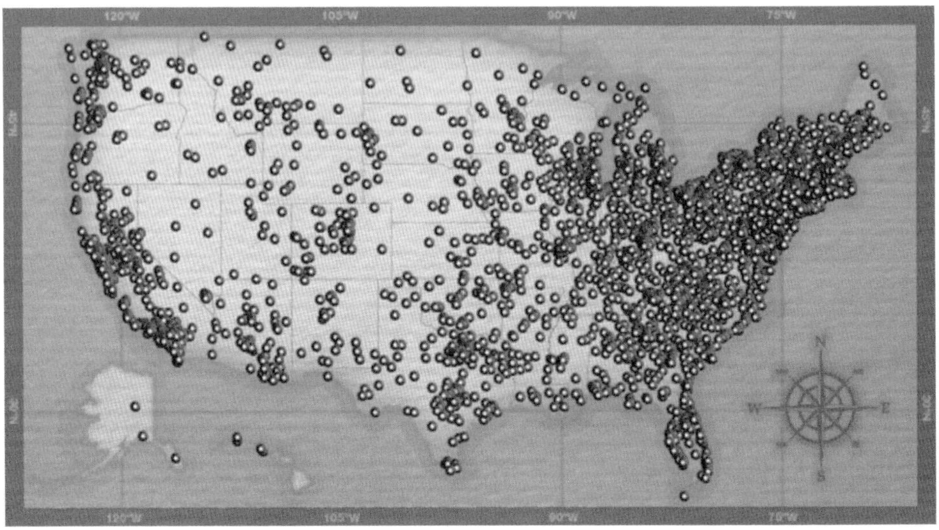